A Pilgrim Returns to Cape Cod

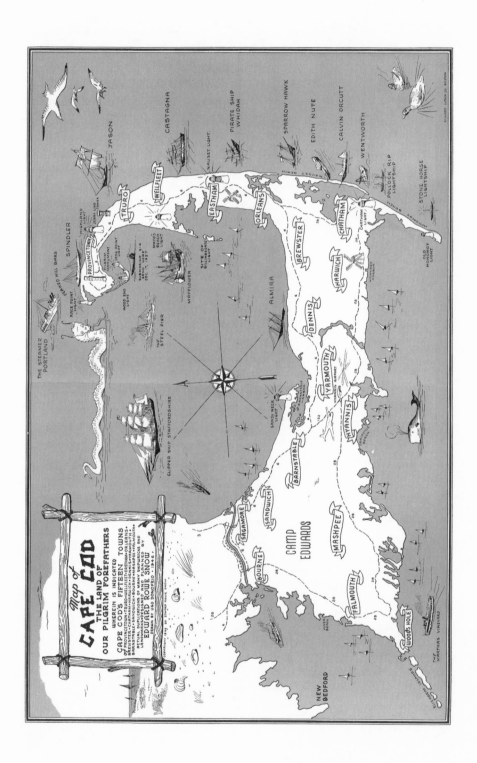

Map of
CAPE COD
THE LAND OF
OUR PILGRIM FOREFATHERS

WHEREIN IS INDICATED
CAPE COD'S FIFTEEN TOWNS
of PROVINCETOWN·TRURO·WELLFLEET·EASTHAM·ORLEANS·
BREWSTER·CHATHAM·HARWICH·DENNIS·YARMOUTH·
BARNSTABLE·SANDWICH·BOURNE·MASHPEE·FALMOUTH·

ACTUAL DUPLICATIONS OF MANY SHIPWRECKS AND
LANDMARKS DESIGNED AND PLANNED BY
EDWARD ROWE SNOW
DRAWN BY UZO DONOFRIO·1946·

A Pilgrim Returns
to Cape Cod

EDWARD ROWE SNOW

Updated by Jeremy D'Entremont

—————————— ∼ ——————————

Issued to commemorate the
centennial of the birth of Edward Rowe Snow

—————————— ∼ ——————————

Commonwealth Editions
Beverly, Massachusetts

ISBN 1-889833-56-8

Jacket and interior design by Judy Barolak.
Jacket illustration from *Truro* by Shebnah Rich (1883).

Printed in the United States.

Published by Commonwealth Editions,
an imprint of Memoirs Unlimited, Inc.,
266 Cabot Street, Beverly, Massachusetts 01915.

Visit our Web site: www.commonwealtheditions.com.

Contents

"A Pilgrim returns to Cape Cod by air," a photo featured in the 1946 edition. Left to right: Edward Rowe Snow, Commissioner Joseph F. Cairnes, Edmund Keville, Lieutenant Governor Robert F. Bradford, and Flight Attendant Margaret Hagerty on the occasion of the first regular 1946 plane flight from Boston to Hyannis, June 1946. (Photo by William Ayoub)

Introduction to the
Snow Centennial Edition

"Cape Cod has universal appeal," wrote Edward Rowe Snow in the preface to the first edition of this book in 1946. Subsequent decades have borne this out to a degree that has been somewhat detrimental to the Cape's environmental health and its status as a quiet getaway. A few years after this book was written, the establishment of the Mid-Cape Highway (Route 6) changed Cape Cod's complexion forever. We'll never again experience the Cape Cod described by Snow and writers like Henry David Thoreau and Henry Beston before him.

Most of Edward Rowe Snow's books can be enjoyed piecemeal, as they're composed of stories loosely linked thematically and/or geographically. You can pick one up and turn to a chapter at random, and then enjoy that particular yarn much as you would a short story. The same applies to *A Pilgrim Returns to Cape Cod.*

But in the case of *Pilgrim,* there's a narrative flow from chapter to chapter that's missing in Snow's other works, as the book follows the length and breadth of his seven-week 1946 hike around Cape Cod's "bare and bended arm." This volume is best appreciated when read from front cover to back. Along with your guide, you start to feel the sand between your toes and the sun on the back of your neck, and the cumulative effect is one of amazement at the sheer volume of colorful, dramatic, harrowing and humorous history and legends that have emerged from this particular sand spit in a few short centuries.

This book was written at a major turning point in Edward Rowe Snow's life. He had taught school in Winthrop, Massachusetts, since the early 1930s. After being wounded in North Africa in World War II, he returned briefly to teaching. But just before embarking on his Cape Cod odyssey, he quit teaching and launched a new career as a full-time writer and lecturer. His newfound freedom seems to have sparked a playfulness in his writing seldom seen previously, and the chatty and engaging style draws the reader in at once.

Much of the appeal retained by today's Cape is reaped from its past, and that past is alive in these pages. The postcard portrait of lobster stew and ocean view celebrated in song by Patti Page is an undeniable part of the picture. But while the history of Cape Cod may be romantic, it's also violent with an assortment of terrible shipwrecks – a subject that was Snow's bread and butter. The wreck and rescue stories told here in typically vivid Snow fashion span the centuries and include one of the most nightmarish of twentieth-century accidents near Cape Cod, the 1927 loss of the submarine *S-4* off Wood End.

Snow visited practically every one of the Cape's buildings and monuments of note during his hike, but it's the people that one remembers most. There are salty and self-sufficient beach dwellers and lighthouse keepers visited along the way, and also historical characters recalled,

Edward Rowe Snow
with pieces of eight

like Captain Lorenzo Dow Baker of Wellfleet, the man who introduced bananas to America, and town crier and sea serpent spotter Professor George Washington Ready.

The text presented here is almost entirely as it was written by Snow, with my notes at the end of the chapters bringing the stories up to the present day or sometimes adding a nugget of information. There have been some minor corrections, mainly to punctuation and spelling.

Most of the photos from the 1946 edition have been included, along with some additional historic photos and a few modern ones. (Some photos and illustrations are uncredited, as they were in the 1946 edition.) Another feature of this edition is a new index.

Besides the authors cited and the various persons and organizations mentioned in my notes, I want to single out those most responsible for launching this new edition. Webster Bull of Commonwealth Editions has an understanding of the timelessness of Edward Rowe Snow's writings and their importance to the region that has kept the project on course, and editor Penny Stratton has done her usual magician's job of keeping the book's structure clear. Bob Jannoni has been a catalyst and vital supporter of the effort to return Snow to print. And Dolly Snow Bicknell – daughter of the man himself – has provided moral support and good humor that means more than I can say.

I hope, like me, you'll find this volume one of the most entertaining and satisfying works produced by the prolific "Mr. New England."

Jeremy D'Entremont
May 2003

Foreword

When Edward Rowe Snow began writing in 1935, I was fifteen years old and madly in love. Besides I hardly knew where Cape Cod was— nor did I care. Then came college and my first real job in New York, with little time for recreational reading. After all, growing up is a serious affair; one is pretty well self-centered.

Then came reality—love and marriage in Provincetown to a girl from Truro. I had a Cape Cod connection, all right. But now I was responsible for someone else, and shortly came World War II. I became a Coast Guard officer and spent my time at sea, ending in Manila. Guantanamo Bay, New Guinea, and Palawan were other ports of call. Edward Rowe Snow was outside my realm of interest.

I became a teacher on Cape Cod, spending some fifty years in the classroom. While I was at it, I began writing books on the Cape's maritime history. Of course by then I knew of the Flying Santa's great work for the lighthouse keepers and their families, but I had no idea of his multifarious other careers. I was simply oblivious.

Now, almost seventy years after the publication of Snow's first book, I am asked to introduce to readers his hundredth-birthday reprint of *A Pilgrim Returns to Cape Cod*. I read the book with growing delight. He's my kind of guy. I discover a master storyteller! Not only that, but I find a wide-ranging scholar, a tireless researcher, someone who not only *reads* his sources but also goes on a thoroughly Thoreauvian walking-tour of Cape Cod to rediscover his own roots and at the same time to cram us marvelously full of the long history of this sand dune.

From a seven-week journey, he not only relates stories of myriad shipwrecks and rescues and other tales but also he speaks with a large number of Cape Codders to reveal the true spirit of this "bare and bended arm of Massachusetts."

For example, Snow tells the harrowing tale of the whaler *Essex,* stove and sunk by an angry sperm whale in mid-Pacific, and of the necessary cannibalism that kept a few men alive. A true horror story. One probably apocryphal tale relates that when Captain Pollard came home, someone approached him, saying, "You must have known So-and-So on your ship." The captain relied tersely, "Knew him? I et him!"

How to do justice to this book? The length and breadth of Cape Cod and its people's spirit include paeans to the Life-Saving Service, the first settlement of the towns, the bravery of the lighthouse keepers and the hardships of the job, the richness of spirit of these hard-bitten people, the disaster of the "Great October Gale" of 1841, when little Truro lost fifty-seven men and boys in seven ships.

One of the most inspiring rescues was that achieved by Boatswain's Mate Bernard Webber and his volunteer Coast Guard crew of three in 1952. In a howling blizzard they set out to find the broken stern section of the tanker *Pendleton* in the rescue boat *G-36500*. Find it they did, and pulled thirty-two men aboard. With the thirty-six men (in a thirty-six foot boat), with a windshield broken in by the waves that tore the compass loose, they made it back to safety. Each of the four-man crew received the gold Coast Guard Life-Saving Medal, the highest Coast Guard honor.

But nearly as exciting as the rescue is the fact that the *CG-36500* herself was rescued and today, fifty years later, is in full operating condition, serving as a magnificent piece of Coast Guard history. This rescue of a different sort was achieved by the Orleans Historical Society, thanks largely to Bill Quinn of Orleans and a host of dedicated volunteers, who spent years raising money and rebuilding the boat. In the summer it is on display at Stage Harbor in Orleans, manned by volunteers—of whom I will be one—to retell the great story.

Not only the thrilling rescue and horror stories are here. *Pilgrim* is full of more mundane but even more important histories: the development of the salt-making works (*twenty-nine acres* by 1802); the growth of the cranberry industry; the Shiverick shipyard in East Dennis, where eight beautiful clipper ships were built; the disgraceful treatment on Cape

Cod of the Acadian refugees from Nova Scotia; the generally friendly treatment of the Wampanoag Indians.

A Pilgrim Returns to Cape Cod is a "must read" for anyone wishing to know the entirety of the Cape and its people.

Admont G. Clark
Captain, U.S. Coast Guard Reserve (retired)
2003

Preface to the 1946 Edition

Cape Cod has a universal appeal. A vacationland of Massachusetts, Cape Cod also attracts large numbers of visitors from Rhode Island, Connecticut, New York, and New Jersey. People from every state in the Union come each summer to enjoy the sandy beaches, the rolling waves, and the great stretches of solitude.

This book, the result of an extended hiking tour around the Cape in the spring of 1946, is intended neither as a history nor a geographical treatise on the Cape. It is merely an account of what I did and what I found out during those seven weeks at the Cape. I did not stop at every house nor did I visit every section of every town, but I did gather enough material to write seven or eight hundred pages. Paper shortages cut the book down to slightly more than 400 pages. Nevertheless, the volume is the largest book on Cape Cod for over half a century.

Stories which I have already told in other volumes have either been omitted or summarized in this book.

Since writing my first volume in 1935 I have received approximately 26,000 letters from almost every country in the world. I am grateful to all who have written, and appreciate hearing from anyone who has either a question to ask or information of importance to give on the subject of New England coastal history.

There were several persons whose efforts helped the volume meet its publication date. Anna-Myrle, my wife, spent tedious hours reading copy. She deserves high praise. Professor Robert E. Moody again generously gave me vital assistance. My mother, Alice Rowe Snow, read many galley sheets and Anna-Myrle's father, Louis Vern Haegg, worked long, weary hours typing and retyping my rewritten manuscript. Lillian Freeman also proved that she was a true friend. Alton Hall Blackington was generous with his advice. Nathan Krock's understanding help and patience were of great value. Channing Howard, with his intense love of Cape Cod history, was an inspiration.

There are others who should be mentioned whose names are inadvertently missing. To those I offer my apologies. I have tried to include everyone. In addition to those whose names appear in the text, I list the following who have helped me:

William Alcott, William Ayoub, Alice Powers Blackington, Dorothy Blanchard, James L. Bruce, Clarence S. Brigham, George S. Chapman, Harry Eaton Damon, Lieutenant John E. Day, U.S.C.G., Paul Dudley, Gertrude DeWager, John E. Ellis, Ruth Madelyn Fill, Ethel Haegg, Maud Hall, Francis F. Haskell, Marion Haskell, Vincent Holmes, Richard Kelsey, William Leshner, Isabell Q. Minot, Kathleen A. Monaghan, Joshua Nickerson, Walter E. Piper, Franklin Pierce, Captain Glenn Estep Prester, U.S.C.G., George Ruddell, Harold Sandstrom, Irwin Smith, John Gilchrest Snow, John I. Snow, Donald B. Snow, Harriet Swift, and John G. Weld.

Institutions which have cooperated include the Bostonian Society, the Boston Public Library, the Massachusetts Historical Society, the United States Coast Guard, the Society for the Preservation of New England Antiquities, the National Archives, the Suffolk Court House, the Boston Marine Society, the Harvard College Library, the Boston Athenaeum, the Peabody Museum, the Essex Institute, and the American Antiquarian Society.

I enjoyed to the utmost my seven weeks at Cape Cod. If the reader's enjoyment of these pages is in any way proportional I shall feel amply repaid for all my hiking, interviewing, and writing.

Edward Rowe Snow
Winthrop, Massachusetts
September 7, 1946

CHAPTER 1

Provincetown, the Tip of Cape Cod

Cape Cod was calling, for it was one of those warm spring days which New Englanders look forward to all winter long. "Why not fly down to the Cape and spend a few weeks hiking along the sandy beaches and winding roads there?" were my thoughts, for it had suddenly come to me that there was nothing to prevent my going. It was April 1946, and I was no longer a school teacher. I was free to do as I wished. Packing cameras, note paper, food, and books into the knapsack, I was soon ready for a springtime journey to the Cape before the summer people, whom Cape Codders call the "health eaters," arrived. I would go to the land of my ancestors at a time when Cape Cod was relatively free from visitors.

An hour later I watched Captain Ed Berndt checking instruments as we sat in the plane awaiting the signal for our takeoff at Boston's Logan International Airport. Then the green light flashed in the airport tower, and we roared down the runway to climb up into the "wild blue yonder," leaving the city of Boston spread out below us in a picturesque design. Flying across historic Boston Harbor, we came down close to Boston Light for good luck, and then began the long steady climb southward for the Cape. Nantasket Beach, Minot's Light in all its majestic isolation, Cohasset, Scituate and her many cliffs—all were left behind. There was Plymouth and the canopy over Plymouth Rock, with the long arm of Duxbury Beach stretching out to old Gurnet Light.

By now we were 3,000 feet in the air, veering out across Massachusetts Bay. There in the distance far below, its sandy shores outlined against the blue ocean, lay my destination—Cape Cod. The bended arm of the great Cape was ahead, with almost every location of importance visible from our plane half a mile in the air. The great bridges over the Canal, the fire towers, Provincetown [Pilgrim] Monument, Highland Light, all seemed to urge us on. Farther away I could see the long bar of Monomoy extending southward from Chatham, and the tiny spots of red offshore which I knew were Pollock Rip and Stone Horse lightships. And there, so distant that it seemed impossible to detect where sea and sky met, lay Nantucket Island itself, with Martha's Vineyard far off to the right. It was a magnificent sight!

A few moments later we were circling for an extremely difficult landing in a field near Provincetown on the tip of Cape Cod. After dropping down between the dunes until our wheels hit, we taxied across the sand-swept field to a stop. I jumped out with my belongings, for Ed Berndt was leaving me there. It was not an ideal airport and we looked over the situation carefully before he decided to go to the very end of the field and try a takeoff. I climbed to the top of a sand dune and stood alert as he raced the engine. Captain Berndt released the brakes and the plane came tearing across the sand, taking a desperate grab at the air as it roared by. Triumphantly the plane rose above the dunes, and then, banking sharply, Ed flew low over the field to give me a final wing flutter of farewell before climbing for his journey across the water to Boston.

The plane was soon a speck in the sky, and the speck eventually disappeared completely, leaving me with a rather lonesome feeling. Although only thirty minutes from Boston by plane, I felt as though I were on my own in practically another world. The descendant of Constance Hopkins, *Mayflower*, 1620, Nicholas Snow, Ship *Ann*, 1623, and William Nickerson, Monomoyick, 1656, was about to begin traveling over Cape Cod, the land of his ancestors. But for a few moments I stood atop the sand dune—the only human being within a mile—breathing deeply of the salt air which the sea breezes wafted inland. The blue of the ocean was in vivid contrast to the white sands and the even whiter foam of the breakers offshore, and the only sounds to be heard above the dull boom of the distant surf were the weird cries of the sea gulls as they settled back to their usual pursuits. In any direction I might face there stretched a road to adventure.

The beach to the north of the airport was a quarter mile away, so I walked toward the shore. Finding that it was easier to hike right across the dunes than to hunt for a path, I struck out for the beach, crossing two faintly defined roads in the sand before coming out twenty minutes later on the shore itself. I reached the Atlantic near a noisy flock of sea gulls. The birds were busily fighting over a great shapeless mass of hide and bones, which I soon discovered was what remained of an unlucky whale stranded there some time before. At my approach the birds flew away, and I found a long, thin piece of the mammal's skeleton, cleaned by the sea gulls and whitened by the sun. A forty-inch piece of whalebone became my first souvenir of Cape Cod.

Happy in the thought that after less than half an hour on Cape Cod I had already acquired a substantial souvenir, my spirits were high enough for a good, long hike. Of course, I knew where I should really head—that curled-up finger tip of Cape Cod's mighty arm known as Wood End and Long Point. These two districts form a tiny peninsula of their own. In fact until the dike to Provincetown was built, their hold on Cape Cod was indeed a slender one, for merely a narrow thread of sand prevented them from becoming an island. A glance at the map shows how Cape Cod curls up within itself at this point.

Years ago there were settlements at both Wood End and Long Point, but for many years now only the lighthouse keepers and the Coast Guard have held sway. I decided to go to Wood End first, so hiked back to the airport to get my bearings. Climbing up on my sand dune, I could make out Hatch's Harbor and Snake Hill in the distance. Starting across the dunes and keeping Hatch's Harbor and its dike on my right, before long I reached Snake Hill and the highway which runs along by Herring Cove. Three quarters of a mile farther on, the highway turns left to go inland toward Telegraph Hill and Provincetown itself, but I left the road and continued faithfully along the beach for my first objective, Wood End Light. The sun was getting hotter, and the great waves, breaking with effortless regularity on the white sands, seemed a perfect invitation to a swim in the ocean. I walked down to a point just above the reach of the sea and took my shoes and socks off. Then I stopped. "How warm is the water?" I asked myself. "Perhaps the season isn't quite as far advanced as it might be," so I rolled up my trousers and waded in a few feet.

Has it ever happened to you? The moment the water was above my ankles, the full effect of the icy, cold seas, which only early April can offer, hit me, and I hastily changed my plans. The sun did not seem as hot now, nor my need for a swim so urgent. My desires for ocean frolicking were indefinitely postponed, and I committed the cowardly act of retreating hastily toward the shore, where I sat down by my shoes and socks, my numbed feet and ankles throbbing violently as I rubbed them to regain circulation. After drying my legs, and putting on socks and shoes, I decided to forget my cowardice and continue hiking toward Wood End Light. At last I saw the square wooden lighthouse building with other houses around it, and knew that I would soon reach my objective. Half an hour later I met Keeper George Grimes of Wood End Light. He had replaced my old friend George H. Fitzpatrick there several months before, and we spent some time comparing notes of various mutual acquaintances we had. Then the talk went to those who have walked around Cape Cod. I spoke of Henry David Thoreau, who hiked the Cape on several occasions. Thoreau tells a story in his *Cape Cod* of a shipwreck at Wood End which occurred in 1849. In his effective style he relates how he met a sailor from the wreck who had escaped drowning by being thrown ashore at Wood End. Without question there have been scores of shipping disasters here. However, regardless of the fact that many lives were lost when countless sailing vessels were wrecked at Wood End, the name means but one disaster in the minds of most seafaring men today, the loss of the submarine *S-4*.

Keeper Grimes sat down with me on the sand. "There's very little I know about the *S-4*," he remarked, "for at the time I was quite young. They say she went down right off here. It must have been terrible that December day when it happened." I pulled out some yellowed newspaper clippings from my knapsack, and spread them out on the sand. Together we read the tale of horror and suffering which took place off that same shore almost nineteen years before when the *S-4* went down in 100 feet of water only eight days before Christmas.

It was on the afternoon of Saturday, December 17, 1927, that the Coast Guard destroyer *Paulding*, under command of her master, Captain John S. Baylis, was proceeding in the waters just off Wood End. Unknown to Captain Baylis, the United States submarine *S-4* was breaking surface directly in the path of the destroyer. Back on shore, Lookout Frank Simonds of the Wood End Coast Guard Station had been watching the periscopes of the *S-4* as they broke surface. Boatswain Emanuel C. Gracie entered the observation room. As the submarine began to surface near the end of the measured mile, Gracie shouted at the top of his voice, "There's going to be a collision," and ran down the ladder to launch the surfboat.

The collision occurred before Gracie could reach the beach. The conning tower of the *S-4* was half out of the water when the *Paulding* smashed into her, crushing her stem into the battery room of the submarine, just forward of the conning tower. The *S-4* filled and sank at once. The *Paulding*, with part of her stem severed, launched her boats, which circled the area in a vain effort to rescue any survivors who might appear. But after the collision, when the sea boiled with bubbles for a brief period of time, the only indication of the wrecked submarine's position was an ominous patch of oil which floated to the surface and slowly spread out over the area.

Boatswain Gracie launched his surfboat almost at once, and soon reached the location where he had seen the disaster. All that day there had been a bitter southwest wind blowing right across the bay, and the waters of Provincetown Harbor were filled with rough, dangerous,

Boatswain Emanuel C. Gracie

white-capped waves. But Gracie was determined to save the men still imprisoned at the bottom of Cape Cod Bay in what was more than one hundred feet of water. Grappling back and forth, he was unable to locate the submarine, although he felt sure he must be close. He had seen the S-4 go down less than three quarters of a mile from his station. The icy December spray froze his hands and made his whole body numb with cold, but he was fighting for the lives of the men who were imprisoned on the sea bottom far below him. Hour after hour passed; still Gracie could not find the hull of the submarine. Could it be that she had continued on a course underwater and was not even in the vicinity? The fact that he had seen the oil slick coming up reassured him, however. Boatswain Gracie kept up his ceaseless dragging. Finally, at 10:00 Saturday night, almost six and a half hours after the collision had occurred, Gracie located the S-4. The disaster had taken place at 3:37 P.M.

It was a terrible ordeal which Boatswain Gracie faced. The southwest wind had been severe in the afternoon. Now that evening had come, it reached almost gale force. The freezing spray and icy wind made his task nearly hopeless, but he clung desperately to the grapnel, praying for the help he knew was on the way. The entire resources of the United States Navy had been alerted. Almost before the S-4 had settled on the bottom, the *Paulding* flashed out a message that she had hit an unknown submarine. Up in Portsmouth, New Hampshire, the submarine mother ship *Bushnell* had been dispatched at once, while from New London, Connecticut, came the salvage ship *Falcon*, later to distinguish herself off the Isles of Shoals in the *Squalus* disaster. Tugs from New York City were towing the pontoons to raise the S-4. In spite of all this, however, a short time before the lights of the *Bushnell* appeared, Gracie's grapnel line snapped. All his efforts had been in vain. He returned to the Coast Guard station and lay down on his cot, completely exhausted.

After a brief rest, Boatswain Gracie got up and went at it again, eventually locating the S-4 for the second time at 10:30 Sunday morning, nineteen hours after the collision. Eight of the Navy's best divers were then on the scene. There were Tom Eadie, Bill Carr, Fred Michaels, and five others who were among America's greatest divers. All had hoped that the gale would diminish with the coming of dawn, but fate decreed otherwise. The eight divers could not go down in the heavy seas. There they stood, on the deck of the *Falcon*, while they had reason to believe that down below them, trapped in the sunken submarine were men, still alive and well, who were waiting for rescue. Finally, at 2:00 that Sunday afternoon, Diver Tom Eadie announced that in spite of highly unfavorable conditions, he could stand the strain no longer and would attempt a dive. A moment later he was over the side.

Eadie slid down the grapnel line to land without accident on the deck of the *S-4*. More than twenty-two hours had elapsed since the disaster. Were any of the men still alive or was he too late? At 100 feet below the surface, visibility was less than a yard, and Eadie was unable to make sure of his position for several minutes. Next he decided that he would try to tap out a message to the men inside the *S-4*, then looming vaguely through the eerie darkness on the bottom. Taking out his hammer, he swung it sharply against the steel hull. Almost immediately there were answering thumps, muffled and dulled, as they reached him, but nevertheless, a distinct signal. He telephoned at once to the men on the surface to let them know that someone was still alive in the submarine then on the floor of the ocean off Wood End Light. Walking carefully, step by step, for diving is one of the world's most dangerous professions, he covered the entire length of the submarine, tapping as he walked. But there was no answering signal except in the compartment he had already heard from. One fact he was sure of, however— there were living men a few feet away from him, who could be rescued if all went well. Surveying the damage, he found that the starboard bow of the submarine had received the full force of the destroyer's keel, and was crumbled and torn for some distance. There seemed to be hope that the submarine might be raised, or that air could be pumped to the men trapped inside the *S-4*.

Returning to the surface, Eadie told the salvage officers what he had seen, and plans were made to connect an air hose with the main ballast tank and force the water ballast out. Diver Bill Carr made the next descent to the ocean floor. He located the valve in the main ballast tank, and a short time later an air hose was sent down to him. Screwing the air hose to the valve, he checked all connections and then telephoned to the waiting officers on the *Falcon*'s deck.

"All O.K.," he cried, "Go ahead."

The air shot down into the submarine, and Diver Carr, watching anxiously for any telltale air bubbles which might reveal a leak in the hull, believed that all was well and returned to the surface. The vessels shifted their positions to allow the *S-4* to rise to the top of the sea without fouling them, and every man aboard waited for the first sign that the *S-4* was about to break surface. But it was not to be. The first air bubbles indicating a leak reached the top of the sea about an hour after Carr affixed the air hose, and every man realized the submarine could not get off the bottom.

Then the weather grew steadily worse, and it looked as though the *S-4* was doomed. It was Diver Fred Michaels' turn to descend. The weather was very threatening, but it was felt that if another air hose could reach the submarine, it might mean the difference between life and death for the remaining men. So Diver Michaels determined to take the risk, although all his previous experience made him realize that he might not come back alive. When he reached the bottom, the lines slacked because of the terrific rocking overhead, and he could not prevent himself from sliding off the deck of the submarine to land in mud up to his armpits. He was imprisoned in the slime at the bottom of the sea! Telephoning his condition to the men aboard the *Falcon*, he waited for them to take action. A dozen men seized his lifeline, and by careful pulling and slacking at the right intervals, eventually brought him up out of the mud. Unfortunately, he was now at the shattered end of the submarine, and a loop of air pipe caught in a fragment of projecting wreckage. When the next wave rocked the salvage vessel far above, Michael's lifeline was trapped on the other side of the submarine, and he was an underwater prisoner in the worst possible predicament. If he tried to disentangle his life line, the air line became tighter, and an attempt to free the air line would bring a similar condition. Finally he told those on the *Falcon* that he was hopelessly fouled. Those above again tried to pull him free, but because of the loop caught in the wreck, all they actually did was to bump his helmet against the deck. The continual smashes of his helmet finally made him groggy and almost unconscious.

Back up on the *Falcon*, Eadie had discovered what was going on. He knew that his pal was losing consciousness on the bottom, and so, in spite of the waves, wind, and icy conditions, he prepared for a dive. A few minutes later he had landed beside the conning tower, and could barely discern the feeble glimmer from Michaels' lamp. Reaching the other diver, he found that his most difficult task would be to keep his own lines from getting tangled while disengaging Michaels' lines from the wreckage. It was a perilous task. As soon as he found that Michaels' air hose was hopelessly stuck, he telephoned for a hacksaw to be lowered, and a short time later he was sawing the fragment of wreckage which was imprisoning his fellow diver.

It was an almost impossible task, sawing down at the bottom of the sea, with a gale on the surface making his every movement a perilous one. Resting time after time from his exertions, he finally watched the metal break loose and then the air line straighten out. But his task was only half over. Michaels floated upwards until the lifeline grew taut and caught him again. Eadie moved across to free it and had just liberated Michaels' line when suddenly his own body went cold and his diving suit filled with water. Only the compressed air bubbling into his helmet kept him from drowning then and there. As he had given a final pull in his effort to send Michaels up to the surface, a fragment of the wreckage had caught his suit and given it a jagged tear, allowing the water to rush in. If he slipped or bent over, Eadie would drown in his own diving suit. He moved cautiously across the deck to separate Michaels' lines from his own, and then telephoned up to the waiting men to haul Michaels out of danger. Not until he had accomplished this did he signal for his own release, and a few minutes later both divers were in the decompression chamber, that vital part of a salvage boat's equipment. Eadie's work that bitter night later won him the Medal of Honor.

Michaels, however, was still in danger, and so early the next morning the *Falcon* rushed him across to Boston in order that he could be taken to the hospital. Back at Provincetown the gale continued.

By this time, another submarine, the *S-8*, and many additional rescue ships and vessels were standing by. All they could do, however, was to send messages to the doomed men by means of the oscillograph. Microphones were attached to the hull of the *S-4*. The imprisoned sailors answered the oscillograph messages by tapping against the walls of the submarine.

"Is gas bad?" was the first question asked of the imprisoned men.

"No," came back the answer, "but the air," indicating that the air was probably foul.

"How long will you be now?" came the vital question from the trapped sailors.

"We are doing everything possible," was the only answer the would-be rescuers could truthfully send, to which came the pleading entreaty, "Please hurry."

"How many are there?" was then asked of the men at the bottom of the sea.

"There are six," came the immediate response, and the names of all six men still alive were slowly spelled out. Lieutenant Graham N. Fitch and his five companions, R. L. Short, R. A. Crabb, George Peluar, Frank Snizek, and Joseph L. Stevens, were all who were alive aboard the *S-4*. The other thirty-four men were dead.

The storm kept on in all its fury, and the relentless hours went by. Messages continued to pass between the trapped men at the bottom of the sea and the would-be rescuers above. Finally came the dreadful word that the last container of oxygen would be entirely consumed by 6:00 that Monday night. Would it be possible for another container to reach them in time?

The salvage officer, Commander H. E. Saunders, consulted with Captain E. J. King, in charge of operations. They agreed that a diver was to be sent to the *S-4* at the first break in the gale. The plan was for those inside the submarine to open the outer port of a torpedo tube where the diver could place a cylinder of oxygen, food, and lime soda to purify the blood. Then the imprisoned men, after closing the outer torpedo port, could open the inner port to obtain the vital supplies, and thus would be able to carry on a few days longer. The storm did not go down in time, however, and it was impossible to descend to the ocean floor with the life-preserving oxygen.

All over the world millions of people were following the efforts which the men aboard the *Falcon* were making to free their imprisoned comrades. Every night hundreds of thousands of prayers were offered for them, but all to no avail. The last communication with the men in the submarine was made at 6:00 in the morning of Tuesday, December 20. Three faint taps could be heard, sixty-two hours after the *S-4* had gone down. It is believed that the last trapped man died before noon that same Tuesday.

The rest of the story, of course, is of secondary importance, for the men had all perished. By Wednesday the gale ended, and divers were able to pump air into the submarine. With great difficulty chains were placed around her hull, but the *S-4* could not be brought to the surface. The bodies of the forty crew members of the ill-fated submarine were later brought out one by one. Each sailor was buried with full military honors.

January and February passed, and still the *S-4* remained at the bottom of the sea. By March 15 three pairs of pontoons were in position, and two days later all was ready. Compressed air began to displace the water aboard the submarine early that morning, and by afternoon the first signs of buoyancy were noted in the pressure gauges connected to the *S-4*'s compartments. Rising steadily, the gauges soon indicated that she was about to leave bottom. Suddenly those watching the water over the submarine saw the first wooden pontoons break the surface. Then the second pair, and finally the third pair of pontoons appeared, followed shortly afterwards by the conning tower of the unfortunate submarine herself. The *S-4* had been brought up from the bottom of the sea.

But the submarine was still in danger, for the barometer was dropping rapidly. Without further ceremony, the salvage tugs affixed their lines and cables, and the long journey to Boston across the March seas began. Time and again before reaching Boston it was a question whether they would make port, but finally the *S-4* reached Boston Harbor and the Charlestown Navy Yard. Repaired and refitted, the *S-4* later became an experimental vessel.

As we sat on the beach that spring afternoon, Keeper George Grimes and I talked of the other great submarine disasters, the *S-51* off Block Island, and the famous *Squalus* catastrophe near the Isles of Shoals. But it seemed a far cry back to those troubled moments of former days, and especially to 1927, when forty men lost their lives on the *S-4* less than three quarters of a mile from the shore where we were sitting.

As I arose, my thoughts were on that still inexplicable subject—why cannot man so govern himself that these weapons of war will become things of the past? But I couldn't supply the answer.

Long Point Light was my next objective, and after a hike of approximately a mile, I reached what is really the extreme finger tip of Cape Cod's bended arm. Keeper Charles Cain was waiting for me, for the coastguardsmen at Wood End had telephoned ahead.

"What's the matter? Why didn't you ride over in the Coast Guard jeep?" he questioned.

I told him I hiked, swam, or rowed around Cape Cod, but I wouldn't ride in a jeep unless there was an emergency. This statement seemed rather ridiculous to him, but I was determined to stick to my plan as long as possible.

"Say, what is that book?" he asked me, as I opened the pages of Thoreau's *Cape Cod*, and sat down to read what the great philosopher had to say about Long Point.

"Would you like to hear what they did here a hundred years ago?" I inquired, and as he readily agreed, I read aloud to him from Thoreau:

> *About Long Point in the summer you commonly see them catching lobsters for the New York market, from small boats just off shore, or*

rather, the lobsters catch themselves, for they cling to the netting on which the bait is placed, of their own accord, and thus are drawn up. They sell them fresh for two cents apiece. Man needs to know but little more than a lobster in order to catch him in his traps. The mackerel fleet had been getting to sea, one after another, ever since midnight, and as we were leaving the Cape we passed near to many of them under sail.

They are still catching lobsters off the shores of Long Point, but as for selling them fresh for "two cents apiece," well, the market for lobsters was about a dollar a pound in Provincetown that week in April 1946, and prices for lobster meat soared correspondingly higher. But I have never been one to begrudge the fisherman any price he may receive for his catch of lobsters or fish, for he earns every cent of his money, risking his life at almost every tide.

Keeper Cain spoke to me of the countless thousands who sail into Provincetown Harbor aboard the Boston excursion steamer *Steel Pier* every season, passing almost a stone's throw from his light on the way into the harbor. As near as he is to all the activity and bustle of the summer excursion crowds, the keeper of Long Point Light very seldom receives a visitor from the *Steel Pier* because it is almost a physical impossibility to get out to Long Point from Provincetown and back before the steamer sails away for Boston.

After examining the jetties around the beach, erected years ago to prevent the sand from washing away, I said farewell to my host, and started back along the outer shore until I reached the Wood End Coast Guard Station. Then I made for the dike or breakwater on which at low tide one may walk to Provincetown. As the tide was out, I crossed over to the first port of the Pilgrims, arriving at Telegraph Hill twenty minutes later.

Walking rapidly down Commercial Street, I was soon on the wharf where the excursion ship *Steel Pier* docks in the summertime. There were several fishing vessels tied up there, and I thought how changed it was from the summer activity later in the year.

For those who participate in the mad, wild scramble which takes place when the *Steel Pier* pours out its impatient thousands in June, July, and August, Provincetown must indeed appear as a bustling town intent only on serving the passengers from the Boston boat. This impression is an erroneous one. If you really wish to see the normal

Provincetown, visit it in the cool of the spring, when this little town, nestling half in and half out of the Atlantic, shows its real self. Of course, I do not suggest that you ignore Provincetown in the summer. By all means take the sail across Massachusetts Bay to see this old fishing town at its busiest. But, come back in the springtime the following year.

As I left the wharf I ran into an old friend, Jot Small.

"What are you doing here in April?" was his question, and I explained that I was hiking around Cape Cod learning its history. I also told him that I was in search of signs of my ancestors, mentioning their names.

"Well, there are plenty of Snows, Hopkins, and Nickersons on Cape Cod to keep you going indefinitely," was Jot's parting remark as he continued walking toward the Anchor and Ark Club.

I walked over to visit Mellen Hatch at the Octagon House, where I found him hard at work on a volume about railroad locomotives. Sitting down by his side, I asked him how it felt to be an all-year-rounder.

"Why, there isn't any comparison," was his answer. "The people who come here in the summer do not find the real Provincetown," he said. "A town or city's reason for being does not depend on the summer tourist, but naturally it helps a lot. Now you take Provincetown— except for the hundred or so trips the *Steel Pier* makes every summer, and those people who come by car and bus—for nine months of the year Provincetown is definitely a large fishing village. Naturally, I know the Portuguese, a fine race of people, have taken over Provincetown. It was bound to come, and we welcome the Azoreans, the Bravas of Cape Verde, and the men and women from around Lisbon."

"How did they happen to come here?" I asked.

"Well, I guess the Bravas came first. You have read of the old days of whalers from New Bedford, Nantucket, and elsewhere. In many cases the crews were dragged aboard while dead drunk, and of course deserted whenever possible. Quite often the desertions were made in the vicinity of the Cape Verde Islands, so it became customary to recruit new men from this pleasant Portuguese seaport. Gradually the sailors from Portugal came to live in America, mostly around New Bedford, but within the last two generations large numbers from the Azores and Lisbon have settled at Provincetown. At present they actually can control the political, social, and economic life of this ancient seaport.

"The Portuguese fisherman from Provincetown, because of improved markets and the general recognition of the working man at sea or on land which has come since 1920, is actually making a fair living by fishing. You might like to know that cod, haddock, swordfish, flounder, bass, whiting, and mackerel are probably the seven varieties of fish caught more often than the others."

Mellen Hatch showed me a few of his railroad engine pictures, and a short time later we were eating dinner, a fine meal prepared in Mrs. Hatch's very capable manner. But I was anxious to reach Race Point Light that afternoon, so after thanking the Hatches for their pleasant hospitality, I started out for the Race Point Road, which I followed until within half a mile of the Coast Guard station. Then I struck off across the dunes to the left, where two miles away I could see Race Point Light.

It was half an hour before I reached Race Point Light. My old friend, Keeper Osborne Hallett, was in the tower when I arrived, and invited me up for a chat. Several years ago I had known and visited him at both Boston Light and Graves Light.

After finishing his work, Hallett took me over to his quarters, where we sat down to coffee and crackers. The conversation went from shipwrecks

Keeper Osborne Hallett and his wife, Florence, at Race Point Light, 1945 (courtesy of Anne Ames)

to pirates and back to shipwrecks again. I asked him if he had ever heard of the strange, mysterious wreck of the *Monte Tabor*, but he said there were no records of any sort then at the station, for all old logbooks and wreck reports had long ago been shipped to Washington.

"What about the *Monte Tabor*?" he asked me. What can you tell me about her?" As it happened, I had been reading about the strange fate of the Italian bark just a few weeks before, and was able to give him an account of what is now considered one of the most melodramatic shipwrecks in Cape Cod history. It was truly an unusual disaster, and could form the basis for several entirely different moving picture scenarios.

The bark *Monte Tabor* sailed from Trapani, Sicily, on June 21, 1896. Bound for Boston with a load of salt, she was in charge of Captain Genero. On the ninth day of the following September, the vessel was struck by a hurricane, which so terrified Captain Genero that he prepared a message to place in a bottle. The communication, later picked up on the beach in the wreckage, read as follows:

> *The Italian bark* Monte Tabor *struck by hurricane on September 9, 1896, in latitude 40° north, longitude 70° west. The captain and crew, after having used all possible means, resigned themselves to the will of Providence. The hurricane originated with a northeast wind on the 7th instant, at 1:00 A.M., two days previous; great lightning, then stormy and black. Then the vessel was hove to on the starboard tack. We tried to go on by force of sails, but it was found impossible to go out from that zone. On the morning of the 9th of September there were great waves, and after proceeding about fifty miles to the northwest we were forced to stop. The captain and crew, all resigned to the will of Providence, gave their souls to God, thanking him for the destiny assigned to them. Our prayer from the finder for their souls.*
>
> The Captain, Genero

Captain Genero then had every crew member sign the statement, and sealed it in the bottle. We cannot tell exactly what happened then, but we may assume that the storm abated, with the captain and sailors regaining their courage, for on the thirteenth of October the lookout sighted Highland Light on a lee shore. The *Tabor* was then carrying her foresail, topsail, fore topmast staysail, and jib, and was still standing to the northward. When the light bore between south and southeast, the bark began to labor considerably. Captain Genero, believing that he had safely passed Race Point, kept off to the westward, planning to anchor in Provincetown Harbor until the storm had let up. Fog was intermittently blowing in, and the captain was in a very dangerous place.

Captain Genero then made his fatal mistake, for he miscalculated the bark's position just enough to send his vessel directly towards the deadly Peaked Hill Bars, where the *Monte Tabor* grounded shortly before midnight. By this time the wind was blowing forty miles an hour, the fog was still thick, and a furious sea was roaring in. Bouncing over the outer bars, the *Tabor* hit again and again, finally stranding herself on the outside of the innermost of the Peaked Hill Bars.

On the Cape Cod beach at this time patrolling the shore was Surfman Silvey, who detected the white light of the *Tabor* off the beach and burned his Coston flare at once to warn the vessel away. But it was too late, for the *Monte Tabor* was already deep in the sand of the Peaked Hill Bars. Silvey ran back to the station to notify Keeper Isaac Fisher of the wreck. It was blackest night, with high surf and gusts of wind which reached hurricane force. Abreast of the wreck, where the gun was to be set up, the waves were hitting hard against the twenty-foot bank, so another part of the shore had to be chosen, a bare level area of sand a short distance away.

Telephone messages were sent to Keeper Charles P. Kelly of the High Head Station and Keeper Samuel O. Fisher of Race Point to dispatch their crews to the scene of the wreck, as difficult work was ahead. Then the light from the *Monte Tabor* disappeared and the bark probably went to pieces at that time, for a hatch and an awning stanchion washed ashore afterwards. But the lifesavers were helpless. Keeper Fisher later remarked there was "nothing to shoot at, and nothing to pull to, even if a boat could have been launched," which of course was at that time impossible. He conferred with Keeper Sam Fisher, who had just arrived, and they spread out their patrols along the beach to watch for men and wreckage.

A short time later Keeper I. G. Fisher detected a Coston flare down the beach and ran in that direction, meeting Patrolman Higgins, who had heard cries coming from the raging surf. As they stood there wondering what to do, a louder shout was heard. All available men then ran down into the water knee-deep, and could faintly see the top of the *Monte Tabor*'s cabin with several men clinging to it about twenty-five yards offshore. Shouting to the men to hold fast until rescued, the surfmen prepared to save them, but the Italians did not understand, and one soon leaped into the sea. He was rescued at once by Surfmen Fish of

Peaked Hill and Edwin B. Tyler of Race Point. Three other shipwrecked mariners then followed their countryman and jumped into the ocean. They were each rescued under similar conditions. The two remaining men still aboard the cabin then threw Tyler a line, which he grabbed and held while they climbed down it to safety. Thus all six members of the Italian crew aboard the cabin were rescued.

When daybreak came, Patrolmen Fish and Cook caught sight of a boy hiding from them in the beach plum bushes along shore. The lad fled at their approach, but as soon as they called to him the boy gave himself up and embraced them. The Italian lad had been afraid that they would kill him, he told them, as he had heard that was the way all ship-wrecked mariners were treated on Cape Cod. Asked where he had received such information, he admitted other members of the crew had told him that such a fate awaited unlucky mariners wrecked there. The lad claimed that he had reached shore by swimming in from the wreck, but the surfmen decided that this was impossible because of the giant waves, and concluded he had drifted in on wreckage.

With the coming of the sun, the area was scanned for signs of the *Tabor,* but except for a few tangled masses of sails, spars, and rigging lying far off the beach, the bark had vanished. More surprises were to follow, however. At 9:00 a Race Point patrolman discovered the body of Captain Genero, and was amazed to find the captain's throat cut from ear to ear. Nearby was found the body of one of his crew, Seaman Biagio, also lying with his throat cut. A half mile away the remains of Steward Olivari washed up on the beach, a bullet hole through his head! The strange discovery of the three men led the surfmen to suspect foul play, but later the other crew members told the ghastly account. It was a queer story. When the *Tabor* grounded for the final time out on the bar, Captain Genero embraced and fervently kissed every member of the crew, and leaving them atop the cabin, descended into it and cut his own throat. The cabin boy Raffaele looked below a moment later and saw Seaman Biagio following suit. Just then the top of the cabin broke loose and the crew floated ashore. It was not known how or why Steward Olivari shot himself, but probably his death occurred at about the same time and for the same reason. He was unable to stand the disgrace of being shipwrecked aboard an Italian vessel.

Thus, of the twelve persons known to be aboard the *Monte Tabor,* six were rescued, one arrived on the beach unaided, three committed sui-cide, and the bodies of the other two were never found. All in all, it was a weird shipwreck, combining suicide, drowning, rescue, and fear of death from the natives.

Lieutenant Frank H. Newcomb, investigating officer, announced later that Captain Genero could have easily avoided his fate had he "used the sounding lead and heeded its warning. The Italian should have hauled offshore in time to avoid all danger." It is a good precaution for vessels which are near Race Point to stay outside of water less than twenty fathoms deep. Lieutenant Newcomb believed that nearly every disaster which this Cape Cod sandbar had caused could have been traced to a disregard of the principle of keeping in water twenty fathoms deep.

After swapping a few other stories with Keeper Hallett, I felt that I should push on toward my next objectives, Herring Cove and Snake Hill, so back I went along the beach and around the airport, crossing Snake Hill to come out on the beach at Herring Cove. It was here in 1886 that Professor George Washington Ready claimed to have seen the sea serpent. By sea serpent I do not mean a typical sea snake, fifty to seventy feet long, as has often been seen at Nahant and Gloucester in the last century, but another creature altogether. Regardless of what others may think, the story as it unfolds seems so fantastic to me as to be unbelievable. It is a sea serpent story to top all sea serpent stories, and should have qualified Professor Ready for membership in any tall story club.

After taking a final look at Herring Cove, I struck inland for Pasture Pond which figures in the sea serpent story. Pasture Pond is the most northwesterly pond on all Cape Cod, having Clapp's Round Pond on the south and Great Pond on the northeast. Sitting down on the edge of Pasture Pond, I pulled out my notes taken from an article which had been originally published in the *Cape Cod Item*. They included some of the strangest statements ever made by an inhabitant of Cape Cod.

One day in 1886 as Professor Ready was walking from Provincetown to the Outer Beach, he crossed a sand dune. Looking over at Herring Cove, he saw a disturbance in the water half a mile from the beach. Spray shot up fifty feet, while the water churned like a whirlpool. Then a huge head appeared above the surface, and pointed for the shore. We read that

> *the head was as large as a two hundred gallon cask, concave on the under side and convex on the upper. Mr. Ready saw the creature coming towards the shore and secreted himself in a clump of beach*

plum bushes, where he got a good view of the monster. The creature swam to the shore with a slow and undulating motion and passed within about thirty feet of where Mr. Ready was secreted. It was about three hundred feet long, and in the thickest part, which was about the middle, he judged as it passed him to be about twelve feet in diameter. The body was covered with scales as large as the head of a fish barrel, and were colored alternately green, red, and blue. They did not overlap each other, but seemed as if they were joined together by a ligature some four inches broad. The most curious feature was the head. The open mouth disclosed four rows of teeth, which glistened like polished ivory, and were at least two feet long, while on the extreme end of the head or nose, extended a tusk or horn at least eight feet in length. The creature had six eyes as large as good-sized dinner plates, and they were, at least, three feet from the head. In the creatures moving along these projections were continually on the move so that the reptile could see before, behind and sideways at the same time. Three of the eyes were of a fiery red hue, while the others were of pale green.

Other news about the serpent noted in the *Cape Cod Item* included mention of a strong sulphurous odor, intense heat which scorched the bushes and grass, and a tail with a sharp cutting edge which sheared off pine and oak trees nearly "one foot in diameter." Ready said that the sea monster headed at once for Pasture Pond, where it submerged, and then the water in the pond disappeared until only an area twenty feet across in the center was left. Ready claimed that men of Provincetown tried to hit bottom in the pond later, but sounding leads 250 fathoms down still did not touch bottom. "Preparations are being made to investigate the matter, and thousands are going to see and examine the track of the huge sea monster." Evidently Professor Ready expected that his statement might be doubted for he prepared an affidavit for all to read:

> *I, George Washington Ready, do testify that the foregoing statement is correct. It is a true description of the serpent as he appeared to me on that morning, and I was not unduly excited by liquor or otherwise.*
> *George W. Ready*

George Washington, who, it is said, could not tell a lie, undoubtedly would have been interested in this Cape Codder who was named for him. Herman A. Jennings published the entire account of Ready and the sea serpent in his Provincetown volume of 1890, and then adds, possibly as an afterthought, "Note, Mr. Ready resides at the head of Pearl Street in this place, and can be interviewed on the subject at any time." The strange Professor Ready died in 1920 at the advanced age of eighty-eight, but he had been able to convince few Cape Codders in the intervening thirty-four years that he had seen the monster. Thus passed a Provincetown character. A traveler of note in his younger days, he had been all over the world, and a "good many other places besides."

Returning to the Outer Beach, I decided to have a swim in spite of the cold water. I undressed on the beach and ran into the waves at top speed, the only way to get into cold water. A few minutes later I was swimming over my head, and as I looked back from time to time the pile of my belongings on the beach grew smaller and smaller. Finally, I had had enough, and swam back to shore, where I raced up and down the beach to dry off. Then I tried my skill at the standing broad jump. Some years before I had leaped more than ten feet in this event, but my meager efforts of little more than nine feet showed me that I was definitely growing old.

Dry and sun-warmed, I dressed rapidly and was soon nearing the Coast Guard station. But dead ahead was something which gave me a definite thrill—a huge timber buried in the sand. Hiking rapidly toward it, I discovered that it was all that remained of the old rumrunner *Spindler*, wrecked in 1922. Since that time hundreds of boys and girls had "played pirate" around this veteran wreck, and scores of picnics had been enjoyed here. Almost every visitor to Race Point in recent years had climbed over the *Spindler*. But after she had weathered twenty-four consecutive winters a few score yards from the Race Point Coast Guard Station, the great Gale of 1945, which began November 29, lifted the *Spindler* off the beach, smashed her to pieces, and gouged out the beach ten feet deep.

Glancing up the high, sandy bank, I saw the head and shoulders of a man who was peering down at me. It was my old friend Manuel Henrique, and I called to him.

"The last winter has done quite a job, hasn't it?" I asked him.

"Yes, we had quite a time down here," was his reply. "But I'm out of the service now. Come on in and meet the fellows." We were soon inside the big, roomy Coast Guard station at Race Point sitting down to coffee.

"By the way," I began, "is there anyone here who knows the whole story of the *Spindler*? I have heard so many different tales that I would like to get it straight. What did happen?"

"I wasn't here when it happened," said Henrique, "but there is someone coming over in an hour or so who was in on the whole affair, only I know he won't let you use his name."

An hour later I was anxiously awaiting the arrival of this man of mystery. He came in an old battered car, and after introductions were over, he told me what I wanted to know. But I had to promise that I would not reveal his name or his connection with the proceedings.

The part of the story which he has allowed me to reveal began on the night of December 29, 1922. During a severe northeaster the rumrunner *Annie L. Spindler*, with a rich and forbidden cargo of Haig and Haig whisky, piled up on the beach opposite the Race Point Coast Guard Station. There were about 600 cases of liquor aboard. Allegedly, the *Spindler* was running between Yarmouth, Nova Scotia, and Jamaica, but those "in the know" later said that her actual destination was near Plymouth, Massachusetts. At any rate, she never did reach port.

Her captain, a small but capable French-Canadian, later told how it happened. The *Spindler* had been caught off the Race by the northeast storm. When the captain tried to square away in an attempt to get inside the arm of the Cape, he couldn't make it, and was forced to take a chance on getting ashore. Soon the *Spindler* grounded, each wave carrying her a little farther up on the beach. The crew reached shore safely, and reported with their captain to the Race Point Coast Guard Station, a few score yards from where they had hit.

All was not lost, however. The captain of the *Spindler* told his story of how he had been caught off the twelve-mile limit by the storm and hurled against Cape Cod. Meanwhile the thirsty inhabitants of Provincetown had already got wind of the disaster, and even then were raiding the *Spindler*. This enraged the captain, who rushed out of the Coast Guard quarters and threw two of the "mooncussers" off the vessel and down on the sand. There was no more looting that night. The next day the Coast Guard ordered every remaining case of liquor stored in the cellar of the station, where it was placed under guard.

The following week another Nova Scotia craft entered Provincetown Harbor. Hailing also from Yarmouth, her captain drove out to Race Point, showed his credentials, and asked that the government help him load the liquor aboard his vessel. All available trucks and men (some of them actually taken off their patrol against rumrunners) were assembled, and

The Spindler, *the morning after she came ashore*

within a few days the entire shipload of liquor was transported across the Cape and loaded aboard the Yarmouth schooner tied up at Railroad Wharf. Then the Nova Scotia captain bade the residents of Provincetown farewell, and sailed for an alleged port in the West Indies. My good friend, who prefers that I do not mention his name, tells me that the cargo was landed that same night, not in the West Indies, but in a port northwest of Provincetown, also mentioned in connection with the landing of the Pilgrims.

"Well, I've told more than I intended," my informant suddenly announced, and with a flourish jumped up from the mess hall table and was out the door. Before we could stop him he was in his dilapidated old car chugging down the road. Perhaps his conscience had suddenly started to bother him; it is possible that he feared later repercussions. At any rate I never saw him again.

"What about that other and more famous wreck, the British man-of-war *Somerset*? Do you see her now and then?" I asked the keeper.

"Well, yes and no," was the surprising answer. "So many people think that it is an easy matter to identify the *Somerset*, but nothing could be harder. All we have to go by is hearsay. After certain storms it does

The remains of the Spindler *in 1945 (photo by Edward Rowe Snow)*

seem that her broken timbers show up for a time, but then the tides wash in and she vanishes again before the experts can arrive here. The last time the *Somerset*, which was wrecked near here in 1778, came out of the sand and stayed out for any length of time was back in 1886, and that is sixty years ago. There are few who saw her then who are still alive, and it is quite a responsibility to say, 'There is the *Somerset* again.' Over 3,000 shipwrecks have taken place at Cape Cod, and to tell which is which takes a clever man."

"I would like to have you walk out with me to the place where you think she is buried," I said. "I'd just like to stand there to say I've been on the location." Half an hour later we had reached that stretch of Cape Cod topography called Dead Man's Hollow, which has always been identified with the shipwreck of the mighty frigate *Somerset*. Many reports have come down through the years about this location. Scores of people have claimed that they have seen ghosts in the vicinity, ghosts of the British sailors lost with the *Somerset*.

We sat down on a log and reviewed the *Somerset*'s career. She was the same vessel mentioned by Henry Wadsworth Longfellow in his "Paul Revere's Ride," and in the early years of the Revolution she had her home port at Provincetown, much to the annoyance of the Cape Cod patriots. When in 1778 a violent storm caught Captain Ourry and the *Somerset* off the coast, Ourry tried to make Provincetown Harbor, but the treacherous seas off the Race caught this proud representative of the British Navy and cast her ashore on the dreaded Peaked Hill Bars. Scores of marines lost their lives as the vessel slid up over the bars and finally came to rest high and dry on the beach.

The people of Provincetown had been waiting. A young blacksmith, William Spenser, organized a small group of Cape Cod minutemen, and they surrounded the frigate. When the tide was dead low, Blacksmith Spenser went aboard and demanded that Captain Ourry surrender. The proud British captain bowed deeply, unbuckled his sword, and presented it to the blacksmith. It was one of the most unusual surrenders in the history of the British Navy. By this time the beach was crowded with people salvaging what they could from the cargo of the ship. Incidentally, goods valued at $150,000 were recovered.

There were now 480 prisoners from the *Somerset* waiting on the beach, and this unwieldy group was actually marched off in the direction of Boston, 120 miles away. By the time the prisoners arrived at Plymouth, however, the Cape Cod captors had tired of their duties as guards and many of them returned home. Others took up the unwelcome task, but great numbers of the British marines and sailors were left to walk unguarded to Boston, where they were soon put aboard a prison ship then lying in the harbor. Later on, some of those same British sailors enlisted in the American Navy.

The ship's surgeon, Dr. William Thayer, well known on the Cape, was allowed to stay in Provincetown. Visiting Truro, he fell in love with Susan Rich there, and shortly afterwards they were married. The couple settled in Truro and had four children, all girls, Anna, Phebe, Susan, and Rachel. Anna married Reuben Rich of Wellfleet, Phebe took as a husband Elisha Newcomb of Truro, Susan became the bride of Simon Hopkins of Wellfleet, while Rachel became an old maid. The descendants of the three married daughters of Dr. and Mrs. Thayer are now scattered all over New England.

After wandering around the vicinity where the *Somerset* was last seen in 1886, we returned to the Coast Guard station. There are many who remember the time in 1886 when the bones of the ship came out, but few are aware that she also appeared about six years before that, around 1880. At that time Captain Henry Cook of Provincetown had several timbers cut away from her. Then the sand covered her over again until the 1886 reappearance, which is so much better known.

A few minutes later I was writing my notes in a Commercial Street lodging house. After going to bed, I opened Thoreau's *Cape Cod* to read, but I felt sleepy and soon turned out the light, for I was to arise early the next day.

When the Provincetown Monument opened the following morning, I was waiting to climb it. It was on this same High Pole Hill that the residents of Provincetown stood as they watched the British frigate *Somerset* lose her fight with the breakers out on the Peaked Hill Bars. It was also on High Pole Hill that a windmill stood as a landmark for years, and probably before the windmill a high pole, the highest the men of Provincetown could obtain, was located there for the guidance of the fishermen at sea. The windmill stood on High Pole Hill for many years, for Timothy Dwight mentions it on his trip during the summer of 1810. When the mill was given up, the fishermen still desired a landmark there, and in 1854 a town hall was erected on the site of the windmill. It was the best landmark Provincetown enjoyed up to that time, with a tower which could be seen, it was said, from Minot's Light. Also employed as a school, the hall was used for town meetings about twice a year, but in 1877 a great fire destroyed this landmark.

Agitation had been growing for years for a proper recognition of the fact that Provincetown was the first landing place of the Pilgrims, but nothing had come of it. Now it was proposed that a Pilgrim Monument be erected on High Pole Hill, with a lofty shaft which could be seen all the way to the rival town, Plymouth. But the years went by, and again nothing seemed to come of it.

The residents of Provincetown were happily surprised one warm June day in 1906 to learn that President Theodore Roosevelt had approved a bill passed by Congress for the erection of a monument, higher than Bunker Hill Monument itself, on old High Pole Hill at Provincetown. The jubilation of the townspeople knew no bounds. At last their importance would be known to the world.

The same carriage which had taken President Grant and President Cleveland around Provincetown was ready for President Theodore Roosevelt when he arrived aboard his yacht *Mayflower* for the cornerstone ceremonies on August 20, 1907. Cy Young was a proud and happy driver as he guided the presidential carriage through the narrow streets on the way to High Pole Hill.

Provincetown's Pilgrim Monument (photo by Alton Hall Blackington)

Although it has usually been agreed that Theodore Roosevelt laid the cornerstone, this is not so. It was actually laid by the Masons of Massachusetts, in the presence of Roosevelt. Not quite three years later, on August 5, 1910, 290 years to the day after the Pilgrims sailed from Plymouth, England, the dedicatory exercises took place, Dr. Charles W. Eliot of Harvard giving the chief address, in the presence of President William H. Taft. The monument itself is 252 feet, 7 inches above High Pole Hill, making it at least 350 feet above the sea, so that it actually dominates every other building in the town. Flying down the coast, one can see it almost as soon as he leaves Boston, and the *Steel Pier* picks it up half way across the bay. It is a structure of which all Cape Codders are truly proud.

For those of you who have climbed Bunker Hill Monument, the Provincetown Monument, although higher, will give you a pleasant surprise, with its gradually inclined ramps and easy resting platforms. And the inscriptions on the blocks of stone set in various places will interest you as you ascend. It probably took me ten minutes longer than I had figured that April morning, because I stopped and examined each of the inscribed blocks.

Finally I reached the highest accessible part of the outstanding landmark. It seemed to me the ideal location to read over Bradford's *Of Plymouth Plantation,* for I had the great tower all to myself. A word about the original manuscript of the book is in order. Quite a long while after the Pilgrims reached America, Governor William Bradford undertook the task of writing this precious history which forms the most important link between the Pilgrims and modern times. It is the story of the Plymouth Colony from its very beginnings to 1647. The volume disappeared from America at the outbreak of the Revolution, and there are those who believe it was taken by Governor Hutchinson when he fled Boston at that time. In 1844 Bradford's work was discovered by Samuel Wilberforce in the library of Fulham Palace, London. Charles Deane, learning of the discovery, communicated at once with Joseph Hunter in England, and after many years of lengthy negotiations the original manuscript was brought back across the ocean in 1897 to America, where the book was written. Making myself comfortable, I opened the copy of the 1928 edition of this unusual book. Of course, I was also historically fortified with a modern edition of that other Pilgrim classic, *Mourt's Relation,* so I felt able to recreate in my mind almost any situation which the authors might mention.

Opening the heavy Bradford volume, I turned to page 3, and began to read. To be honest, page after page didn't interest me too much. There were accounts of the religious history of England, and the journey of the Pilgrims over to Holland. My interest returned when I read of the Pilgrims setting sail in the *Mayflower* on her successful voyage. Page 93 gave me a strange thrill.

> *But to omite other things (that I may be breefe) after longe beating at sea they fell in with that land which is called Cape Cod; the which being made & certainly knowne it be it, they were not a little joyfull. After some deliberation had amongst them selves & with ye mr. of ye ship, they tacked aboute and resolved to stance for ye southward (ye wind & washer being faire) to find some place aboute Husons river for their habitation. But after they sailed ye course about halfe ye day, they fell amongst deangerous shoulds and roring breakers, and they were so farr intangled ther with as they conceived themselves in great danger.*

I could see the whole drama unfold itself before my eyes, the sturdy little *Mayflower* making a landfall probably somewhere near Pamet River, the happiness aboard which is always present whenever a vessel sights land, and then the disappointment when the dreaded Pollock Rip prevented further progress to the southward. I read on:

> *& ye wind shrinking upon them withall they resolved to bear up again for the Cape, and thought them selves hapy to get out of those dangers before night overtooke them, and by Gods providence they did. And ye next day they gott into ye Cape-harbor wher they ridd in saftie. A word or twoo by ye way of this cape; it was thus first named by Capten Gosnole & his company, (Because yey tooke much of yt fishe ther). Ano: 1602, and after by Capten Smith was caled Cape James; but it retains ye former name amongst seamen. Also yt pointe which first shewed those dangerous shoulds unto them, they called Pointe Care, & Tuckers Terrour; but ye French & Dutch to this day call it Malabarr, by reason of those perilous shoulds, and ye losses they have suffered their.*

Having watched the Pilgrims rattle their anchor down in what is now Provincetown Harbor, I got up and stretched for a while. Outside the sun was still steadily climbing in the eastern skies, while a few soft fluffy clouds, the delight of all photographers, glided by in seemingly effortless motion, pushed along by the gentlest of winds. It was a perfect spring day.

Returning to the story of the Pilgrims, I found that they had spent the following day, Sunday, November 12, aboard ship in worship and prayer, but early the next morning, America's first washday, the women and children were put ashore. The entire group frolicked on the beach at first in happiness. Then the women set to work in earnest, and soon they were scrubbing and beating huge piles of clothing and bedding which they had brought across the Atlantic with them. For safety the men stood guard nearby. I could see the site from where I sat reading, an area between the Wharf Theatre and the place where Atlantic Avenue meets the water. While the washing was going on, the men brought ashore the shallop for repairs, as they wished to explore the coast. Meanwhile plans were made for an overland expedition, and volunteers were called for. I was pleased to read the name of my own great-great-great-great-great-great-great-grandfather, Stephen Hopkins, in the list of sixteen who volunteered, and doubly happy to find he was chosen among the four leaders, the others being Myles Standish, Edward Tilley, and William Bradford himself. I could picture this expedition as it set out along the great beach, ready to explore the unknown. All the men wore their heavy armor and were well prepared to meet hostile natives.

Continuing along the sand, they fell in with a party of Indians, who vanished into the woods. This excited the curiosity of ancestor Hopkins and his fifteen companions, and they foolishly plunged into the woods after the red men. Luckily, they ran into no danger. Several miles later they came out of the woods to find a clearing near the beach, where the Pilgrims located a sandy hill, in the back of which was a meadow. Digging into one of the heaps of sand there, they uncovered an Indian corn cache. Without further thought, they pilfered the cache of as much corn as they could carry, and then reburied the rest. In spite of the ignominy of their theft, it was lucky for them that they did steal the Indians' food, for otherwise they would not have been able to plant corn the next spring.

Their second expedition was even more interesting. Ten days later another group set out, this time in the shallop. Reaching Truro, they explored along the coast until they arrived at the Pamet River. In their estimation it was merely a tidal estuary, so they decided it was no place for a settlement. They then went over to the meadow where they had taken the corn, and removed all of the remaining corn. While digging up the rest of the corn, "some others found another heap of corn, which they digged up also," thus compounding their felony.

It was then that they made an unusual discovery The next day they found the skeleton of a child and that of a man, who had fine yellow hair still on his skull, and part of the flesh remaining. In the grave were fragments of a man's clothing and a knife, needle, and several other articles. The Pilgrims also found an Indian settlement in the vicinity, and this made many wish to colonize at this location. But the majority voted against the idea, and Truro just missed becoming the Plymouth of America.

Then, as everyone knows, the Pilgrims sailed across the bay and explored Plymouth Harbor and Clarke's Island, and their connection with Provincetown and Truro practically ends. But Plymouth cannot, no matter how she tries, take away from Provincetown the honor of being the first place which we can truthfully call the location where the Pilgrims first landed.

When the first permanent settlers of Provincetown came to the tip of the Cape they made their homes up along and down along the beach. Few chose to live back from the beach in the sand dunes and hills they called "up-back." Down through the years the old names have clung, and even today if you go to the westward on Commercial Street your direction will be "up-along." If you journey eastward it will be "down-along." Should your travels carry you as far as Gull Hill you will be going "way-up-along," and a correspondingly lengthy trip westerly is called "way-down-along."

Sitting there in the tower, I thought of some of the vessels which had plied between Boston and Provincetown through the years. Those steamers and packets which are names of the past include *Yankee Clipper, Romance, Governor Cobb, Dorothy Bradford, Cape Cod, New Brunswick, Longfellow, George Shattuck, Naushon, Acorn, Express, Olata, Northern Light,* and *Truth.*

Climbing down from the tower I headed across to Commercial Street and indulged in a chocolate frappe at the drug store. After visiting Paul George Lambert at the *Provincetown Advocate* office, I walked along to call in and say hello to John Fisher Rosenthal of the Mayflower Shop. Rosenthal was named Fisher for Reverend Caleb Fisher of Lowell, and his father, Irving Rosenthal, was a well-known photographer and sheriff of Barnstable County. Many fine pictures of shipwrecks are still preserved by the son.

The old excursion steamer *Longfellow*, which carried so many happy summer tourists to Provincetown from Boston, figured in a strange shipwreck in the year 1904. I have never included the disaster which befell the *Longfellow* in any of my previous books, and consequently several years ago S. Osborne Ball of Provincetown wrote to me about the shipwreck. He told me so much about it that I decided if I should ever write the story of the *Longfellow*, S. Osborne Ball was the man to interview.

Going to Mr. Ball's Provincetown office, I found him deep in legal matters.

"I have come to hear the story of the steamer *Longfellow*," I began. "I'm Ed Snow, the fellow you wrote to about the disaster."

"Oh, yes," Mr. Ball answered, "you left out one of the best stories of all from your shipwreck book, didn't you?"

I agreed, but explained that he hadn't written to me until two years after the book had been published, so there wasn't much I could do about it then. "That's why I'm here today—to get your story," I said.

"Well," began Mr. Ball, "I don't know much more than what I wrote to you. The *Longfellow* was a small, single screw vessel, probably about five hundred tons smaller than the excursion boat *Steel Pier*. Built back in the seventies, she had finally been retired from the tourist trade to transport a load of dynamite to Portsmouth, New Hampshire. But the *Longfellow* ran into one of the early fall northeasters soon after leaving Wilmington, Delaware, and the storm so loosened her seams that she started to leak when off Orleans.

"The storm increased in intensity, and the leak grew worse. There the crew was, carrying a cargo of 300 tons of dynamite aboard a leaking vessel which they could not beach for fear of an explosion. The easterly blow was steadily getting worse, with the wind then hitting about thirty to forty miles an hour. She was pitching and rolling, and the *Longfellow* might take a lurch any time which would tumble the cargo around and blow them all up."

"When did they think of taking to their boats?" I queried.

"Well, about the time the *Longfellow* reached a point off our summer home at Ballston Heights, the crew were so frightened that they decided they could never keep her afloat as the water was gaining rapidly. They launched two lifeboats into the high waves then rolling ashore, and started to make for the beach. Back on the shore the life-savers from both the Pamet River and Highland Stations were waiting for them, and lit Coston flares to warn them against attempting a landing, for the breakers were much too high. I remember that Surfman Ben Paine was the first to light his Coston flare that night.

"By waving lanterns and shouting, the lifesavers indicated to the ship-wrecked mariners that they should row toward the south. The Highland crew paced the two lifeboats along the beach until they reached the halfway house, at which place they turned the task over to members from the Pamet River crew, who continued to guide the lifeboats along the shore.

"At dawn one of the lifeboats started for the beach but capsized, and the lifesavers quickly launched their boat to rescue the floundering seamen. Surfman James Morris was among those who saved the sailors, and he told me later that there were some very narrow escapes before the last man was pulled to safety."

"Did the other lifeboat also attempt to make a landing?" was my question.

"No, I guess that what they saw happen to the first lifeboat was enough for them. They waited until the Highland crew launched their surfboat and rowed over to take the second boat of the *Longfellow* in tow. Rowing steadily, the Highland crew pulled the shipwrecked men to the westward. Then the members of the High Head Station launched their boat, and joined in towing. Reaching the bar and passing it in safety, the lifesavers brought all three boats in on the relatively calm beach."

I remembered from the official report I had read at Washington that the sixteen shipwrecked men were all given fresh clothing and supplies which were on hand for just such an emergency. These comforts were furnished by the Women's National Relief Association, an organization which devoted itself to the aid of all shipwrecked mariners.

I was yet to hear Osborne Ball tell of the aftermath of the *Longfellow*'s sinking, and waited while he checked a few items in his record book. Then he looked up with a smile.

"I just wanted to make sure when it did happen, but now I have it," he continued. "The following December during a southeast gale there was a terrific explosion off the Ballston Beach. For a moment we wondered what it was and then we all realized what had happened. The *Longfellow* had been pulled off the ledge by the gale and had blown up in some inexplicable way. We went down on the shore shortly afterwards and found dead fish piled up two and a half feet high! The earthquake seismographs all recorded the explosion!"

"Did much material come ashore that you could salvage?" I asked.

"Oh, yes, but we missed the best souvenir, the pennant of the *Longfellow*. Jim Morris's sister Carrie dove into the surf and brought it up. We boys had ignored it, for we were afraid it might be a corpse. Then there were chairs, empty dynamite boxes, kerosene drums, and stateroom doors. We still have the stateroom doors on our cottage."

"I have quite a few other souvenirs out at the cottage," said Mr. Ball. "There is a flagstaff made from two wrecks. The mainmast is off the barge *Oakland*, from which two men drowned, and the topmast from the yawl *Sleepy Girl*, wrecked because a Harvard professor fell asleep. That was an odd wreck. Sailing from Marblehead to Woods Hole, the lone mariner fell sound asleep and the craft sailed and luffed twenty-five miles without human guidance to tear into the breakers at Pamet River. Yes, the professor awakened in time to leap to safety from his appropriately named *Sleepy Girl*."

I expressed my gratitude to Lawyer Ball for his interesting stories, and asked him if he could direct me to Chip Hill, where some interesting ruins had been found during the middle of the nineteenth century.

At least fifty localities up and down the New England coast claim for their own the romantic legends of the Norsemen. Though I run the risk of offending those who believe these legends, I hereby state that there is no authoritative proof that the Norsemen landed at even one of these many places. We can imagine that the tip of the Cape at Provincetown, jutting out as it does into the ocean, would have attracted the Norsemen if they really reached the vicinity. This supposition has led many people to try to find some connection between the Norsemen and the ruins of a strange wall found on Chip Hill during the middle of the nineteenth century.

Much has been made of these ruins. In 1805 Chip Hill had been cut down twenty-five feet when salt works were built there. As salt was mined commercially in New York State a short time later, the local works could not compete, and one by one they went out of business. In 1853 a house for Francis A. Paine was built on the hill where the salt works had been. While the cellar was being dug, the workmen came across a red wall, and were surprised to find that the mortar for the wall contained fish bones, and the stones were blackened by fire. When the house was repaired in 1895, another view of the wall was possible. Nothing could be found in the entire history of Provincetown to explain the wall, so when the known history was exhausted, attempts were made to associate the discovery with the ancient Norsemen, about whom so little is actually known. And that is about all it has amounted to. It is said that the wall probably was built from the ballast taken ashore from Leif Ericsson's vessel and left there to build a fort against the natives. Trying to prove this assertion is another matter. The wall has various titles, with the Norsemen's Fireplace and the Norsemen's Fort the most popular.

Definitely interested in the wall itself, I decided to walk down Front Street until I recognized Tremont Street, and there at the corner of Tremont and Cottage Streets I found the object of my search, the Norse Wall Cottage at Chip Hill. Francis E. Rogers and his wife, Eugenia, now own the building. Rogers is one of Provincetown's mail clerks, and I was anxious to ask him questions about the house.

"I wonder if I could see your famous Norse Wall," I began.

"No, you can't," was the answer. "The wall is now under cement, and cannot be seen at all. About ten years ago a group of M.I.T. men came down and began digging around to uncover the ancient relic, but it seemed as though the house might collapse, and so they gave it up. The cellar was cemented over at the same time, and the remains of the wall are under the cement."

"Did any Harvard men ever explore the ruins of the wall?" I inquired.

"Why, yes, about 1900 there were some Harvard scientists who came down here and wanted to examine the wall. All they had to promise was that they would put the wall back, just as they had found it, but that didn't seem to interest them, so they had to return to Cambridge without getting anywhere."

"What do you think the wall really is?" I asked.

"It is all up in the air as far as I am concerned," said Francis E. Rogers. "Anyone can guess, but no one knows." With the sensible comments of Postal Clerk Rogers in my thoughts, I bade him farewell and returned to Commercial Street. As I walked, there came to my mind the Icelandic sagas of almost a thousand years ago, when Thorfinn Karlsefni, Leif Ericsson, and Thorwald roamed the New World. It would be interesting to know definitely whether Kjalarnes, and the land of Furdurstrandir, the great sandy beaches of their stories, really were located at Cape Cod. We shall never know for certain, however, one way or another.

Although artists are not present in Provincetown in large numbers until later in the summer, I was able to visit several studios during my stay there. It is said that summertime Provincetown now has one of the largest art centers in the United States, although it was not until 1900 or so that the devotees of the brush and palette really discovered that the end of the Cape was ideal for their requirements. Perhaps a brief history of the movement would not be amiss at this time. The early artists include Halsall, the marine expert, Marcus Waterman, who came to Provincetown to use the sand in a painting of the Sahara Desert, and Charles W. Hawthorne, who in 1901 opened his art school. In 1914 Mrs. John Herring was the guiding light in the organization of an Art Circle. Hawthorne, however, remained the dominant figure in Provincetown art history. Although he died some years ago, there are many stories and legends still told about this great man's methods of dealing with his pupils.

Hawthorne, a stern taskmaster, despised the so-called pretty-pretty school of painting. He had seen many of his promising students attempt to paint Highland Light and the results to him were always disappointing, for they seemed to get into that particular style which he detested. He was unusually caustic when he detected that his best student had fallen by the wayside to attempt the impossible according to his ideals—a good painting of Highland Light.

Jeremiah Digges tells us that one day Hawthorne was particularly sarcastic in his criticisms toward the students. Going from canvas to canvas, he broke the heart of one student after another, ridiculing the efforts of everyone. Finally he reached the painting of one of his most promising students, who, unfortunately, had chosen that particular day to show Hawthorne his painting of Highland Light, done in the detested "pretty-pretty" style. Hawthorne stood in front of the canvas for a full minute. Then he stepped back, and announced that he was thinking of an appropriate title for the masterpiece so that it would be fully appreciated when hung in the Metropolitan Museum. Suddenly opening his arms as if to embrace the canvas, he cried, "I think I've hit on a good name—'Papa kiss Mamma.'"

In spite of his eccentricities, it is safe to say that Provincetown art would not be where it is today were it not for Charles Hawthorne's efforts.

In recent years there seems to be harmony between the many schools of artistic thought at Provincetown, but for a time around 1935 open dissension was in evidence, the modern school scorning the academic school to such an extent that two separate exhibitions were necessary. Let us hope that the Provincetown Art Association, which has its building at 460 Commercial Street, will continue to operate as a united group for many years to come.

The annual Artists' Ball is one of the peak attractions which close the busy summer of painting activity. Without question, it is well worth a trip to Provincetown and return just for the chance to see this great festival. Incidentally, there is something about the familiar and picturesque figure of a middle-aged man or woman sitting relaxed in front of an easel, which has always made me wonder whether they became artists because of the opportunity to enjoy the scenery or were enjoying the scenery because they were artists.

One of the truly admirable figures living in Provincetown today is Donald B. MacMillan, whose home is at 473 Commercial Street. Anthropologist and arctic explorer, MacMillan is a great scientist. He is one of the best known authorities on the North Pole regions. Born in Provincetown in 1874, he went to sea at an early age with his grandfather, attended Bowdoin College, and was a teacher for several years at Worcester Academy. MacMillan attracted the attention of Admiral Peary by rescuing a group of young people in Casco Bay, where Peary summered. Because of the rescue, Peary and MacMillan met, and from that time on MacMillan developed an intense interest in the northern regions of the world.

His trip of 1913 lasted four years, and it has been said that no other explorer ever equaled this journey in length of time spent in the frozen North. One of the most unusual events of his life took place aboard his ship *Bowdoin*, where in the presence of an amazed group of Eskimos, a special program was given. MacMillan has told me that the Christmas program of 1923, when because of his efforts the Eskimos were able to enjoy the radio, phonograph, and movies, affected him as have few other episodes of his strenuously active life.

Provincetown should well be proud of her great son, Donald B. MacMillan. As I visited the place of his birth he was even then preparing to journey north on another expedition to continue his chosen work, exploring the Land of the Midnight Sun.

As MacMillan has placed many of his priceless relics in the Historical Museum on Commercial Street, that was my next objective. After visiting the first and second floors, I started for the top of the museum. In spite of previous visits, I am always startled when I reach the third floor of the museum, for at the top of the stairs is a stuffed polar bear which seems to be waiting for his next victim. As you reach the landing it is quite a shock to discover him standing there seemingly alive and ready for you. I like to look at the brant's nest and eggs which MacMillan brought back from his northern travels. Then there is an extremely rare white wolf and a walrus head.

In other parts of the museum I enjoyed seeing again the Bible from the *Somerset*, a chair made from the ship's wreckage, and a cannon from the War of 1812. Women visitors, of course, are interested in the ancient dolls, the dresses of our grandmothers, and the samplers of a century ago. The town crier's bell, a pearl shell carving of the Last Supper, a collection of Sandwich glass, and Admiral Dewey's pewter teapot comprise another series of exhibits I viewed before leaving the museum.

Passing the theater on my journey along the street, I thought of the many great playwrights who have done part of their creative work around Provincetown. Wilbur Daniel Steele, George Cram Cook, John Dos Passos, Mary Heaton Vorse, and Susan Glaspell are a few of the important names. Probably the best known of them all is Eugene O'Neill, who came to Cape Cod and lived for some time in the battered remains of an old hulk out on Truro Beach. His first New York play was given by the Provincetown Players in New York during November 1917, and was based on the story of a Provincetown whaler whose wife went out of her mind in the frozen north. The Players, organized in 1915, included many great names of stage and screen. It was George Cram Cook who was the guiding genius of the movement.

Eugene O'Neill is still seen from time to time at Provincetown. Some years ago he moved out beyond the reach of the hero worshippers by taking over and refitting the old Peaked Hill Bars Coast Guard Station, where he lived in the relative security which three miles of soft, deep sand offers. But he had not reckoned with the ocean, for in the great storm of March 4, 1931, still remembered for its ruthless destruction up and down the Massachusetts coast, the old Coast Guard station toppled over the bank and quickly went to pieces.

As I walked the sands one afternoon, I came across a sticky substance washed up by the waves, which seemed to weigh fourteen or fifteen pounds. It interested me strangely, and after I had gone ten or twelve miles up the Cape I began to wonder whether or not it might have been ambergris. It was just a little too heavy to carry it all the way up the Cape, so I shall never know just what it was. But the chances, I have since been told, were very much against the object's being ambergris which does not usually float. Ambergris is worth twice as much as gold, pound for pound.

Provincetown has long been a center for ambergris activities, thanks to the business done there by a man who for many years was known as the Ambergris King of America, David Stull. The whalers and fishermen would bring their ambergris from all New England and the South to Provincetown, where King Stull would value it, pay the finders, and ship the ambergris across the ocean to far-away Paris to be made into a base for perfumes. The whalers usually found the precious substance in hard bunches in the whale's intestines, secreted there because of something the whale ate. Cutting away the dark, chocolate-colored mass, they carried the not-unpleasant-smelling material at their earliest opportunity to David Stull at Provincetown, and received their reward. The record catch is said to have been brought in around three quarters of a century ago by a Nantucket captain whose 900-pound find was worth $125,000.

David Stull died in 1925, but long before he passed away the ambergris business had slackened, as the whalers gave up their professions one by one and took up other, more profitable occupations. Specimens of the material are still preserved at Provincetown, and it is said that David Stull left an unusual collection of it to his daughter when he died.

I decided to rest from the hike. Finding a huge log, I sat down with my back against it, and pulled from the knapsack two books written by Thoreau and Drake. Henry David Thoreau and Samuel Adams Drake, two outstanding writers of their day, visited Provincetown, Thoreau for the first time in 1849 and Drake about a quarter century later. Thoreau hiked over to a fish house at Provincetown one morning, and was fascinated by the method of drying the fish. Three or four men were engaged in "trundling" out pickled fish on barrows and spreading them to dry. A vessel had lately arrived from the Banks with 44,000 cod aboard, which recalled to Thoreau a visit of Timothy Dwight to Provincetown some years before, when 56,000 fish had been brought into town aboard a schooner whose main deck was eight inches under water.

Thoreau's attention was taken by the men standing on the fish, just removed from the pickle, pitching them out with an instrument which had "a single iron point." One tobacco-chewing boy spat repeatedly on the fish. Thoreau thought that the boss would speak to the boy when he noticed what was going on, but presently the boss followed suit. Thoreau soon walked across to the hotel for breakfast, where he was given a choice of dried fish hash or beans. "I took beans," said Thoreau, "though they were never a favorite dish of mine."

Thoreau remarked on the fact that the further inland you travel, the more the potato predominates in the fish hash. He also noticed that no fresh meat was slaughtered in Provincetown in 1849, and the Boston steamer brought the only meat to reach town.

Many of the houses in Thoreau's Provincetown were surrounded by fish flakes close up to the sills on all sides, with a narrow passage less than three feet wide to the front door, so that instead of looking out on a flower garden, you glanced through the window to see rows and rows of codfish drying in the sun.

Provincetown itself impressed the famous writer as a flourishing town, and some of the residents asked him if he didn't think they were prosperous. He agreed, and later went to visit a native by special invitation. Finding the inhabitant awaiting him in his front doorway, Thoreau was taken aback by a gigantic circular cobweb which guarded the gateway, and so he went all around the house to enter. Thoreau's rambles about the Provincetown area were many. One Monday morning he walked out to Shank Painter Swamp, where he found a high sand dune. He kept glancing off in the direction of Wellfleet, where the first appearance of the steamer could be noticed. Philosopher Thoreau mentioned the wonderful ability of the Provincetown inhabitants to notice ships at sea. One day, while at Highland Light he wondered aloud if the Boston yacht *Olata* had entered Provincetown Harbor, some seven miles away, when a ten-year-old Provincetown lad who had overheard him announced that he had just recognized the *Olata* sailing into Provincetown at that very moment. Let us read his account:

This was the very day one would have chosen to sit upon a hill overlooking sea and land, and muse there. The mackerel fleet was rapidly taking its departure, one schooner after another, and standing round the Cape, like fowls leaving their roosts in the morning to disperse themselves in distant fields. The turtle-like sheds of the saltworks were crowded into every nook in the hills, immediately behind the town, and their now idle wind-mills lined the shore. It was worth the while to see by what course and simple chemistry this almost necessary of life is obtained, with the sun for journeyman, and a single apprentice to do the chores for a large establishment. It is a sort of

> *tropical labor, pursued too, in the sunniest season; more interesting than gold or diamondwashing, which, I fancy, it somewhat resembles at a distance. . . .*
>
> *From that elevation we could overlook the operations of the inhabitants almost as completely as if the roofs had been taken off.*

Thoreau was told that as almost no fresh water emptied into Provincetown Harbor, it was practically the best place in the world to locate saltworks. But he noticed that the works were all being torn down and the lumber sold for what it could bring. It was another great Cape industry lost "on the rocks of discovery," for new salt mines had been found elsewhere which were much cheaper to operate.

Thoreau's remarks about the sand getting into his shoes should interest all those who have walked a beach. Believe it or not, there is a certain knack about walking in the sand (though I never attempted to master it) whereby you can hike almost ankle deep in sand even in slippers without discomfort. A certain Provincetown gentleman announced that he walked in sand all day long and scarcely had six grains of sand in his shoes when he took them off at night. The girls and women also are experts in the art of sand walking, having a peculiar movement with each step which empties their shoes as they walk along.

The sand made its conquests on the buildings, however. In former times the houses were built on piles, to allow the sand to pass under them. One old abandoned schoolhouse was visited by Thoreau, who found the room filled with sand up to the tops of the desks.

Of course, with the modern improvements such as streets and automobiles, Provincetown residents are accustomed to watching vehicles go by, but it is said that not more than 100 years ago a boy well-versed in the ways of the sailor came ashore in Provincetown. A wagon passed him on the street.

"How can you steer so straight without a rudder?" was the question the perplexed sailor lad asked the amused driver, who promptly explained the method of horse propulsion to the astonished boy.

Three travelers—Timothy Dwight, Henry David Thoreau, and Samuel Adams Drake—have spoken of the great harbor of Provincetown. Dwight in 1810 called Provincetown the only harbor "on a windward shore within two hundred miles." Thoreau in 1849 said it was "deservedly famous," while Drake commented that the harbor was completely landlocked, with "good anchorage for vessels of the largest class."

The observations of Samuel Adams Drake are extremely interesting. Coming to Provincetown as he did a quarter century after Thoreau, Drake fills a vital place in Provincetown annals. His remarks follow:

> *Provincetown was originally part of Truro. Its etymology explains that its territory belonged to the province of Massachusetts. The earliest inhabitants had no other title than possession, and their conveyance is by quitclaim. For many years the place experienced the alternation of thrift and decay, being at times well-nigh deserted. In 1749, says Douglass, in his "Summary," the town consisted of only two or three settled families, two or three cows, and six to ten sheep. The houses formerly stood in one range, without regularity, along the beach, with the drying-flakes around them. Fishing vessels were run upon the soft sand, and their cargoes thrown into the water, where, after being washed free from salt, the fish were taken up and carried to the flakes in hand-barrows. Cape Cod Harbor, by which it is also familiar to the readers of Pilgrim chronicles, was the earliest name of Provincetown.*
>
> *There are two principal streets in Provincetown. One of, I should imagine, more than a mile in length, runs along the harbor; the other follows an elevated ridge of sand-hills, and is parallel with the first. A plank-walk is laid on one side of the avenue by the shore, the other side being occupied by stores, fish-houses, and wharves. No sinister meaning is attached to walking the plank in Provincetown; for what is the whole Cape if not a gangplank pushed out over the side of the continent?*

Thoreau and Drake give us the landlubber's report on Provincetown, but we have preserved for us a delightful account of a New England sea voyage by Robert Carter which includes a visit to Provincetown.

When Robert Carter sailed into Provincetown Harbor aboard his sloop, July 6, 1858, he was piloted by Captain Widger of Swampscott and accompanied by Francis W. Underwood (the first editor of the *Atlantic Monthly*) and Henry Ware. They anchored in Provincetown Harbor about 4 P.M. Carter called his comrades, Underwood and Ware, the Assyrian and the Professor. Ware took the dory and rowed over to a lobsterman, from whom he purchased twelve good-sized lobsters for three cents each. Recalling that Thoreau mentions the market for 1849 as being two cents a lobster, we can see that the cost of living by 1858 was slowly rising. I especially like the informal style of Robert Carter's

book, and since the volume is an exceedingly rare collector's item and
has been out of print for over eighty years, I will quote from it.

> *The Assyrian, who despised flounder-fishing, however big the floun-*
> *ders, said the heat made him thirsty, and that furthermore he never*
> *ventured to eat lobster unless he had previously fortified what he called*
> *his "atom-jack" by some preventive of colic or cholera-morbus. Accord-*
> *ingly, while we were getting ready our lines and bait, he persuaded the*
> *Skipper to row him ashore at the town, in order that he might quench*
> *his drouth with a cocktail, or something of the sort.*
>
> *When the dory returned, the Professor, the Artist, and I rowed to*
> *within a hundred yards of the shore, opposite the town, and dropped the*
> *boat's killock in deep water. We had strong codlines, with two large*
> *hooks each, which we baited with pieces of lobster—a very difficult bait*
> *to keep on. The lines hardly reached bottom before the flounders began*
> *to bite so rapidly that they kept us actively employed in putting on bait,*
> *they took it off so easily. Nevertheless, in the course of an hour we had*
> *caught twenty or thirty—all large ones, weighing several pounds each.*
> *The largest was twenty-eight inches in length by eight in breadth. They*
> *bit so eagerly that twice we caught two at one haul of the same line.*

A horn then sounded out over the waters of Provincetown Harbor
from the Carter sloop to announce that supper was prepared, and so
Carter rowed toward the wharf to pick up the Assyrian, who announced
that Provincetown was indeed "dry and dreary to the last degree, with a
very repulsive-looking set of inhabitants." Underwood proceeded to
relate his experiences. He had tried to find a tavern, and reached the
Union House, where a dentist offered to pull his teeth. The dentist, finding that the Assyrian was in search of liquid refreshments, directed him
to a neighboring apothecary, where Underwood demanded a cocktail.
This astounded the apothecary, who replied, "I do not know what you
mean by a cocktail." In turn, Underwood was astounded by the fact that
anyone could not understand what a cocktail was, and told the apothecary that a cocktail was something to drink.

The druggist then suggested lemon, strawberry, pineapple, or sarsa-
parilla soda, but the Assyrian shook his head. Was there nothing else
the apothecary could offer? "Nothing," came the very definite answer,
and then Underwood had an idea. He would describe to the druggist
how to make a cocktail. Slowly he unfolded the method of concocting

such a drink, and the druggist listened as a man who is learning a new science. A light began to dawn, and he retired to the back of the drug-store, whence he triumphantly produced a dusty bottle of sherry bitters. Quoting Carter, "In the absence of anything better, cocktails could be made with sherry bitters. The other requisites were on board the sloop." A few hours later the Assyrian had satisfied his craving for cock-tails, and was fast asleep.

The next morning they awoke to a cloudless sky and a gentle breeze, and Provincetown stood before them with its long line of white-painted houses. At the time Carter described it as having 3,000 inhabitants who lived in five or six hundred houses, "nearly all of which stand on one narrow street," which ran between the shore and a ridge of sand hills. Carter went ashore to see a dentist, and found one who combined the callings of an auctioneer, hardware man, and furniture dealer with his dentistry, but the man finally chosen was a dentist and nothing else. The troublesome tooth came out in a hurry.

Then it was agreed to visit a beach some four or five miles away, probably in the Race Point area, and so the party hired a small boy to drive them out there. Carter's comments follow:

> In a few minutes we had left behind us the single street of the vil-lage and merged into a desert of white sand, that looked as if it had been sometime rolled into high waves by a raging tempest, and then suddenly arrested and fixed before it had time to subside to a level. Here and there in the dells and hollows were patches of vegetation, alders, huckleberry-bushes, low pitch pines, scrub oaks, and clumps of wild roses, glowing with the brilliant hues which the sea air gives to flowers. But outside of the village there were no houses, fences, paths, or any traces whatever of man or beast. It was a wilderness, as it was when it first met the eyes of the Mayflower pilgrims. The horses that tugged us onward had the muscles of their rumps unusu-ally developed from working always fetlock deep in sand. . . .

A great flock of terns flew away as the party approached, and kept wheeling around in the air nearby, their piercing cries making quite a disturbance. Far in the distance were a few white sails, but "signs of death" were visible around them on the beach in the form of fragments of wrecks thrown high on the shore. Carter picked up a piece of bam-boo which had possibly floated from some vessel on the way back from

China or India. All the others soon left Carter except the "urchin of a driver," who busied himself in replanting the roots of the dune grass so that it would grow and spread, halting the march of the sand over the highway. Carter sat down on a timber from an old wreck and thought of Whittier's lines on Hampton Beach:

> What heed I of the dusty land
> And noisy town?
> I see the mighty deep expands
> From its white line of glimmering sand
> To where the blue of Heaven on bluer waves
> shuts down!

The tide then began to come in, and the long lines of surf were slowly hitting the beach with a dull, continuous roar. Carter started to help the boy transplanting the beach grass, but sank to his ankles in the sand and gave it up. A short time later the red shirt of the Professor came into view, and soon the entire party was ready for the trip back to Province-town. Back in the town, Carter walked from one end of Provincetown to the other on the narrow plank sidewalk. They spent the afternoon in dredging the harbor for the marine life that could be found at the bottom of the sea, and that night listened to yarns about "money-digging and privateering," and then all turned in. The next morning at 8:00 they sailed out of Provincetown Harbor for Swampscott, Massachusetts.

Whether or not Robert Carter ever visited Provincetown again, we do not know. But if he had met the town crier of Provincetown, I am sure the ancient costume of this character would have intrigued him.

The town crier appears only in the summer months. Dressed in the traditional Pilgrim costume, Amos Kubick, the present town crier, stands on the wharf and rings his bell as the Boston boat unloads its daily thousands. After he rings the bell he announces the various activities of the day. Of course, in these times of newspapers and radios, the town crier is more or less a publicity stunt, but in days of old he had a vital part in the activity of the village. The most spectacular town crier of modern times was George Washington Ready of sea serpent fame, while the last official town crier was Walter Smith, who retired around 1928. [*The position was officially revived in 1935.—Ed.*]

Next I wandered over to the old Provincetown Cemetery, where the first stone to attract my attention was that of Eleazer Young, who died in 1832. On the same stone was an inscription to the memory of William

N. Young, lost at sea in 1831 at the age of twenty-four. Then I noticed the grave of the Reverend Samuel Parker, the first regular minister of Provincetown, who was ordained in 1769. His wife is remembered as the "best of Wives, tenderest of mothers." What finer sentiment could anyone have expressed toward his loved ones? There are sixty-four Nickersons buried in the Provincetown cemetery, and as one of my ancestors was William Nickerson, I was particularly interested. Many of the family were drowned at sea.

The Hopkins family have an obelisk in honor of Scammons Hopkins, who died in 1837. Being the tenth descendant in line from Stephen Hopkins, I scanned the graves to find as many descendants as I could of my forebears in the Provincetown Cemetery. Other familiar Cape Cod names on stones in the graveyard were those of Allerton, Atkins, Collins, Cook, Dyer, Freeman, Mayo, Paine, Rich, Small, Smith, and Whorf.

I set out again for the outer beach, for I could imagine the surf was roaring in that afternoon. And it was a grand sight, for when I had scrambled down the bank by Al and Dorothy Fearing's cottage near the old Peaked Hill Bars Station, I found that the seas were rolling high on the beach. Sitting down on the edge of the dune, I looked out toward the bars, then white with angry surf which was breaking over them. I thought of the night when the *Elwood Burton* was wrecked.

On October 14, 1904, a three-masted schooner, the *Elwood Burton*, hit the dreaded Peaked Hill Bars during a wild storm which threw heavy seas against the Cape. The *Burton* had left St. John, New Brunswick, several days before, with a crew of seven and a great load of laths. A surfman from the Peaked Hill Bars Station, while making his night patrol along the beach, was the first to discover the *Burton* at 11:00 that night. He saw the vessel rapidly drifting ashore on the lee beach. Although the surfman burned his Coston flare, there was no answer from the schooner. The schooner shivered to a stop, and he could tell she had hit the bar. Hurrying back to the Peaked Hill Station, he reported the schooner's position to Keeper William W. Cook, and all hands were called out.

The faithful old station horse was placed in harness, the apparatus hitched on, and the wagon started along the beach. Sinking down into the soft, deep sand, the horse was soon having a hard time of it, and the surfmen pitched in and helped man the heavy cart. Finally they reached that part of the shore closest to the wreck of the *Burton*. In a short time they had the gun set in place ready to fire; the line shot out over the water, but there was no response from the schooner. Keeper Cook sent one of the surfmen back to the station to telephone the Race Point Life-Saving Station for help. The men waited there, as the seas were too heavy to launch a lifeboat at that time.

It was not long before the cargo began to float up on the shore. Masses of laths soon pushed themselves up into a pile four or five feet high all along the beach. It was a peculiar sight, with the long thin strips of wood piled helter-skelter in such a fashion that one could not tell where the shore ended and the ocean began, as both sand and sea were buried under the debris.

Keeper Cook then ordered one of the crew to stand on top of the pile of laths with a lighted lantern to signal out to the schooner. When there was no response, it was decided all the crew were either drowned or drifting ashore on the wreckage, and lifesavers were sent along the beach to watch for seamen or wreckage in the waves. Then the keeper cut the shotline, as it had been across the *Burton* for half an hour without being hauled aboard. By this time the Race Point crew reached the scene, headed by Captain Samuel O. Fisher. Fisher had been the first Cape Codder to hear the blasts from the ill-fated *Portland* foundering near his station six years before.

There was still no sign of life from the *Burton*. Shortly afterwards, the wreck seemed to be moving toward the shore. When it reached a position not more than 200 feet from the inner line of breakers, Keeper Cook ordered a second shot fired over the *Burton*. Both keepers agreed that without question it had successfully reached its mark. No answering tug indicated that anyone aboard was attempting to secure the line, however.

Every surfman on the beach then heard cries for help, but strange as it was, the shouts seemed to be coming from the great piles of laths along the beach. In places, the wood had reached the almost unbelievable height of fifteen feet. Anxious to find the crew of the schooner, Keeper Cook cautiously made his way out over the half-floating pile of jumbled laths and lumber until he reached the outer ridge of the mass, and then directed his men to follow him. They finally located the cries of a man coming from under a huge mass of laths, and all the lifesavers began to dig feverishly. After several minutes of furious digging, a terrified sailor was uncovered. When he was brought ashore to safety, more shouts of distress were heard, this time from a heaving, waving, shapeless mass of laths a short distance offshore.

The two head keepers, Cook and Fisher, clambered out over the dangerous mass of lumber to locate and rescue another poor sailor, who had decided to give up hope just before he was rescued and brought ashore. Still another pitiful cry for help was heard, this time seemingly from the vessel itself. After crawling for the third time out on the thin pieces of wood, which each wave caused to rise and fall, they located a man swimming in the water just beyond the mass of laths. The surfmen threw him a heaving line, which the sailor quickly grasped to be hauled ashore. All three rescued men were then taken to the Peaked Hill Bars Life-Saving Station, where they revived to tell their part of the story.

The mate of the *Elwood Burton* announced that the captain and three crew members had drowned. The mate admitted that the captain had made him a mate just for the voyage, for he knew little of the sea. He had sailed on one voyage before, as a steward! The mate said that the warning Coston flare had been observed while all seven men had been in the rigging, but not one of them knew what it meant. When the shot line came whizzing out at them, the captain and three sailors had already been swept overboard to their death, while the three survivors were just about to leave the *Burton* on a small raft. As the schooner was very rotten and old, it broke up almost at once, and soon became unrecognizable.

Although over forty years have passed since the wreck of the *Burton*, there are many who still remember her. Scores went down on the beach after the storm to view the huge piles and masses of laths spread in every direction all along the shore, and the memory of the strangely disordered Cape Cod shore always remained with them.

Hiking along that same beach, I watched the cliffs reaching higher and higher the further I went. Finally I neared the vicinity of the Clay Pounds, and could make out the top of the Highland Station radio mast and the lighthouse. I found the path, if we may call it that, and climbed laboriously for fifteen minutes before I came out fairly near the golf course and had my first look that day at Highland Light from the top of the cliff.

Today's summer visitors to "P-Town" can take a variety of tours of the town and surrounding beaches—on foot, or by trolley, boat, or four-wheel drive vehicle. You can check on what's available by contacting the Chamber of Commerce (www.ptownchamber.com, 508-487-3424). Much of the town has been designated the Provincetown Historic District, with blue and white plaques on many of the houses explaining their significance. You can get walking tour booklets/maps at various locations.

The breakwater Snow crossed to reach town from Wood End was once a sandbar called House Point Island, where farmers grazed their cattle on salt marsh hay. The lighthouses at Race Point, Wood End, and Long Point are all still active aids to navigation, and all three are cared for by the Cape Cod Chapter of the American Lighthouse Foundation under a license with the U.S. Coast Guard. The keeper's dwellings at Wood End and Long Point were removed years ago. The keeper's house at Race Point, which was abandoned for many years, has been beautifully restored and is open for overnight stays. See www.lighthousefoundation.org for details. Also, the old fog signal building at the Race Point Light Station is now a field station used by the Center for Coastal Studies and other organizations.

The area upstream of the dike at Hatch's (or Hatches) Harbor is now subjected to regular, controlled tidal flooding as part of a plan to restore about ninety acres of salt marsh. The National Park Service has installed four large culverts and control gates at the dike, which was originally constructed as a mosquito-control device in the 1930s.

Among the devices tested on board the *S-4* in its days as an experimental vessel was the "Momsen Lung," which would allow crewmembers to escape from a sunken submarine. Also tested were telephone buoys designed to allow anyone trapped inside a submarine to communicate with rescuers on the surface. The *S-4* served until 1936, when it was towed out to sea and sunk in 2,000 fathoms of water off Pearl Harbor.

Each year a ceremony at Provincetown's Church of St. Mary of the Harbor (the "Outermost Church") commemorates the anniversary of the *S-4* tragedy. A wreath tossed into the ocean symbolically marks the watery grave. Outside the church stands a cross erected in the memory of those lost on the *S-4*, with the names of the forty men who died listed on a bronze plaque.

According to Amy Whorf McGuiggan, author of *My Provincetown: Memories of a Cape Cod Childhood*, Mellen Hatch, visited by Snow at the Octagon House, wrote a "very interesting little book" called *The Log of Provincetown and Truro on Cape Cod*, published in 1939.

George Washington Ready, town crier and sea serpent watcher, was born in Provincetown on January 1, 1833. It isn't known exactly how he earned the title "Professor," but he liked to say he had traveled all over the world and "a great many other places besides." His fantastic sighting was one of a long line of sea serpent reports in the vicinity of Provincetown. In fact, Benjamin Franklin's grandfather was one of those who reported spotting an unusual sea creature during a 1719 rash of sightings.

Almost three decades after he wrote this book, Edward Rowe Snow finally got his chance to see the timbers of the *Somerset* protruding through the sand. He was one of those who visited the beach near Provincetown to see the rare attraction in the summer of 1973.

Marjorie Hubbell Gibson's book, *H.M.S. Somerset 1746-1778: The Life and Times of an Eighteenth Century British Man-O-War and Her Impact on North America*, disputes a number of oft-repeated *Somerset* stories. The log of the Somerset contains no mention of visits to Provincetown Harbor, which means that either the log was incomplete, or later writers (before Snow) had colorful imaginations. The story about the romance of the ship's surgeon and a local lass has also been called into question. It seems the *Somerset*'s surgeon was actually Henry Watson, not William Thayer. Thayer was a Truro doctor who salvaged some of the materials from the *Somerset*, a fact that might have contributed to the birth of a legend. Thayer was married to Susannah (not Susan) Rich. But some legends die hard, and this one has been repeated by many authors.

The correct name of the Provincetown Monument is the Pilgrim Monument. This monument, based on the tower of the Torre Del Mangia in Siena, Italy, is the tallest all-granite structure in the United States. President Theodore Roosevelt was actually one of several people who ceremonially used a trowel to spread cement on the foundation for the laying of the cornerstone, so it can be truthfully stated that he "helped" lay it.

The Provincetown Museum next to the monument today has an extensive exhibit on Eugene O'Neill and the Provincetown Players.

Ambergris is a gray, waxy substance formed in the intestines of sperm whales. Its prime use was as an ingredient in perfume; it helped slow down evaporation. It is no longer used for this purpose, of course, as the killing of the endangered sperm whale is now outlawed. It's said that virtually all the ambergris collected in the twenty-five years before his death passed through the hands of David Stull, the Ambergris King. He had a beautiful home on the corner of Commercial and Cook Streets in Provincetown.

Robert Carter's account of his 1858 cruise was serialized in the *New York Tribune* and later published as a book, *A Summer Cruise on the Coast of New England*.

Amos Kubick, Provincetown's first town crier to wear a Pilgrim costume, was said to be somewhat temperamental after having his photo taken by thousands of tourists. Gene Poyant was Provincetown's last town crier, serving until the position was eliminated in 1986.

Captain Lee Woodman Williams of the *Elwood Burton* was twenty-eight years old, with a wife and one child, when he died in the 1904 disaster off the Peaked Hill Bars. His body, found by Surfman Collins of the Peaked Hill Bars Station, was returned to his native St. John, New Brunswick, for burial.

CHAPTER 2

Truro, Its Hills and Highland

Regardless of what other attractions Cape Cod offers the summer tourist, nothing should mean quite as much as a visit to Cape Cod Light, better known as Highland Light, which stands overlooking the highest part of Cape Cod's coast line. Its nightly beam of 4 million candlepower gleams out across the ocean from a height of 183 feet above the ocean. Twenty miles out to sea the alert mariner can see the single white flash which illuminates the sky every six seconds, while on clear nights even sailors aboard vessels over the horizon fully fifty miles away have detected a slight glow in the sky where they know Highland Light is flashing.

The officer in charge of the lighthouse station here is William Joseph, a member of the Coast Guard, but the man whose duty it is to light the beacon is Charles F. Ellis, still officially listed as a lighthouse keeper.

Walking over by the giant outdoor fog signals, I hiked toward William Joseph's residence, which is connected by a covered way to Keeper Ellis's home and the lighthouse itself. I rapped on Joseph's door, but there was no answer. Then I heard a voice: "You won't find anyone home there," it shouted, and I turned my head to see a most interesting character. It was my old friend, Keeper Charles F. Ellis, who was standing outside the back door of his house with his black shaggy dog, Trudy, who was barking half-heartedly as if wondering whether or not she should accept me. Walking over to Trudy, I ran my fingers through the curly hair on the dog's head, and all was well.

Keeper Charles F. Ellis and his wife, Louella, at Cape Cod Light (photo by Richard Kelsey)

"Come on in the house," invited Charles Ellis, and then shouted at the top of his voice, "Louella, look who's here." I stood in the dark hallway and waited for his wife. In a moment she appeared. "Here's the man you listen to on Sundays," Keeper Ellis told her.*

"Why, for heaven's sake, it is, isn't it," she ejaculated, sinking into a chair. The suddenness of my arrival had been too much for her, and it was several moments before she continued. "I listen to you faithfully every Sunday," Mrs. Ellis told me, and naturally I was pleased. "But where do you find time to look up all the stories you tell?"

I explained that when you don't do much else you have plenty of time for the thing you like to do.

"Well, I'll tell you a story," began Keeper Ellis, but his wife interrupted.

"Don't tell him anything, or you'll hear it on the radio some day," she warned, but neither Keeper Ellis nor I was worried. We sat down at the kitchen table and I got out my notebook.

"Did you start in the service as a lighthouse keeper?" I asked him.

"Well, I am really a lightship man, you know," was his reply. "When I entered the service in 1919 my first ship was the *Hedge Fence No. 9*. But that wasn't my first taste of the sea. Born in Brewster, I still have my home there. I married Louella in 1898, the year the *Portland* went down five miles out in the ocean from here. Two years later I started going to sea. The first vessel was a two-masted fishing schooner, the *Mertie and Delmar*, named for twins. Then I shipped aboard a schooner yacht named *Shyessa*, which is the Indian name for winner. She was a real racer, and many's the tussle we've had aboard her. I was mast headsman—know what that means? I changed sheets and tacks—and many times she was heeled over so much that had I fallen I'd have gone into the water.

"Then my next thrill was the *Zuzzia*. Be careful how you spell it because it's a Chinese word which means water wagon. I've never met anyone who could really translate it. The nearest was a professor from Harvard who called it a water cart. He didn't come too far away, you see. Well, by that time the first World War had ended and I had a chance to go on a lightship.

"I always liked the lightboat *Hedge Fence No. 9*. I had about the narrowest escape ever at that time, too. One day a schooner ran into us and loosened our plates. She was a three-sticker and misstayed at the wrong

---

*Snow told his stories on a variety of radio programs over the years.—*Ed.*

time to crash us. It was a head wind and head tide, and we were out of luck. After sheering off, she dropped anchor nearby, and our old man, Captain James Frizell, told me to row over with him and investigate. We launched a small fourteen-foot dory, and he had the stroke oar. We started rowing for the schooner, and then it happened. I saw a big fin coming for us, and all I could think of was that it was too late for sharks to be in the sound, November thirteenth. I yelled at the captain. 'I see it,' he cried. Then the shark came up right in front of us, rolled over, and tried to nudge us so that we'd go over. 'Hit him with your oar,' I yelled, and the old man brought his oar down on the shark's head. It must have hurt, for the shark then gave up and swam off. But not for long, for after he got about fifty feet away he turned and I could see his big fin cutting through the water like a knife as he came after us again.

"Then there was a soft thump and we were actually lifted out of the water. But the old man was ready this time, and whanged his oar time after time on the shark. Finally the shark decided to call it a day, and sank out of sight. We were both scared stiff, and rowed as fast as we could to the other vessel. But the fish didn't show up when we rowed back an hour later, and we were very thankful. It isn't any fun swapping punches with a fifteen-foot shark at any time. I'll never forget that November thirteenth."

After a few more stories, I bade farewell to this happy couple, and left New England's brightest lighthouse. I set off across the golf course in the general direction of a tower I had seen on many occasions from the air, but had never visited. When I looked down at it from above, the tower always seemed prominent, standing in a section of undergrowth half a mile to the southeast of Cape Cod Light, approximately a hundred yards from the cliffs. It reminded me of the First Corps Cadet Armory Tower in Boston. Years ago I had obtained the real history of this fascinating bit of transplanted Bostonia. The edifice is actually a tower of the old Fitchburg Terminal Building, which was erected a century ago at what is now Causeway, Beverly, and Haverhill Streets, next to the Boston Garden.

As I forced my way through the thick undergrowth which covers practically every approach to the tower, I looked for a path in vain. The branches tore my legs, penetrating the skin. I kept on, however, and after a ten-minute battle with the undergrowth, emerged at the base of the old Norman-styled tower. On the other side of the building was a well-defined path, which I could have used had I been patient in my

The old Fitchburg Terminal at Boston (photo by Alton Hall Blackington)

explorations before entering the thicket. My battle scars were honorable, nevertheless, and I threw myself exhausted at the foot of what remained of the old Fitchburg Terminal and reviewed its history.

On the first day of November 1847, in Boston, the cornerstone of the new Fitchburg Terminal had been laid. Many people, however, considered that the plans for the new building were far too pretentious for a railroad running scarcely fifty miles from Boston. In spite of much opposition, Alvah Crocker, president of the road, speeded up the enterprise so that by August 9, 1848, the first train entered the new station. Above the terminal, as is true of the present North Station, a large auditorium was built, the biggest in all New England at the time, seating 3,000 persons.

When Phineas T. Barnum brought the immortal Jenny Lind to Boston in 1850, two concerts were arranged for Depot Hall, as it was then called, on October 11 and October 12. Barnum's methods of salesmanship

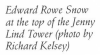

Edward Rowe Snow at the top of the Jenny Lind Tower (photo by Richard Kelsey)

allowed hundreds of extra tickets for the October 12 show to be sold by speculators, who, incidentally, made their first appearance in Boston at this time. The hall was filled hours in advance of the concert and late-comers milled in Causeway Street, furious at Barnum's duplicity. Finally windows were smashed and the bolder unseated ticket holders forced their way into the hall. It was a tense situation, and still forty minutes remained before the scheduled concert.

Jenny Lind was told what was going on so she hurriedly ordered the orchestra into the pit. The lights in the auditorium were dimmed, and the world's greatest singer strode out on the Depot Hall stage. Raising her hand, she signaled for attention. A miracle then occurred. When her beautiful voice singing the first few notes of "I Know That My Redeemer Liveth" reached the thousands packed in the hall, anger became admiration and the noise and tumult gave way to silence. Later she sang from one of those towers to the many who could not get into the hall. Jenny Lind saved the day and completed her conquest of Boston. Her sincere personality and her wonderful voice always caused a powerful emotional reaction in her audiences, and this was one occasion when it actually prevented what might have become a dangerous panic. Boston has heard many outstanding female voices in the past hundred years, but it is doubtful if anything quite like the scenes in Depot Hall have been equaled since.

As I sat there at Cape Cod a few feet from the Jenny Lind Tower, I tried to imagine the singer's voice as it had echoed in that same tower Columbus Day night in 1850, but only the fitful sharp-throated chirp of a sparrow disturbed my tranquility. I thought of other incidents in the tower's career. Once a southern belle had approached the station to take a train for the west, but refused to enter the building, as she called the edifice a "Northern Bastille." On another occasion Cashier Stover of the railroad was set upon by thugs on the stairs of the tower, and while he scared them away by shouting, was dealt such terrific blows that he became hopelessly insane because of his injuries. During the War of 1861 recruits drilled in the great hall, but at the command "double quick" they shook the floor so violently that the building inspector condemned the hall shortly afterwards. In 1864 the hall was abandoned. When later the floor was removed, those who had originally called the edifice Crocker's Folly felt that they were vindicated, but the hall had fourteen years of activity. The Fitchburg Terminal Building was demolished in 1927.

One day while it was being torn down Mr. Harry M. Aldrich, a well-known State Street lawyer, passed the site. He decided that it was a definite shame that one of the towers could not be saved for posterity. Visualizing it on his hill in Truro, he made the necessary arrangements which culminated in the tower's being moved to Cape Cod. There are those who like to believe that one of the Aldrich family group was captivated by Jenny Lind's voice, and this influenced Harry M. Aldrich years later to move the tower to Truro, where it now enhances the beauty of the last land Jenny Lind saw on her return to Europe. I asked Samuel Nelson Aldrich, a classmate of mine at Harvard and the son of the late Harry M. Aldrich, for information on that point. Aldrich replied that the tower's connection with Jenny Lind "in no way motivated my father to transport the most perfect of the four towers of the old North Station piece by piece to the Cape and re-erect it."

Rested sufficiently, I walked over to the entrance of the tower which, naturally, I wanted to climb. The doorway was open, for the door had either been forced in by the storms or broken open by vandals. The floor was littered with wood, and a circular iron staircase led toward the top. Several of the iron braces, however, had rusted away, and when I reached the top of the staircase, another problem presented itself. The entire top landing had collapsed, and the only way from the top of the staircase to the turret was by means of a heavy marine-type hatchway ladder which originally rested on the top landing but which now hung precariously from two small brackets attached to the roof. I tried part of my weight on the ladder and it gave ominously. As it would have been a sheer drop of almost fifty feet had the ladder fallen while I was climbing it, I decided a coward's fate was better than a dead hero's eulogy. For the moment I had been defeated, but I determined to return at a later date.

Leaving the Jenny Lind Tower, I walked back by the well-defined road and turned left. Five minutes later I was again on the shore, heading south for Truro. As I trudged along the Cape Cod beach, I thought of the countless shipwrecks which had occurred at this Massachusetts outpost, and my mind focused on the Coast Guard itself. The Coast Guard has taken over the duties which were first thought of in this country by a blind man, a Dr. Moyes. In 1785 Dr. Moyes entertained at his lodgings in Boston three Bostonians, the Reverend James Freeman, Royall Tyler, and a man identified as A. Dexter, and discussed with them plans for forming an organization similar to the British Royal Humane Society, which was established in 1774. Because of Dr. Moyes' urging, the first meeting of the group which became the Massachusetts Humane Society was held at the old Bunch of Grapes Tavern at the corner of King Street and Mackerel Lane, now State and Kilby Streets.

Among the earliest activities of the society was the building of huts for shipwrecked mariners along the Massachusetts coast. By 1806 there were seventeen such huts. In 1807 the first lifeboat in America was put in service by the society at Cohasset. The year 1840 was a turning point, for it was then that the society definitely decided to establish a chain of life-saving stations. By 1896 the Massachusetts Humane Society's activities had grown until there was actually a total of ninety-two stations. The government gradually assumed control of the life-saving activities along Cape Cod and the Massachusetts coast. In 1872 nine life-saving stations were built and manned between Race Point and Monomoy. By 1900 this number had been raised to thirteen stations for the entire Cape. They were Wood End, Race Point, Peaked Hill Bars,

High Head, Highland, Pamet River, Cahoons Hollow, Nauset, Orleans, Old Harbor, Chatham, Monomoy, and Monomoy Point. In 1915 the entire life-saving organization was combined with the revenue service and taken over by the United States Coast Guard. Two stations, High Head and Pamet River, were given up, and a few years later the Peaked Hill Bars and Old Harbor also, leaving only nine regular Coast Guard stations now in operation at Cape Cod.

It is only by walking along the beach dead tired that one can really understand what the lifesaver, surfman, and coastguardsman have suffered and endured since the first lifeboat station was established more than a century ago. At times the men have to crawl on their hands and knees because of the terrific force of the storm. But they do not complain. The lifesavers of Cape Cod have been known all over the civilized world for their bravery in times of danger, their gallantry and intrepidity whenever the occasion demanded. Every night for years they walked their lonely miles, whether it was a northeast gale or thick fog. Blinding snow and cutting sand made their task doubly hard; surf and quicksands made their path terrible and dangerous. Many a stout lad perished in carrying out his duty; scores of others have had their careers cut short by injury and sickness brought on by their strenuous work. Hundreds of city-bred Temporary Reserves deserve great praise for their patrol work during World War II. We should all honor and respect the men who have guarded the Cape's shores, and those who still watch along the same beaches today.

I was getting tired and thirsty when I sighted the Pamet River Valley showing up ahead. I cut across to the Pamet Road North, and followed it inland until I met the Grand Army Highway, and headed up the abrupt hill leading to the Snow graveyard.

There are three books which are most valuable in learning the history of Truro, and I was carrying one with me as I hiked. In 1796 the Reverend Dr. James Freeman, well known for his sermons at the King's Chapel in Boston, wrote a short sketch of the town. This was followed by two large volumes written by the Reverend Mr. Frederick Freeman of Sandwich, who in 1861 published his work on the history of Cape Cod in general and of the thirteen towns in particular. Truro received a substantial share of attention in the volume. In the year 1883 Shebnah Rich gave to the citizens of Cape Cod his rightfully famous volume, *Truro—Cape Cod, or Land Marks and Sea Marks*. This book is one of the most outstanding volumes ever written on Cape Cod, and in my knapsack I had a copy to which I referred many times as I made my way toward Truro.

The only easy way to Cape Cod in the old days, of course, was by the weekly packet, and for nearly 150 years there was no important variation in the customs and manners of the Cape Cod communities. Wars would check their enterprise, destroy their business, and completely discourage them, but back they came after every setback to carry on their efforts for existence. Mighty gales swept in out of the Atlantic time and again to decimate their numbers, but the survivors carried on as best they could. Worldly unhappiness seemed strangely missing from their lives, however, for there were few murders and fewer divorces, and drunkenness was rare. Education was meager but effective. As Rich tells us, "Modern education is a beginning of many things," so there were quite a few Cape Codders who went to greater heights.

There are two graveyards of extreme interest in Truro. One is located on the Hill of Storms in North Truro, where the old meeting house formerly stood. The other is located on the Hill of Churches in Truro itself, but both have many old gravestones which tell their own story of shipwreck and disaster on the high seas. My first visit was to the Hill of Churches, and after reading a few of the inscriptions on the tombstones I decided that either graveyard could be called the Hill of Storms, for there were countless graves recording the fact that a loved one had been lost in a storm at sea.

It is always with a feeling of deep reverence that I approach this burial ground, so closely associated with Truro of old. There were many descendants of my two good Pilgrim ancestors, Nicholas Snow and Constance Hopkins, mentioned in the commemorative stones and inscriptions which I found on every side as I entered the graveyard. The cemetery itself is called the Snow Burial Ground. The most impressive stone of all is a tall marble shaft, surrounded by an iron fence, which stands in memory of Truro's worst marine disaster in October 1841. Fifty-seven men and boys sailed away from their homes, never to return. I pulled out my notebook and copied the inscription:

SACRED to the memory of 57 citizens of Truro who were lost in seven vessels, which foundered at sea in the memorable gale of Oct. 3, 1841

"Then shall the dust return to the earth as it was; and the spirit shall return unto God who gave it."

"Man goeth to his long home and the mourners go about the streets."

The untold suffering represented in this mute testimonial almost staggers the imagination. The extreme youth of many of the boys indicates the ages at which they were sent to sea. Andrew W. Cordes and Thomas C. White were only twelve, while Charles Nott was eleven!

In addition to the great number of Snows mentioned on the memorial, there were the families of Cook, Wheeler, Smith, Atkins, Rich, Bible, Anderson, Paine, Mayo, Boyle, and Cordes which I listed. The names of the seven vessels from which the entire crews perished were the *Arrival, Altair, Cincinnatus, Pomona, Prince Albert, General Harrison,* and the *Dalmatia.*

I remained in that restful Truro cemetery for two hours more. When I finally packed my papers, books, and cameras, I somehow felt at peace with the world. There are those who do not like to visit ceme-

Unlike many of her descendants, who were buried in Truro, Constance Hopkins Snow was buried in Eastham. (Photo by Jeremy D'Entremont)

teries, but I always pity them, for there is so much they miss, stories of other days that they will never know, and delightful inscriptions and sayings of a past generation. Each stone is like a different page of a book.

But the sun was setting, and I hiked to Truro to make sure of a room for the night. After breakfast the next morning I started back for the old church near the cemetery on the Hill of Churches. Sitting down on the lee side of the building, I undid my knapsack and pulled out several volumes—Thoreau, Rich, Kittredge, and Tarbell. I had fortified myself for the day with four apples, three bananas, and a dozen oranges, and my canteen was full of water. Actually, I spent the next six hours without leaving the shelter of the church more than once or twice. But how I enjoyed it!

My first thoughts were naturally of the first inhabitants of Truro, the Indians. Governor Thomas Hinckley tells of the red man's interest in strong drink. Hinckley wrote that the Indians' ungovernable appetite for strong drink was a great hindrance to their improvement. The tip of the Cape was often used to traffic with the Indians illegally in liquor, and without question many of the red men gave away their last articles of barter to satisfy their cravings. A paragraph from Hinckley's writings follows:

> *When they had nothing to give, they did not consider it out of place to obtain their liquor by stealth. Before the Court at Plymouth, 1667, were Simon, Monchase, and Assooat, for going on board the boat of Simon Stevens at Cape Cod, and taking away a cask of liquor, and having a hand in embezzling and spending the same. They were ordered to be whipped at the post in Plymouth, which was done accordingly.*

Rich tells us that the Indians had a hereditary love for rum. Mr. Stone, the Provincetown minister, hammered constantly at the Mashpee Indians when he preached before them about the evils of strong drink. One day a deacon asked an Indian how he liked Stone's preaching. The answer was that "Mr. Stone one very good preacher, but he preach too much about rum. When he no preach about rum, Indian think nothing about it; but when he tells how Indian love rum and how much they drunk, then I think how good it is and think no more 'bout the sermon, my mouth waters all the time so much for rum." Another day he was asked to compare Mr. Stone and blind Joe, a Baptist minister. His answer was, "Mr. Stone he make best sermons, but blind Joe, he make best Christians."

Sitting there on the Hill of Churches, I thought of the day when John Billington, Junior, the seven-year-old son of John Billington, Senior, had been found by the Indians wandering not too many miles from Truro itself. He belonged to that notorious Billington family which made so much trouble for the Pilgrims. The Billingtons were known as "one of the profanest families" of all the Pilgrims. When the *Mayflower* was anchored in Provincetown Harbor, Francis Billington, another son of John Billington, shot off a fowling piece near the powder kegs, and this prank nearly blew up the *Mayflower* then and there.

Later, after the Pilgrims were settled at Plymouth, young John Billington, Junior, wandered off into the woods to become hopelessly lost on Cape Cod. He was found by the Nauset Indians, and taken way up to what is now Truro. The Pilgrims hunted for the lad, but after a week they gave up the search, considering the child dead, but to their surprise word came from Massasoit that young John was alive and well. A party of Pilgrims landed at Cummaquid, and were warmly welcomed by Sachem Iyanough, who told them that the lad was in the land of the Nauset Indians, which then extended almost to Provincetown. Iyanough offered to journey with them. Arriving at Nauset, the Pilgrims dispatched Squanto to find Aspinet, the sachem of the local Nauset tribe. Just before dusk Aspinet made his appearance with the boy and a great number of the Indians. After an exchange of gifts and presents, the Pilgrims landed again at Cummaquid, where Iyanough had his Indian girls join "hand in hand" to dance around the Pilgrims, and Iyanough removed a bracelet from his neck and presented it to the Pilgrims. Young John Billington then went back with the rest of the Pilgrims to Plymouth. This journey and the Indians' friendly hospitality made a lasting impression on the Pilgrims.

However, the Billingtons went from minor troubles to major ones. In 1622, young John's father, John Billington, was tied up by the neck and heels for swearing at Myles Standish. Without question he was in on the so-called Lyford-Oldham mutiny in 1624, but his real crime occurred in 1630.

In that year, John Billington, the elder, who according to Bradford "shuffled into our company" by methods Bradford knew not, engaged in a controversy with John Newcomer, waylaid the said Newcomer, and blew him apart with a blunderbuss. This amazing act of one of the Pilgrims shocked the rest of the company, and it was some time before action could be decided upon. Then Billington was given a trial and found guilty of murder, but the Pilgrims wondered whether theirs was the right to carry out a death sentence. It was only after Governor Winthrop, up in Boston, had agreed that death was the only punishment possible, that the Pilgrims acted. John Billington was hanged by the neck until dead, taken down, drawn, and quartered.

I learned that the original name of Truro was Payomet. As the years went by, the natives cut out the middle syllable of Payomet and it became Pamet. Its settlement is of interest. In the year 1640, the Old-comers, those who had arrived at Plymouth in the first three ships, the *Mayflower*, the *Ann*, and the *Fortune*, received a grant of land from the General Court, but they did not remove to the area until several years later. In 1643 they purchased Nauset from the Indians, but finding it too confined for their numbers, obtained an enlargement of their original grant in 1644, so that those who "go to dwell at Nauset" were to have "all that tract of land lying between sea and sea from the purchaser's bounds at Nanskeket to the Herring Brook at Billingsgate with the said Herring Brook and all the meadows on both sides of said brook, with great Bass Pond there, and all the meadows and islands within said tract."

Name origins are a fascinating study. For many years after the Civil War there was a tradition, apparently well founded, that Revolutionary British soldiers had given the name of "Hog's Back" to the peculiarly shaped hill down near the shore, covered with a ridge of pine trees, because of its strange resemblance to the contour and bristly back of a hog. It is a good story, but the only discrepancy is that in the old records I found an item dated 1703 which referred to Thomas Mulford's land as being "next Hog's Back, " and another item of 1725, wherein John Lewis of Barnstable kills a whale "near at a place called Hogg's Back."

The names of the early Cape Cod children were, to say the least, unusual, but they were typical of the period. Armemaryvetta Rogers, born in 1714 at Sandwich, Cape Cod, can be matched by Mahershallal-hashbaz Dyar, who arrived at piratical Newport, Rhode Island, in 1661. Seaborn Cotton, Reliance Hinkley, and Wrestling Brewster were three other early Massachusetts dwellers. The son of my grandfather seven times removed, Stephen Hopkins, born at sea on the *Mayflower*, was appropriately named Oceanus. Other names include Love, Fear,

Patience, Resolved, Humility, Remember, Shining, Desire, and Faith. A Truro girl had the following scripture names in her family, which she recited in singsong fashion:

> *Hezekiah, Jedediah, Shebnah, and Eliakim, Sarah and Mary, Hannah, and Penina.*

There is an amusing anecdote about the Reverend Nathaniel Eells, who declined to accept the offer to minister unto the people of Pamet for reasons we shall never know. His wife, the former Hannah North, was a relative of Lord North of England. One day their children were unusually active, and Hannah North Eells remarked, "How can so good a man as my husband have such wayward children?" His answer was that of a typical male: "True, and you seem to be sensible that the mischief all lies on the North side of the house." Their nine children however, grew up to become "well settled in life." In 1704 Nathaniel Eells was at Scituate, Massachusetts.

The Reverend Samuel Treat was a wonderful preacher to the Pamet Indians and their good friend as well. His daughter, Eunice Treat, became the mother of Robert Treat Paine, the Revolutionary patriot who signed the Declaration of Independence. The Reverend Mr. Treat, who had a powerful voice, had no trouble making his congregation hear him, for it was said he could be heard "a great distance from the meeting-house; even above the howling winds of the Eastham plains." Dying on the day of the Great Snow of New England, on March 18, 1716, he could not be buried until a path was tunneled more than four hundred yards to his grave. He was carried to his tomb by the mourning Indians of Cape Cod, to whom he had preached in their native tongue.

Peering through the old records, I was delighted to find that my ancestor, Isaac Snow, born in 1678, was selectman of Pamet in 1709, along with Benjamin Small and Humphrey Scammon. These three men were the last officers of Pamet. Isaac Snow also represented Cape Cod at the General Assembly in Boston.

Another item which caught my eye concerned the crows and blackbirds. They must have caused serious loss at Pamet, Eastham, and Truro in the early days, judging from the following legislation. The first act was passed in 1711, and provided that "whereas crows and blackbirds do much damage by pulling up and destroying the young corn, every housekeeper shall bring or cause to be brought . . . to the selectmen, eight blackbirds' heads, two crows' heads, or proportionally thereto or forfeit 3s. 8d." Another decree forbade the young men of the town from marrying until they killed "six blackbirds or three crows."

The wolves, however, should have filled every young heart with fear. One old wolf was so important and had committed so many depredations on the Cape that he was referred to as "the Wolf." What a record he must have had, to be known up and down the Cape with such special designation!

This particular wolf roamed at will all over the Cape, killing and causing widespread damage everywhere. Finally, however, age crept up on him, and one afternoon he was spied by George Braley, a farmer who also worked for the Sandwich Glass Company.

It was August 14, 1837. On that day Braley was driving through Sandwich Woods, and as was his custom, he carried his gun on the seat by his side. Suddenly, in a clearing he saw the wolf. It was but the work of a moment to aim and fire. His aim was good, and the wolf fell dead on the spot. So many years had elapsed without the wolf's being caught that the bounty was then worth $100, composed of a town bounty of $85 and a state bounty of $15. In addition, Braley received $20 for the hide of the wolf itself.

The pelt of the wolf seemed to satisfy many persons in the vicinity who had actually refused to believe in the existence of such a large animal at Cape Cod. Even Zenas Nye, writing in his journal that night, said that "he was really larger than I expected from what I had seen of his track. He was tall and long-sided. Perhaps it would be no exaggeration to say that he has destroyed 3,000 sheep in this town within the past five years." Zenas inspected the "monster," for such he proved to be. When measured, the wolf was found to be four feet long, exclusive of his tail, and two feet, four inches in height. He weighed seventy pounds. The creature was of a light brown color, with darkish grey jaws and short ears standing upright. I was very happy that the wolf was around in 1837 instead of that April day in 1946.

The Province Lands, from which Provincetown received its name, were regarded as part of Truro until 1714, and constituted a district known as the Precinct of Cape Cod. On September 24 of that year, a line was clearly settled which separated the Province Lands from Truro. This line would be interesting if we could trace it today. According to contemporary description, it started at the easterly end of a cliff near the Cape Harbor, which the Indians called Hetsconyet and the English called Cormorant Hill. The landmark there was the jawbone of a whale set in the ground by the side of a red oak stump. Then the line ran along range trees suitably marked to a single tree standing by a reedy pond, and then to a high hill on the north side near the North Sea (Atlantic) with a cedar post in the hill, and from there the line was continued in the same direction to the sea. By June 14, 1727, the number of people living in the Province Lands was sufficient for the area to be incorporated as a township, having the name Provincetown.

Perhaps my boyhood interest in whales and whaling can be traced to my Cape Cod ancestry. But as a matter of fact, almost any boy, whatever his ancestry, is interested in thrilling adventures of the old time whalers. When my mother was a girl sailing on the bark *Russell* with her father, she dropped a belaying pin on the back of a whale to prove that she was a true sailor. I remember particularly my Aunt Annabel's hired man named Charlie Smith, an old whaler who had made many voyages before his shipwreck on the sea of intemperance. He would talk to us children by the hour about his adventures. He interested me in whaling at an early age, and I would often visit the library to take out volumes on whalers and their experiences.

Whaling was one of the principal industries of the Cape. When the English first came to America, they noticed that the whales habitually swam in Massachusetts Bay near the shore where they were able to find the best food. Often, however, the ebbing tide would strand them, and then the Indians and white men would kill and cut them up. These were the drift whales which have so often been part of the division of the poor minister, whom Thoreau pictures sitting on the cliffs anxiously watching the beach for a whale to be cast ashore. Legislation passed in 1662 decreed that a "part of every whale cast on shore be appropriated for the support of the ministry."

Gradually the whales worked offshore, and the smaller boats of the Cape Codders gave way to large sloops which could follow the whales far out to sea. Early in the nineteenth century Truro had nine whaling sloops and one of them was the *Lydia and Sophia*, probably the first vessel ever built in Truro.

An interesting whaling record was registered by Town Clerk John Snow in February 1720. For some reason Joshua Atwood's lance, with which he dispatched finback whales, had a three-square head marked W. R. Evidently he was afraid that a person finding a whale with W. R. on it would never associate the initials with Joseph Atwood, so

Atwood made sure there would be no mistake by registering the initials of his lance.

Writing in 1794, Dr. James Freeman told of the long whaling voyages necessary in that time to remote parts of the ocean. He mentions the two Truro men, Captain David Smith and Captain Gamaliel Collins, who reached the Falkland Islands in 1774.

Cape Cod sailors were so far ahead of the rest of New England in whaling around 1690 that Ichabod Paddock was asked to visit Nantucket and instruct the people there in the art of whaling. His visit actually began the Nantucket whaling industry, which then spread to New Bedford and across to England. Yes, it was a Massachusetts man, Captain Jesse Holbrook, who killed fifty-four whales on one voyage, and was later asked to teach the English how to become successful whalers. When we realize that at one time 193 Nantucket sea captains hailed from English ports, we can get some idea of the widespread character of the whaling industry.

Around the middle of the century Mr. Richard Paine told Shebnah Rich that he could remember when there were lookouts stationed at Pond Landing to watch for whales. As soon as a whale hove in sight, the lookout would cry out "Towner," an Indian word which originally signified that the lookout had seen the whale twice. There are definite records in Truro that a lookout's shout in the excitement of the discovery was actually heard two miles away!

In 1810 a South Truro whaler fastened his lance to a right whale off Truro itself, and the whale violated all the ethics of whaling by promptly standing on her nose, thrashing the water with her flukes to prevent anyone's getting close. Captain Tom Atwood, a famous whaling captain who had recently retired from the sea, was summoned to handle the emergency. They found him at home reading his Bible. "Yes, I'll come and kill her," said the old man, and shut up his Good Book. An hour later he was in the whaleboat nearing the whale. Ordering the oarsmen to come up on the safe side, he skillfully sent his lance into the whale's vital organs and killed her. Then Atwood ordered the delighted whalers to row him ashore, and he walked home in triumph to continue his reading of the Bible.

An interesting anecdote concerns the ship *Milton*, cruising at the time in the Northern Gulf. The lookout sighted a whale, which emitted a whistling sound as the ship approached him. After killing the whale, the headsman climbed aboard the whale's body to find a harpoon running transversely through his spout holes. The peculiarly situated lance had produced the whistling. By the date stamp, the headsman discovered that the whale had been carrying the harpoon fourteen years!

The blackfish, known as *Globicephalus melas,* are not fish at all, but full-fledged members of the mammal group. From earliest times they have been known to inhabit the waters around Cape Cod.

Although my personal connections with the subject of blackfish do not qualify me as a blackfish expert, I assisted in bringing to shore one of the great black creatures some years ago. But the days of the black-fish runs seem to have passed. In the last century many active Cape Cod men fast enough to be among the first at the scene netted tidy sums from the blackfish they caught. Hundreds of blackfish, from eight to twenty feet in length, would swim into shallow water after herring or squid. Then men and boys in boats would frighten them up on the beach, where they thrashed about until slaughtered. Tryworks were set up close at hand, and each fish averaged more than a barrel of valuable oil. As much as $15,000 has been realized in this way by one Cape Cod town alone. Oil wells later ruined the market value of blackfish oil, and now, as in the case of my blackfish, they are not worth cutting up and are towed out to sea.

Thoreau watched a large school being captured at Great Hollow in July of 1855. Thirty blackfish had been killed just as he arrived, and far-ther north another school was being chased ashore. It was an exciting race as they drove the beasts before them. If they were stranded, each boat took one share of the catch, but if the men were compelled to kill the blackfish offshore, each boat's company took what they were able to strike. Thoreau met a blind old fisherman who eagerly asked where the blackfish were and if they had been taken. It was an extremely exciting sport, and nearly as dangerous as whaling itself, according to one of the fishermen.

A few days before this, Thoreau says, 180 blackfish had been driven ashore at Eastham. The keeper at Billingsgate Light went out one morn-ing to find a fortune in fish stranded around his lighthouse. Before any-one else was aware of his good luck, he had initialed every blackfish to sell them later to Provincetown butchers for $1,000, making much more in one day than he had made in a full year's work at the lighthouse!

In 1874 the largest school of blackfish ever known to have been dri-ven ashore at Cape Cod came up on the Truro beach, 1405 in number. They lay all along the shore from Great Hollow to the Pond Landing, a distance of about a mile. The blackfish yielded 27,000 gallons of oil. Around the middle of the century Captain Daniel Rich, who lived on Bound Brook Island, drove his cows to pasture one day, and then walked over to the bank where he looked down on the beach hoping to find some blackfish ashore. To his pleasure, he detected a great number of them thrashing about in the shallow water, and before going to breakfast that morning, Daniel Rich had cut his initials into seventy-five of the largest blackfish anyone could hope to catch. Before the sun went down, Rich had made $1,900!

But don't go down to Cape Cod and hope to follow the example of the Billingsgate lightkeeper or Captain Daniel Rich. If you caught blackfish today and brought them ashore, or even if you cut off the head of one on the beach or cut your initials into it, you would probably be summoned by the local board of health to take your property a suitable distance from land and sink it before it began to decay. Since the oil is relatively worthless, you would have the trouble of towing your possession far out to sea.

Thrilling stories from time to time have been told of Cape Cod sailors, but the account of the voyage of Captain Sylvanus Rich of Truro is a strange legend of terror on the high seas. Leaving a North Carolina port with a load of corn some time in the last part of the eighteenth century, he was becalmed, and so took advantage of the situation by rowing ashore for some fresh milk. What happened ashore is a matter of conjecture, but when Captain Rich returned to his vessel with a pail of milk, he declared in a frightened voice that the old woman who sold him the milk was bewitched. That very night, according to Captain Rich's story, the woman came aboard his ship and entered his cabin through the lazaret. Saddling and bridling the poor captain, she drove him ashore in some mysterious fashion and rode him all the way up to Truro, where he was forced to carry her on his shoulders around Bound Brook Island and through the woods surrounding Truro. Every night, the captain declared, she repeated the performance.

Meanwhile the vessel, commanded by an apparent madman, lost her sails and was blown far off her course, drifting nearly to the Grand Banks. The captain, originally a stout man, lost weight until his skin hung in bags around his weakened body. He said that he couldn't stand it much longer, and the crew, muttering to themselves, agreed with him. A beautiful ship had become a helpless derelict, all because of a supposed witch.

Finally, another vessel in charge of his own son, Captain Sylvanus Rich, Junior, fell in with the derelict and went aboard. This seemed to break the spell, as the captain forthwith straightened out his mental condition, accepted fresh sails from his son, put his vessel in order, and finished his voyage, thinking no more of the strange old woman he believed had bewitched him.

Down on the Cape one hundred years ago it was the custom for friends to drop in on one another to spend an evening. In each community there was a separate gathering place where a room full of neighbors would meet. Here were told the old stories of Cape Cod, the unwritten masterpieces practically all of which have been lost to the world forever. Many a young boy decided his life career should be the sea, as he sat entranced by the exciting adventures told by the sea captains of a former day.

On a certain evening one lad in particular was attentively listening to a breathtaking ghost story told by a white-haired veteran of many round-the-world sailings. Although he knew that a long walk awaited him before he could reach home, the lad stayed on and on until he became afraid to leave the warmth of the chimney corner where he was sitting. Finally, the last story finished, the boy forced himself to get up, say his farewells, and walk out into the night. There were no stars visible overhead and the air seemed to be full of vague, shadowy forms. When he was within a relatively short distance of his house, he reached a narrow part of the road with a high fence on the left and a steep bank on the right. In the center of the road he saw what seemed to be a coffin, scaring him almost out of his senses. Unable to get up the steep bank or climb the fence, he decided to make an attempt to jump over the coffin. As he was only ten years of age, he realized it would be a hazardous attempt for a boy of his years, and so backed a short distance down the road for the effort. He ran with all his might. When he reached the spot just in front of the coffin, the boy gathered himself for the leap, and sprang into the air. As he sailed over the terrifying object, a hand came out of the coffin and grabbed his leg, causing him to be catapulted into the cavernous object. There was silence. He lay still at the bottom of the box for several seconds, unable to move in his fear. Then, letting out a terrified cry, he sprang to his feet. To his amazement the coffin resolved itself into a long two-bushel corn basket which had accidentally rolled from a neighbor's cart some hours before. The hand which had tripped him was one of the basket handles which he failed to clear in his desperate leap for life. Had it not been for this handle, he would probably have told the story for the rest of his life that he had jumped over a coffin in the road near his home one dark and starless night.

Between Eastham and Pamet lies a small region the General Court voted in 1709 should be called Dangerfield. This name seems to suggest a bold group of pioneers living in a precarious fashion, but, strange as it may be, I have been unable to find any other contemporary reference to Dangerfield. Then, there was a plan for a town to be called Poole, which would be located near Billingsgate Beach, but this, also, never achieved reality. Both names, although mentioned in rare cases by historians, seem to have faded from use.

Many years ago the *Massachusetts Gazetteer* printed a reference to the world-famous meeting house at Truro, Massachusetts, saying that it stood alone "on the hill of storms! It is seen afar by the mariner as he passes by on the dark-rolling wave." Commenting on it in 1883, Shebnah Rich remarked that the meeting house no longer stood on the Hill of Storms, but he could still see in spirit "its high walls and double row of windows." Continuing his thoughts about the meeting house, Rich says, "I tread its aisles; I gaze upon the sounding-board suspended like Mohamet's coffin; I hear the hymn of David, and listen to the tender prayers and 'sweetest mind' of Christ's servants. . . . I see the ruling elders and deacons, and the Christian mothers."

This old Truro meeting house, standing on the high, windswept plain, was the Cape Cod landmark for 120 years. For generations, even before a lighthouse had been erected at Cape Cod, the Truro church guided mariners by day, and also at night gave out its feeble help whenever possible. This memorable edifice stood near the southwestern corner of the graveyard and faced south, following the custom of the day. Its heavy oak frame, tradition says, was cut and hewn on the spot. When the venerable meeting house showed signs of age in 1840, it was demolished, but the large timbers were still sound. The old edifice had been erected sometime before the earliest known interment in the cemetery, which occurred in 1713.

During the service one of the duties of the sexton was to turn the hourglass. I can well imagine the eyes of the congregation watching him as this good man strode forward to carry out his task. Possibly they were wondering how much longer the minister would continue, or if the sexton's activities would have any effect on the length of the sermon. Yes, the sermons of yesteryear were almost always of substantial length. A certain minister from Scotland thought nothing, it was said, of preaching for five hours. On the other hand, did you sit through the moving picture *Gone with the Wind* or the play *Strange Interlude*?

Tobacco was recognized as an evil early in Cape Cod history, for in 1669 a law was passed prohibiting smoking "on the Lord's Day, going to, or coming from the meeting, within two miles of the meeting house." Of course, there were those who interpreted the law as allowing smoking in the meeting house itself. One year Joshua Lombard and Jedidiah Lombard were fined for smoking just outside the Yarmouth church. Members of the early juries were not allowed to chew tobacco.

It seems that as early as 1745 there were actually mischievous boys on Cape Cod. A tiding man was appointed to watch them in church, and for this purpose the tiding man used effectively a long pole which had a knob at one end and feathers at the other. He administered a punch with the knob in handling the unruly boys, and used the feathers to arouse the ladies if by chance at the end of the second hour of the sermon they appeared to doze. One day the sermon brought agreement from one of the men parishioners, who gave a vigorous nod, when suddenly there came a blow from the knob. The alert tiding man had taken the nod for a doze and had acted accordingly.

The children were at first "corrected," in 1748, and then in 1752 "a man was appointed to take care of and chastise the boys who play in meeting." A few years later, a committee of three men was appointed to "correct and whip" the disorderly boys who sat up with the young girls in the gallery of the meeting house, apart from their parents. Rich suggested that the boys or girls who could sit still through two of the long services without playing probably died young and went straight to heaven. The seats, hung on hinges, were lifted at appropriate times during the services to give more room, and when the hymns were announced the youngsters made the most of it by banging the seats when they rose to sing. The pews had a balustrade ten inches high, and through the loopholes the children watched each other.

Making my way to a location near the back of the cemetery on the Hill of Storms, I reviewed the notes I had taken covering the location. Three unusual events are connected with the old graveyard meeting house, and the first, which occurred many years ago during a wild northeast storm, concerns a man returning from Provincetown to Truro.

Overtaken by darkness, he sought shelter in the meeting house to rest. While he was gathering his strength, he thought he detected a child's cry coming to him from the graveyard even above the roar of the storm. Again and again he heard the plaintive shout, until he was certain a young child was lost not too far from the place where he was standing. Finally he could endure the uncertainty no longer, and vaulted over the fence to search for the voice among the gravestones. Bumping into tombstones and torn by the wild brush, he searched the area, guided by repeated cries.

Suddenly a terrifying thought entered his mind, for the sound seemed to be coming out of the ground. Had someone been entombed alive? Reaching the place from which the sound was coming, he bent down to find a hole in the ground whence came a warm breath! Desperate but determined, he thrust his hand into the grave's opening and encountered a soft, shivering body which was making the weird cries. Carefully pulling it out of the tomb, he found that it was a little fleecy lamb which had been lost and had sought shelter in the old grave. When the storm let up, the relieved traveler, with the little lamb snuggled to his breast, finished the journey to his Truro home.

The second story is about Cynthia Gross, who was said to have taken a short cut across the graveyard and run into a person who claimed that he was the Devil. Cynthia, one of ten devoutly religious sisters, leaned weakly against a gravestone and said, "If you are the Devil, poor soul, I pity you." The man, overcome by the brave reply, then disappeared without bothering her further.

During another storm a woman, lost in the snow, forced open a window in the church in her efforts to find shelter, and made a ghastly discovery. The poor soul started to sit down in a pew, but it was already occupied by a dead man! Terrified, she forced her way out of the church, fought her way through the drifts, and finally reached home. It was several hours, however, before she recovered sufficiently to tell her experience. The following week she learned what had happened. Several bodies had come ashore from a shipwreck in the gale, and they had been carried to the church to await the end of the storm. The woman had encountered one of the bodies in the pitch blackness of that winter night.

As I sat there I thought again of the October 1841 gale, and of the two sea captains who lived through the storm to relate their experiences in that great hurricane. They were Captain Joshua Knowles and Captain

Matthias Rich. Those out in it who lived through 1898 believed that it was every bit as bad as the Portland gale of the latter year.

Captain Joshua Knowles left Provincetown aboard the *Garnet* on Saturday, October 2, shaping his course for the Georges with all sails set. The wind soon began to breeze up, and Captain Knowles ordered light sails taken in. At midnight, since it was blowing a gale, the mainsail was taken in. It was worse than ever by 4:00 Sunday morning, and so they took in the jib. Two hours later the foresail was double-reefed, but it soon parted the leachrope and tore to the luff. There was nothing left to do except to crossbar the sail and put on a preventer leachrope as soon as possible, setting it close-reefed.

The foresail soon gave out, was repaired, but blew to ribbons again. The mainsail suffered the same fate. By 8:00 Sunday night, there was only the jib left. Soundings were then fifteen fathoms, and all knew they were drifting into shoal water. Twelve, eight, and then only six fathoms were registered. When the seas began breaking fore and aft, Captain Knowles ordered all members of the crew below except his brother, Zach, whom he needed on deck. It was decided to swing her off before the wind, and Captain Knowles put up the helm. Just as she began to fall off, a great billow with a giant crest hit them, and over the Garnet went on her beam ends.

In the confusion Zach was washed overboard, but he grabbed at the mainsheet and hauled himself to safety. The foremast had broken off fifteen feet up, and the mainmast was unstepped, with the galley, bulwarks, and everything else on deck swept overboard. The ballast also shifted. Captain Knowles was barely able to reach his hatchet to cut away the rigging. The men crawled through the lazaret into the hold and threw the ballast to windward, partially righting the *Garnet*, which was now only a helpless wreck. The captain noticed that after the giant wave which capsized them passed, the sea became quieter, and by afternoon the gale moderated. The night came and went without further danger.

Finally, the next morning, a jury mast was rigged, the staysail set for a foresail, the gaff topsail for a jib, and so the crew were able to steer the vessel. By 10:00 Tuesday morning, October 5, 1841, the weather was fine. The sailors found some potatoes floating in the hold, and were able to recover the teakettle. Although the galley had gone by the board, the boys built a fire on the ballast and boiled a few potatoes, which was the first food any of them had eaten since Sunday morning.

A long pole was then sent aloft with the flag as a distress signal, and just before sunset Captain Knowles observed a sail making for them from the east.

The sail proved to be the Liverpool packet ship *Roscius*, the finest merchant ship of her day. Long before they were overhauled, the yards and rigging of the *Roscius* were crowded with men interested in the wreck of the *Garnet*. Then came the hail from Captain John Collins of the *Roscius*, a Truro man himself. "What assistance can I give?" was his question.

Captain Knowles had already decided on his answer: "I am abandoning my vessel, will you take us aboard?"

The *Roscius* quarterboat was soon alongside, and Captain Knowles, with a few accurately placed blows of his hatchet, knocked a hole in the bottom of the *Garnet*. As he stepped aboard the waiting quarterboat, down went the *Garnet* out of sight. Thus Captain Knowles and his crew of ten men were rescued 200 miles out to sea from "Neversink," New Jersey, and were aboard a passenger ship on which 400 persons were sailing to America. After landing later at New York, they all reached home to be greeted as souls back from the very gates of death.

The account of Matthias Rich, Captain of the *Water Witch*, also out in the same wild gale of October 1841, gives us definite evidence of how the vessels which were lost met their fate. At 4:00 in the morning of Sunday, October 3, he sailed by the Truro fleet, then lying comfortably to the northwest under foresail with two or three vessels carrying bob jib. He sailed so close to the *Dalmatia* and the *General Harrison* that he could have hailed either. Several hours later, he passed the *Pomona*, and recognized Captain Sol Dyer on board. Dyer immediately followed the *Water Witch* in toward land, for he sent a boy forward to loose a part of the jib, which they hoisted at once.

Captain Rich realized that the storm was then so bad that he would have no chance of tacking, and would either have to make a harbor or run ashore. At this time another vessel, probably the *Bride of Dennis*, was sighted, and joined them. The storm increased until it blew a hurricane. At 1:00 in the afternoon land was sighted under their lee and well along to windward. Captain Rich's story continues in his own words:

> *Our desperate condition was at the first moment a terrible shock, but quickly recovering, I sprang on deck, called up my crew, ordered the jib set. Under the pressure of the jib she fell off so far that the land was windward of the bowsprit. I knew we had a good sea-boat; I had*

tried her in a hard scratch, and knew that our race was life or death.
The mainsail had been balanced reefed before laying to; this I ordered
hoisted; the sail was small, but before half-way up, our vessel lay so
much on her broadside, that the halliards were lost, the sail came
down by the run, and blew to pieces, the main boom and gaff going
over the lee rail. We first tried to cut them away, but fearing the main
top-in-liff would carry away the mainmast, got on a tackle and pulled
the boom and part of the mainsail out of the water. Then righted and
came up to the wind, making good headway.

Thus Captain Rich saved his vessel. He and the others had been so
busy on the *Water Witch* that they had no time to look for the other two
fishing craft, but when they had a moment's rest, those on the *Water*
Witch peered in vain for the other two vessels. Both vessels had disappeared, evidently having capsized. Some time later the *Pomona* drifted
into Nauset Harbor, with three drowned boys in the cabin. All were lost
aboard the *Bride of Dennis* as well. Captain Rich brought his vessel into
Herring Cove to anchor at 6:30 that eventful day. He had been lashed
to the helm for twelve solid hours, with the brief exception of the time
that they were laying to, removing the wreckage.

Another amazing event of this same wild October Gale of 1841 was
the remarkable accomplishment of the vessel *Reform*. Laying under bare
poles, with a drag-out to keep head to the wind, the *Reform* was being
swept by the seas, which made a breach fore and aft. All hands were
fastened below in the cabin awaiting whatever fate had in store for
them. Elisha Paine went up on deck.

Suddenly a terrific sea completely swallowed them up; they went
many fathoms below the surface. A moment later they were all thrown
against the deck, upside down, and then the ship continued to turn,
finally coming upright again. Two or three of the men crawled out on
deck to discover that the masts were gone and the hawser of the drag was
wound around the bowsprit. The *Reform* had turned completely over to
come up on the opposite side! Poor Elisha Paine was never seen again.

Aboard another Truro vessel in the storm, two brothers had gone
down to their death. For days, weeks, and even months afterwards, a
lonely, heartbroken father would climb on top of the Hill of Storms
with his telescope, where he scanned the ocean in all directions, searching for the sail he knew in his heart he would never see.

Over eighty years before the October Gale of 1841, another Truro captain had sailed into the far north. In one of Governor Francis Bernard's letter books there is an item dated February 16, 1761, which tells an amazing story of the adventure of Captain Henry Atkins, of Truro, Cape Cod. Sailing from Boston in 1758, Atkins made a voyage to the Davis Straits in the far north. Going ashore at several points in latitude forty-six degrees, the Truro captain was unable to discover any signs of explorers having visited there before him. Only the native inhabitants greeted him, and they indicated that he was the first white man to visit them in history.

Captain Atkins decided to barter with the natives and carried ashore some trinkets, which were exchanged with the Indians for whalebone. Apparently both sides were happy, for the natives seemed highly pleased, and Atkins obtained £120 value in sterling for his investment of 10 shillings in trinkets. An item from the book of Governor Bernard follows:

> *The Indians were chiefly dressed in beaver clothing of the finest fur, and some in seal skins. He could not distinguish their sex by their dress, but one of his seamen approached one of them, who opening her beaver, discovered her sex, which pleased the Indians greatly.*

The entire region at Davis Straits was named for places and friends back at Truro and Cape Cod. Gull Sound and Cape Cod were both bestowed on lonely regions of the far north. Sailing for home September 29, 1758, Atkins reached Fortune Bay in good time. On October 20 he arrived at Newfoundland, where it was so cold he could not fish, although if he had remained at Fortune Bay, fishing would have been possible. He eventually reached home in safety.

I found a very ancient stone, the monument to Mrs. Hannah Paine, who died in 1713. It was the oldest stone in the entire graveyard, and I hunted for several hours to make sure.

My search was successful along other lines as well. For some time it had been my hope to locate the final resting place of the captain and crew of the unfortunate schooner *Rachel* of Sullivan, Maine, but I had not been able to find it. I was particularly anxious because of information which should be placed on the gravestone of those who perished with the Rachel in 1798. The story follows.

Captain John Simpson, a prominent citizen of Sullivan, Maine, sailed from there for Salem, Massachusetts, in the middle of the month of

November, 1798, as master of a new 100-ton schooner, the *Rachel*. He sailed in company with another new schooner, the *Diana*, commanded by Simpson's brother, Captain Josiah Simpson. The two vessels continued together down the coast until they reached Herring Gut Harbor, now Port Clyde, off St. George, some ten miles from White Head, Maine.

Threatening weather made the two brothers discuss the situation, and Josiah decided to make the harbor, while John believed that because of the fair wind he would try to reach Salem. Then the storm hit with all the unleashed fury which a northeaster can muster. Twice during the storm the gale seemed to relinquish its hold, only in both cases to start again worse than ever. The *Rachel* was blown all the way across Massachusetts Bay to Cape Cod. The storm proved so severe that when it ended, from four to six feet of snow had fallen on level ground and traffic on all post roads was suspended.

The gale was one of the worst of the entire eighteenth century. On Cape Cod alone there were twenty-five bodies recovered from the wreckage of ships which came ashore. When the roads were ploughed, the Cape Cod men went down to the beaches. At Highland Light the keeper found seven vessels ashore, among them the *Rachel*. She had hit the beach between the second and third sand hill south of the light, and not a soul remained alive. The body of every member of the *Rachel*'s crew was recovered, however. The personal belongings of Captain Simpson and the other sailors were carefully taken from them and

Captain John Simpson's grave at Truro (photo by Edward R. Snow)

saved; their bodies were interred. Some of the possessions saved at the time, including a sealskin trunk, a pearl-handled knife, and a handkerchief, have been preserved by Captain Simpson's descendants to this day. The handkerchief has a special significance, for the captain's five-year-old daughter had placed it in his pocket the day he sailed away from home never to return.

The story of the tragedy was told and retold in front of many firesides for several generations. Over three-quarters of a century afterwards, John S. Emery and Erastus O. Emery journeyed to Cape Cod to find the final resting place of Captain John Simpson, their grandfather. There they were aided in their search by Miss Polly Collins, whose grandfather helped bury the captain and crew in 1798. In 1878 a marble tablet was erected over the graves, set in granite quarried at Sullivan, Maine, where the *Rachel* sailed from.

Several years ago I had first read this story while looking up information for my *Storms and Shipwrecks* but found no one who knew where the graves were or who could volunteer additional information. Therefore I did not include the shipwreck in my volume. Since that book was published, however, I learned the complete story and was anxious to see the stone, for which I had looked in vain for years.

I discovered the stone in an odd way. First I noticed one of the monuments had been tipped over, probably during a storm, and was then lying flat on the pedestal. On closer examination I found that stone to be the one for which I had been searching. Although partially covered by a yellow fungus such as often gathers on old marble, I was able to read it.

> *This tablet marks the burial place of Captain John Simpson, of Sullivan, Maine, aged 38 years, Master of sch. Rachel, of that place, who, with his entire crew, consisting of the following persons, viz., Paul Dudley Sargent Jr. passenger, William Abbott, Stephen W. Merchant, Zachariah Hodkins, and one other, were lost on the wreck of the above vessel near this place, in the Memorable Snowstorm November 20, 1798, and afterwards buried here. Erected in 1878, in memory of Captain Simpson, by his grandson, John S. Emery of Boston.*

I knew the name of the "one other" lost on the wreck. It was James Springer, and before the sun had set that afternoon, I made arrangements to place his name, missing from the grave for 148 years, on the tablet where it rightfully belonged.

————————— ⌇ —————————

Highland (Cape Cod) Lighthouse is open to visitors from May to October; see www.trurohistorical.org/lighthouse.htm for more information. In 1996 the tower was relocated about 450 feet back from its former location close to the edge of the eroding bluff, and it stands today close to the seventh fairway of the Highland Golf Links.

The Jenny Lind Tower was deeded in 1961 to the Cape Cod National Seashore by the daughter-in-law of the man who brought it to Truro, Harry M. Aldrich.

Regarding alcoholism among Native American Indians, it is now accepted that this tendency is not hereditary. Alcohol abuse and alcoholism are today the leading causes of mortality in the Indian population, but the reasons are believed to be cultural and socioeconomic.

Captain Jesse Holbrook, who as Snow mentions was credited with fifty-four whales killed on one voyage, was described by Jeremiah Digges in *Cape Cod Pilot* as a "strong athletic man, weighing 350 pounds." Holbrook spent twelve years in England as an instructor in the art of whaling.

Blackfish are better known today as pilot whales. Pods of pilot whales still occasionally beach themselves on Cape Cod. In July 2002 dozens of the animals came ashore in Dennis and Wellfleet. Some of the whales were helped back to safety by rescuers, but most stranded themselves again and eventually died or were euthanized. On Cape Cod, some attribute whale and dolphin beachings in part to the sickle shape of the peninsula that acts as a trap for marine mammals. The commercial killing of pilot whales continues in some parts of the world, but they are officially protected in the United States under the Marine Mammal Protection Act.

CHAPTER 3

The Town of Wellfleet

The next day I started my walk to the Pamet River, but it wasn't much fun in the pouring rain which had greeted the dawn. After waiting in a shelter some time for the rain to stop, I hiked back to the GAR Highway Number 6, and resumed walking southward toward my destination. By the time I had crossed Pamet River I was wet and miserable and began to wonder if I hadn't better ask for shelter again at the next lodgings I came to. But I was stubborn and kept walking, and eventually the sun came out to reward my efforts. By that time I had sighted four of Truro's well-known ponds—Great Pond, Snow Pond, Round Pond, and Ryder Pond—as I headed for Wellfleet. Reaching that town, I quickly made arrangements for a room for the night, but arose early the next morning, rested and refreshed by my extra sleep.

The afternoon of the next day I hiked along the Outer Beach, or the backside, as Cape Codders like to call it. Reaching the shore by following Pamet Road south from Truro, I proceeded in a southerly direction. My objective was the home of the Wellfleet Oysterman, Uncle Jack Newcomb, mentioned by Thoreau almost a century before. I had tried to find it on several other occasions, but this time I had a very definite hint from my good friend, Miss Elizabeth E. Freeman of Wellfleet. She assured me that the house still existed, and gave me definite directions on how to find it. But, thinking I could find it by my own methods, I was hiking the beach southward from the end of Pamet Road rather than coming up through Gull Pond Road to Higgins Pond as had been suggested.

It was a cold April day, and I felt that the gods had forsaken me. I was actually very uncomfortable in my light sweater and sweatshirt, but I wouldn't admit it. So I trudged away along the sand, sinking in five or six inches at every step, and continuing that necessary uphill lurch of my gait, so important to keep from walking into the sea. An hour passed, and finally I climbed the bank to find myself near the boundary line which divides Truro and Wellfleet. There I knew that I was within striking distance of the house itself. I had been told that old Uncle Jack's homestead was now owned by the Powdrell family of Wellfleet.

However, I had also been told that the house had been torn down years ago, so was wondering just what I would find there. First I came across a series of autopaths through the woods, but there was no indication that I was near my destination. Then I found a sign nailed to a tree—Powdrell—and I knew that I was taking the right turn. After many curves and twists I came out into a clearing, and there was the house itself, with the name "Mt. Thoreau" visible to all. I had reached my goal. I knocked on the front door, but there was no answer. Walking around the building, I peered through the windows to make out the old fireplace. Now, why was that fireplace of unusual interest to me? Well, for the answer to that question, let us go back to the year 1849.

One evening in that year Henry David Thoreau himself was sitting with William DeCosta by the fire in this same house. The eighty-eight-year-old man, Uncle Jack Newcomb, who had heard cannon fire coming across the bay during the Battle of Bunker Hill, was telling of the strange wreck of the *Franklin*. The *Franklin* was too far inshore, heading for the bar. Wishing to watch the vessel wrecked, Uncle Jack had gone over to the cliff to seat himself comfortably there while a disaster took place before his eyes, a shipwreck which cost the lives of eleven people. It later developed that Captain Charles Smith of the *Franklin* had purposely wrecked his ship, but as he lost his own life in the disaster, his plans to get insurance backfired. Newcomb told of the day when the British steamer *Cambria* went aground and the English ladies played pranks with his scoop nets in the ponds.

That night Thoreau slept in the house with the wind rattling the fireboards and the casements. When early morning came, Newcomb's wife arose before her husband, for she was only eighty-four.

Thoreau, after running down to the beach cliffs to watch the sun come up, had again resumed his seat facing the fireplace across the room. The old Wellfleet Oysterman, standing with his back to the fire, began to tell stories again. Thoreau admits that the ancient mariner had one weakness, tobacco chewing. His favorite location for relieving himself of the tobacco juice was the fireplace, where the breakfast was being made ready. And it was quite a breakfast—eels, buttermilk cake, cold bread, green beans, doughnuts, and tea. Every so often Uncle Jack would half turn around to expectorate into the fireplace, but sometimes his attempts to hit the fire met with only partial success. Thoreau admits that the Wellfleet Oysterman was "ejecting his tobacco juice right and left into the fire without regard to the various dishes which were there preparing." Thoreau sat down with the others to breakfast, and ate applesauce and doughnuts, "which I thought had sustained the least detriment from the old man's shots, but my companion refused the applesauce, and ate of the hot cake and green beans which had appeared to him to occupy the safest part of the hearth." Later they compared notes, and Thoreau tried to prove that "the buttermilk cake was particularly exposed," but his companion DeCosta was definitely sure that the "applesauce was seriously injured, and had therefore declined that."

Uncle Jack Newcomb and his wife, Thankful, both died in 1856, and are interred in the Wellfleet graveyard. I hiked over the hill and found their graves after quite a hunt. The Wellfleet Oysterman's marble tombstone has a jagged crack. From the cemetery I struck across the fields for Robert Powdrell's home. He and his mother are the present owners of the Newcomb property. A short time later we went back to Mt. Thoreau, and Robert Powdrell allowed me to inspect the chimney.

"The original bricks are still there," said Powdrell, "but we have taken out the oven. The building was unoccupied for some time, and we purchased it from the Baker estate. Probably the Bakers got it from the Newcombs, for we bought it in 1919."

"Have you ever stayed in it all the year round?"

"Yes, for two years, but we haven't tried it lately. You may be interested to know that the room with the wooden shutters, which rattled in the wind the night Thoreau slept there, is just as it was originally. We try to keep it looking much the same as it was in the days when he visited here."

Leaving Robert Powdrell at his summer home, I hiked southward, finally doing some dry land navigation which brought me out around Gull Pond and onto Gull Pond Road itself. Half an hour later I was knocking on the door of Miss Elizabeth E. Freeman.

Miss Elizabeth Freeman's home in Wellfleet has much to interest almost anyone. Priceless china dishes brought home by her sea captain relatives, paintings of barks and ships, a panel from Donald McKay's famous clipper ship *Glory of the Seas*, and an amazing coal hod that will mystify you are just a few of the many treasures in her 200-year-old house tucked back in the woods.

For many years there lived in the house a wonderful lady, Aunt Drusilla Laha, who had twenty-two children, two of her own and twenty who were adopted. Her husband was shipwrecked soon after their marriage and drifted on a raft for a long period of time before being rescued. He never recovered from this terrible experience, and remained an invalid for the rest of his life. She took care of him and did very well at it, running a general store at the same time.

The exact age of the house is unknown, but the fact that it is well over 200 years is attested to by the discovery of ancient buckle shoes found buried in the soil in the cellar.

Years ago Mrs. Mary Manson Freeman, Elizabeth's mother, obtained a pistol from the British frigate *Somerset* while in Provincetown. Mrs. Freeman presented it to her son-in-law, Admiral Chester Nimitz, and this famous American naval hero now has in his possession a relic from the first war this nation ever fought.

Miss Freeman often spoke of the fact that she had uncles, great uncles, grandfathers, and great-grandfathers who were sea captains, and now with Admiral Chester Nimitz in the family she must indeed be more proud than ever.

I was fascinated by the panel of the *Glory of the Seas*. It was a distinct thrill to carry it out into the yard for a picture, for I had in my hands part of the last clipper ship Donald McKay ever built. I thought of the occasion of her launching in 1869 when Donald McKay's daughter, Frances, christened her, of the ninety-six–day run to San Francisco from New York which was the ninth best on record, and of her record run to Australia. The *Glory of the Seas* left San Francisco to arrive at Sydney, Australia, in thirty-five days, a record which no other sailing ship has ever equaled! And I was temporarily in possession of a panel of that famous vessel! The photographs made, I carried the panel carefully back into Miss Freeman's home.

The panel had been designed and painted by Thomas L. Manson, Miss Freeman's grandfather. One day he had it removed from the clipper ship to do a small amount of work on it, but the *Glory of the Seas* sailed unexpectedly and never returned to America. He retained the panel and it was later given by his daughter to Miss Freeman.

Elizabeth E. Freeman directed me to the part of the Wellfleet grave-yard I was eager to visit, where the drowned victims of the ill-fated *Franklin* are interred. Half an hour later I stood in the Wellfleet Ceme-tery at the yucca-covered burial plot there for several minutes before continuing my journey. There were many other shipwrecked sailors in that pleasant Wellfleet graveyard, but none met death so unnecessarily as those poor people who drowned because the captain willfully wrecked his vessel for insurance. No stone marks their grave.

Leaving Wellfleet's Pleasant Hill Cemetery, I headed south until reaching Gross Hill Road, which I followed until I was in the center of Wellfleet. Finding Lake Road Pond, which runs out to Cahoon's Hollow Coast Guard Station, also known as the Wellfleet Station, I soon passed Long Pond on my right, and fifteen minutes later I had reached the shore again. I am always thrilled to visit the sea near the Cahoon's Hollow Station, for it was near this point that a real pirate, doomed to die in the surf, first sighted the shores of Cape Cod!

The pirate's name was Samuel Bellamy, and his ship was the *Whidah*. After cruising up and down the Atlantic Coast, preying on shipping, he and his crew of 145 bloodthirsty buccaneers found themselves on a lee shore one night during a gale. All except two of the pirates drowned in the disaster which befell the *Whidah* when she hit the beach during the great storm. It was the third greatest loss of life in any New England shipwreck. One hundred thousand dollars in gold and silver are believed to be buried in the wrecked hull of the *Whidah* two miles south of the Cahoon's Hollow Coast Guard Station. Alton Hall Blackington, however, believes that the money may have been left in Maine at a secret location there just before the disaster occurred.

I went down the bank for two miles, hopefully peering into the water, but I did not see Bellamy's ship, the *Whidah*. In 1923 John Howard Nickerson not only located the hulk, but at dead low water stood waist deep on the wreck to remove part of the cannon he found there. The exact location is two miles south of the Wellfleet or Cahoon's Hollow Coast Guard Station.

I sat down on the bank to rest and reviewed Wellfleet's history. Before 1644 the Pilgrims had purchased this territory of Pononakanet from Sachem George, who had succeeded Aspinet. The legend goes that the Pilgrims were discussing the area now called Wellfleet with the Indians, and they asked, "Whose lands are those?" to which the Indians replied, "Nobody's." That was all the information the good white people needed.

"Then they are ours," the Pilgrims replied, and Wellfleet came into being as a territory owned by the English.

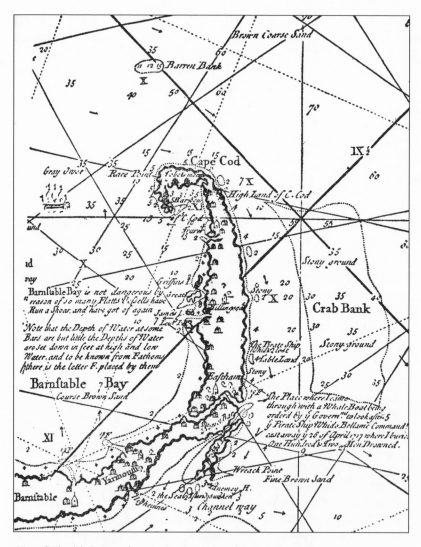

Map of Whydah *location (from Snow's* True Tales of Buried Treasure*)*

When the seven first settlers arrived at Nauset, they included both Wellfleet and Orleans in their claim. Later they changed Nauset to Eastham, a name the area still retains.

In its early history this region was known as Billingsgate. By 1722 the inhabitants of Billingsgate asked permission to become a separate church parish, and in 1723 the court granted the petition. Thirty-eight years later the citizens decided to attempt forming a new town, and Captain Elisha Doane and nine others sent a petition to Eastham. Finally, on May 25, 1763, an area eight miles in length from north to south, averaging three miles in width, was set off from Eastham to become what is today known as Wellfleet. The first lighthouse was erected in 1822 at Billingsgate Point, where Myles Standish had landed on his way to the mainland. The light stood for many years before washing into the sea, along with all the land around it.

When the early inhabitants of Wellfleet settled there they made their homes on the islands and on Billingsgate Point itself. The word Billingsgate was brought over from London, where Billingsgate Market has been the chief fish depot since 1461. The shores and islands around Wellfleet made it an ideal location for the first comers, as birds, fish, oysters, and clams abounded in the vicinity. It was easy to catch birds in those days without shooting them, for the old gull houses could trap forty or fifty birds in an evening.

Without question the Pilgrims learned the idea of the gull house from the Indians. A gull house was built from crotches fixed in the ground and covered with poles. Seaweed and beach grass were then suspended from the poles, on which was placed lean whale meat or fish. When night came, a light was exhibited on the gull house, and the curious birds would fly down to discover the meal, whereupon a man concealed inside grabbed the bird by the legs to wring its neck.

The schoolmaster of Wellfleet suffered humiliation during the activities concerning tea importing just before the Revolution. John Greenough had procured two damaged chests of tea up at Provincetown and brought them to Wellfleet, where he was publicly criticized for his act. One of the chests he claimed was for Colonel Willard Knowles of Eastham, but both were taken from him and confiscated. Schoolmaster John Greenough signed a written confession of the error of his ways, but was under a cloud for years afterwards for what was apparently an innocent act.

One of the earliest records of blackfish concerns Wellfleet Bay. In 1793 the Reverend Levi Whitman saw 400 blackfish lying on the shores here. A full-grown fish at that time weighed five tons. Blackfish Creek was so named because of the many blackfish stranded there.

Another source of Wellfleet income besides blackfish was the oyster industry. In fact, Wellfleet owes its very name to its association with oysters. Everett Nye tells us in his History of Wellfleet that Wellfleet's name comes from the Wellfleet oysters of England. Before 1750 a wall was built on the north side of Blackwater Bay, Essex County, England, and the oysters found nearby became known as Wellfleet oysters. When the "wall" was changed to "well," Nye does not suggest.

In the year 1908 there died at Wellfleet the man responsible for bringing bananas to America, Captain Lorenzo Dow Baker. When he made a voyage to South America in 1870, he stopped at Jamaica on his way back to Boston. After loading a cargo of bamboo, he threw a few bunches of bananas aboard to carry as a deck load and started for home. Although he ate many of them, they ripened too fast and were soon thrown over the side. The next year he picked a cargo of green bananas, which he brought to Boston. In this manner Dow became the first man in history to sell bananas in any quantity in America. The demand was soon so great that Captain Lorenzo Dow Baker formed his own company for the sole purpose of bringing bananas to Boston and called it the L. D. Baker Company. In 1885 the business became the Boston Fruit Company and after fourteen years passed, the United Fruit Company. The familiar white ships with the diamond markings on the stacks are a well-known part of American shipping activity.

Once in a while the ships either come in too late or for some other reason the bananas arrive fully ripened. I recall going up on the wharf in Boston with several hundred others years ago to receive free bunches of the golden fruit. It was wonderful, shouldering a full bunch of bananas and starting for home with them. There were so many in the crowd on the wharf, however, that by the time I reached Atlantic Avenue I had not more than half the bananas I started with, for hand after hand would come out of the crowd to grab a banana from my stalk. Some of the more unfortunate men arrived outside the wharf with an empty stalk on their shoulders, but I did bring home to my surprised mother a stalk with forty or more bananas still clinging to it.

Incidentally, the people of Jamaica did not forget Captain Baker, who brought economic prosperity to their island. In 1905, when Captain Baker was sixty-five years old, they presented him with a silver service in gratitude for what this Cape Cod shipmaster had done for them.

Lorenzo Dow Baker sleeps in the Pleasant Hill Cemetery at Wellfleet, but because of his foresight and industry millions of Americans are able to enjoy that delicious fruit, the banana.

In the year 1901 Guglielmo Marconi went to Wellfleet to build the first wireless station in America for the transmission of messages overseas. Twenty sturdy wooden poles were erected in a circle, but during the winter a sleet storm brought them all crashing down, and the sum of $50,000 was needed to repair the damage. The next year four latticed steel towers, 200 feet apart, were built, and by December the wireless system was ready for a test. Marconi hurried to Wellfleet, and the work progressed to such an extent that by January 19, 1903, all was in readiness to send President Theodore Roosevelt's message of greeting across the ocean to King Edward VII of Great Britain. The message was successfully communicated to England on that epochal Sunday night in 1903, and the wireless telegraph was a reality.

I walked down the beach to the ruins of the old Marconi Station. What was left of the station, which was dismantled in 1930, slid down the bank some years ago, and now all that can be seen are the cement floor slabs almost at the base of the cliff. The ocean began to wash away the sand cliff, and there is no telling when the process will stop.

Clambering up the bank, for it was over a hundred feet high at this point, I threw myself over the edge to rest before hiking across to what is still called Wireless Road. I left Wireless Road shortly afterwards to follow a trail southward, veering sharply to the right after a quarter mile to cross the railroad tracks. There between the tracks and the main highway was the South Wellfleet Cemetery. An hour later, following the old King's Highway Road, I had reached the town boundary line separating Wellfleet and Eastham, its mother province.

After satisfying my desire for food, I started eastward again, and arrived at the outer beach, where I noticed a strange, ugly fish washed up on the shore. I decided it was a baby cousin to the ninety-pound molligut I had hooked a year before off Deer Island Light in Boston Harbor. This little fellow probably was only about ten pounds in weight, although the extended mouth with ferocious teeth was eleven inches across. After taking his picture, I left him on the beach.

It wasn't warm enough that April day to enjoy a swim; I didn't even feel like trying it. I just kept plodding along the sand. Occasionally an extra-high wave would wet my feet and run up my legs to my knees. It was a pleasant sensation, and I enjoyed it.

⸺⸺⸺⸺⸺ ∼ ⸺⸺⸺⸺⸺

The eighteenth-century Cape-style home of Jack Newcomb, the old Wellfleet Oysterman, still stands on the east shore of Williams Pond. Wellfleet's Newcomb Hollow Beach is named for "Uncle Jack."

Alton Hall Blackington's opinion on the *Whydah* (now the accepted spelling) treasure was based on material in the book *The General History of the Pirates* by Captain Charles Johnson (now believed to be Daniel Defoe). This source had Bellamy establishing a fort in the area of Machias, Maine. According to pirate historian and Whydah Museum director Ken Kinkor, this "could not have occurred given what we know about Bellamy's movements in the weeks before the wreck from more reliable, primary-source, evidence."

According to Kinkor, what John Howard Nickerson actually recovered in 1923 was "a dead-eye, which was used for adjusting the tension of the ship's rigging. Given that dead-eyes did not change much over time, and the number of wrecks which occurred 'two miles south of Cahoon's Hollow' there is no way of knowing whether or not Nickerson actually recovered the dead-eye from the *Whydah*."

Searching for the lost treasure of the *Whydah* later became a favorite pursuit for Snow. He built a diving platform at what he believed to be the wreck site, but all diver Jack Poole was able to recover was an encrustation containing a few pieces of eight. The operation was halted when a storm smashed the diving platform to pieces. Today it is impossible to determine whether Snow and Poole actually explored the remains of the *Whydah*, as there are many other wrecks in the vicinity.

Underwater explorer and Cape Cod native Barry Clifford has now spent nearly two decades bringing up an estimated 200,000 individual items from the *Whydah* wreck site, including a bell inscribed "The Whydah Galley 1716." A selection of the artifacts recovered by Clifford and his team are now displayed in a museum on MacMillan Wharf in Provincetown.

Bananas, the fruit introduced to the United States in the late nineteenth century by Lorenzo Dow Baker, are now the most consumed fruit in North America at over twenty-four pounds per capita. Remembered chiefly for his fruit-related pioneering, Baker also bought Wellfleet's Mercantile Wharf and built a hotel 400 feet offshore, the Chequesset Inn. The hotel was staffed with Jamaicans. The pier was eventually undermined by ice, and the hotel was destroyed in 1934.

The strange fish referred to by Snow as a "molligut" is the *Lophius americanus*, best known today as the monkfish. Other nicknames for the fish include "angler," "allmouth," and "fishing frog." Monkfish can reach six feet in length, reportedly eat prey up to half their own size, and can capture water birds swimming at the surface of the ocean. The monkfish was formerly regarded as a "trash fish," but in recent years it has been realized that the tail portion is quite tasty—it has been called by some "poor man's lobster."

Bell from the pirate ship Whydah, *recovered by underwater explorer Barry Clifford (courtesy of the Whydah Joint Venture, Inc.)*

CHAPTER 4

Eastham and Nauset Beach

On the sandy shore opposite the Nauset Beach Light, I rested for the climb I knew was ahead. Then I began to ascend the bank. Struggling up the last few treacherous feet of sliding sand, I grabbed for the beach grass at the top and pulled myself to safety. It was quite a climb. There before me, vivid in its coloring, was the famous Nauset Beach Light. Its red top and white base were in striking contrast to the blue sky and white, fluffy clouds overhead. But I was looking at it from a prone vantage point, for I had thrown my exhausted body down on the edge of the cliff.

After a few minutes I walked over to Keeper Coleman's residence beside the light. When I knocked on the door, his affable wife, Amanda, responded.

"Why, Lieutenant Snow, what a surprise! Come right in. Gene is up in the tower and I think he'll be down soon. Sit right over there and tell me what has happened since I saw you last."

"Well," I offered, "when did you see me last?"

"Now don't tell me you didn't see us waving our heads off as you dropped your package the day before Christmas. Why, you flew right over us at about fifty feet above our house in that beautiful blue and red airplane! And do you know, it was so pretty that we just stood there watching it until it was out of sight, and forgot all about where the package was going to land and where it did land, so as a result we spent the next few hours trying to find it. But find it we did and everything had landed safely. Here's the book now," and Amanda Coleman passed me my *New England Lighthouses*. I looked it over carefully, and although it had been dropped from a plane traveling at far better than 100 miles an hour, the book looked as though it had just arrived from a bookstore. It did give me quite a thrill.

Just then steps were heard on the porch, and Keeper Eugene Leslie Coleman of Nauset Beach Light opened the door.

"What's going on around here? Why, hello, Santa Claus," he greeted me. "So you're the cause of all this excitement. How'd you arrive? Where's your car?"

"What do you mean, car?" I queried. "Do you think I've got your money?" After that sally we both sat down to talk things over. During the conversation it developed that all the three former wooden towers of Nauset Light were still in evidence around the neighborhood. Two of them, known as the Towers, were back in the woods a quarter mile and were owned by Mrs. Helen Cummings. The third, just across the road from the lighthouse, served as the cupola of a dwelling known as the Beacon, where Mrs. A. H. Hall lived. The lighthouse station was originally started in 1838 and was then a three-light station affectionately called by the inhabitants the Three Sisters of Nauset. The stone towers all went over the bank and were buried in the sand at the bottom of the cliff, as the surf and the wind ate away the Nauset cliffs at that location.

The Three Sisters of Nauset (photo by Henry K. Cummings)

The glass and framework of the lights had previously been buried on the lighthouse reservation by government order. Reconstructed of wood, the three towers were placed a safe distance away from the edge of the cliff, but in 1923 were removed altogether. The present metal structure, brought up from Chatham where it had served as the north tower of Chatham Light, was painted red and white, which made it stand out from other lighthouses along the coast. The bank is still being eaten away here, unfortunately. Just two years ago the government marker was undermined sufficiently to cause it to slide down the incline, and no one knows where it is today.

Our conversation turned to my find of buried pirate treasure the year before at Chatham. "Quite a lot of money has been found around here," said Coleman. "I never found even a cent, but I'm still looking."

A few years ago Captain E. H. Larallee of Cranston, Rhode Island, picked up several gold coins fairly close to the light. They probably washed ashore from the wreck of the old pirate ship *Whidah*, whose bones still lie submerged a few rods off the beach not many miles from the Nauset Beach Light Station. Captain Larallee also found some other small discs which may be coins, but the metal is so corroded and worn that identification at this time seems impossible.

After an hour spent visiting the lighthouse itself and looking at the many lighthouse pictures in the parlor, for Coleman had been in the Lighthouse Service at both Boon Island and Cape Neddick Nubble, I bade farewell to the Coleman family and their dog, Stubby. Soon I was down on the beach again hiking toward the Nauset Coast Guard Station. As I pushed along through the sand, I remembered two wrecks which had occurred in the general vicinity, the *Castagna* and the *J. H. Eells*.

On December 1, 1913, the 843-ton Italian bark *Castagna* sailed from Montevideo, Uruguay, bound for Weymouth, Massachusetts, with a load of guano. It was summertime in South America, and neither captain nor crew members seemed to realize that they were proceeding into northern waters where snow, ice, and sleet were common occurrences of the winter season then about to reach its height. Nearly every member of her crew was used to fine, warm weather, and was not prepared to withstand misfortune, having clothing suitable only for the tropics.

Until they arrived in the vicinity of the West Indies, nothing of consequence happened to indicate the fate in store for the captain and his crew, but about the first of February the weather grew steadily worse.

Day after day the rains and winds hit the bark, until by the night of February 16, 1914, every man aboard the *Castagna* was cold, discouraged, and bewildered. They were not accustomed to operating icy lines, or furling frozen canvas which handled like boards. They had no extra clothing to don when the snow squalls hit, nor could they realize the dangers into which their vessel was taking them.

On that night of February 16, the captain, Guiseppe Gevi, realized that he was closer to the Cape Cod shore than he had reckoned, and made an effort to wear ship. Because of the physical condition of the crew members, and the icy sails, rigging, and lines, the effort met with failure. The desperate captain now ordered the anchors let go, but to the astonishment of everyone on board, they discovered that the ice had so frozen the forecastle that the anchors could not be moved! Here, indeed, was a serious situation. Unable to wear ship and unable to anchor, the captain and crew thus found themselves at the mercy of a Massachusetts winter, as ill prepared for it as any sailors ever were.

The bark drifted aimlessly before wind and sea, and at 5:00 the next morning struck bottom at a point actually three and a half miles to the southward of Cahoon's Hollow Life-Saving Station. Captain Gevi then ordered a distress signal lighted, and had the momentary satisfaction of seeing a Coston flare burned by some alert patrolman on the Cape Cod beach.

At the time, heavy seas were hitting right up to the sand bluffs, and they soon swept over the slowly settling bark, which swung around side-on to the beach. Several smashing billows ripped the two deck-houses off the bark, and the lifeboats disappeared shortly afterwards. The crew, by this time perched in the rigging, were not clad in any way for the torture which lay ahead. One poor man had nothing over his body but an oilskin, which was little protection against the freezing spray and icy wind which hit him. Most of the crew were bareheaded and barefooted! Many had on only undershirts and trousers. An hour or so later, watchers from the shore saw the captain of the *Castagna* lose his grip and fall into the sea to his death, followed a short time later by a crew member.

The *Castagna* had been sighted by a patrolman at 5:20 that morning, and he telephoned the news at once to the Cahoon's Hollow Station. The members of the Nauset Station were then notified, and by quarter of 6 that morning two crews were on their way to the scene, one from each station, each with parts of the necessary apparatus hauled by a horse. A boat was not brought down to the beach at this time because of the high waves, which made launching impossible.

As soon as they reached the scene, the surfmen set up the beach gun and shot out two lines over the wreck. They fell across the topgallant brace, too far for the frozen sailors to climb. The third attempt was more successful, the rope landing on the mizzen topmast stay. One of the sailors aboard tried to reach the line before it slid off into the sea, but he was too late and watched it hit the deck when he was only a few feet away. Then the waves washed along the vessel, making it impossible for anyone to descend to the deck. Finally, a sailor grabbed the line, after which the tail-block was drawn aboard with the whip line rove through it. Several of the sailors then made the block fast to the bitts aft, but their rapidly failing strength would not permit them to carry the block high enough above the deck before they made it fast. Therefore the line would not run clear.

The watchers on shore saw the weakened condition of the sailors and decided they were unable to help themselves. The lifesavers then determined to attempt to launch a surfboat, and five husky patrolmen were dispatched to the nearest station, Cahoon's Hollow, for the Monomoy surfboat. By 8:30 they had pulled the heavy boat to a position abreast of the wreck, and were pleased to find the seas had moderated slightly.

The surfboat was launched and took in little water. The lifesavers pulled for the inshore side of the bark, which lay parallel to the beach, but they found no chance to reach the unhappy sailors, for the great seas roared around both stem and stern to meet again just inside the *Castagna*. However, one of the alert surfmen noticed that the current

The wreck of the Castagna

and waves had piled up the sand so high that every time a wave receded it was actually bare between the vessel and the shore in several places. Anchored to the sand, the lifeboat was carried by the southward current to a position abeam of the wreck. Several of the surfmen jumped out of the lifeboat to wade over to the bark, where they shouted to the bewildered men to slide down a line into their arms.

The first sailor slid down the rope and was rescued by the surfmen. One by one the freezing members of the crew of the *Castagna* left the doomed craft. In a short space of time the lifesavers of Cape Cod carried eight sailors to their anchored lifeboat. It was a strange rescue. Finally, believing all those still alive had been taken off, the surfmen decided that if they were to save the frozen men from dying, they should rush them to the hospital.

As soon as the eight victims were safely ashore, the patrolmen turned them over to willing residents of Cape Cod, who hurried the frozen men to the Marconi Wireless Station at South Wellfleet where first aid was applied. But it was seen that they were rapidly weakening, and plans were made to send them at once to the Carney Hospital in Boston.

Meanwhile, another crew went out to the *Castagna* in charge of Keeper Tobin and Keeper Walker of the two life-saving stations to search for more victims. Arriving at the bark, they threw a grapnel over the side with a line attached and went aboard hand over hand. Before going up to the frozen bodies in the rigging, they carefully searched the vessel for possible survivors. On the poop deck they found a poor, frozen, bare-footed sufferer clad only in trousers, shirt, and vest, still alive but moaning piteously in his unconscious state. Carrying him to the side, they lowered the sailor into the lifeboat and rowed him ashore, but the man died before they could get him off the beach.

While conducting the rescue, Keeper Tobin almost lost his own life by stepping into the quicksands. He was rapidly sinking when two of his comrades rescued him. When extricated, he was so chilled and weakened that he also was sent ashore and up to the Wireless Station for treatment.

After Keeper Tobin and the sailor were landed, the crew went back to the bark for the unpleasant task of cutting down the lifeless victims of the disaster. An hour later all dead bodies had been removed, and the abandoned ship lay alone in the ocean, its icy rigging glistening against the background of surf and sea.

The sailors at the Marconi Station were rubbed with snow and ice water for several hours while waiting for the train which was to take them to Boston, and finally they were all removed to the railroad station and carried aboard the waiting passenger car. Arriving in Boston, they were soon made as comfortable as possible at the Carney Hospital. The steward, Luigi Bianchi, died on March 3 from the effects of his experience, but the other men eventually recovered, although in at least one case amputations were necessary. It had been a terrible experience both for the sailors of the *Castagna* and the lifesavers of Cape Cod. The *Castagna* became a total loss.

The other shipwreck near this point was that of the schooner *Eells*, which also hit Nauset Beach. On March 15, 1887, the schooner *J. H. Eells*, of Camden, Maine, in command of Captain Frederick Wallace of Rockport, Maine, was proceeding from Perth Amboy, New Jersey, to Boston with a load of railroad ties and pig iron. A heavy northwesterly gale accompanied by snow had made her captain decide to run for the nearest shelter, as the *Eells* had sprung a leak. Trying to beat around the Cape, she stranded at 9:30 that morning on the edge of the outer bar off Nauset, about 350 yards from the low-tide mark.

Keeper Walter D. Knowles of the Nauset Station had already seen the *Eells* at 9:00, and had walked along the beach following her as she steered south. Then he lost her in the swirling snow as the storm shut in. He returned to the house and was about to enter when the snow let up for a brief instant; through the opening in the storm he sighted the schooner, this time in the breakers, with her head toward shore. Sounding the alarm, he ordered the crew out. Just as they were about to start, the south patrol came running up the beach with the news that the *Eells* was on the edge of the bar a mile and a half to the south.

The lifesavers, with the wind at their backs, made good time as they pulled the beach apparatus along the sand, and were opposite the wreck by 10:00. As the waves were sweeping right along her decks by that time, preparations for the launch were made at once.

The launch was successful, but the current swept the men southward and away from the schooner as they tried to reach the wreck. The surfboat headed to windward and almost capsized in the breakers. Fast bailing saved them, and again they started for the wreck. The wind was too high, keeping them from reaching the schooner for the second time. When still another attempt ended unsuccessfully, the thoroughly discouraged lifesavers determined to attempt the rescue by using beach apparatus, for the combination of strong current and high wind made the lifeboat helpless to aid the shipwrecked men. By this time the crew were clinging to the rigging of the *Eells*.

On their return to shore, four of the men went to bring back the gear, and at 11:30 they placed the Lyle gun in position and fired. The line fell short. No less than ten other attempts all ended the same way. For some reason, the lighter number four gun was not used, although, as later tests proved, it would have reached the schooner. While the firing was in progress, one of the men left his perch in the rigging of the *Eells* and went out on the bowsprit, where he lashed himself to the jibstay.

All during this period people were gathering on the shore. The super-intendent of the Cape Cod Life-Saving District, Benjamin C. Sparrow, got up from a sickbed to be on hand. Scores of fishermen were walking up and down the beach, and one of them suggested trying the new Hunt gun of the Massachusetts Humane Society, which was then in charge of Captain Jabez Snow of East Orleans. Men went to bring back Snow and the new Hunt gun.

Meanwhile, the schooner's deck was completely under water as the tide was rising and the craft was settling into the sand. The waves had reached the foot of the bluff, so all apparatus had to be moved to higher ground, increasing the distance of the schooner from the would-be rescuers to 400 yards. Because of this the new shot fell short, when fired, by about seventy-five yards. After another futile attempt, Captain Snow suggested that Keeper Knowles fire the Hunt gun by his own method. Knowles loaded the gun with six ounces of powder instead of three, and used a number four line.

A great shout went up from the massed hundreds on the Nauset cliffs when Keeper Knowles landed his shot successfully across the schooner between the two masts. There were three sailors huddling in the starboard forerigging, and two of them climbed up to secure the line to the crosstrees, and then hauled out a larger number seven line which had been attached. Next the keeper sent out his whip, but the current was so strong that the two sailors could not pull the whip out, and Keeper Knowles had it drawn back to shore. Although another method was tried to make it easier, the sailors were still unable to draw out the block because of the current. After hours of experiments, the line parted and communication with the wreck was ended. The new gun was then brought forward again, and another shot landed successfully in the rigging. The third member of the schooner's crew in the rigging joined his comrades aloft, but the three were unable to accomplish anything. The man down on the bowsprit, later identified as the captain, did not attempt to reach the rigging.

Darkness soon came to send the multitude of citizens on the beach to their homes. Nevertheless the station men stayed at the scene, waiting for whatever was ahead. When dawn arrived, it was seen that the captain had been washed off the bowsprit to his death and that one of the three in the rigging was dead. A terrible sea continued to rage, making all communication impossible. A large crowd had gathered on the beach to await the low tide and a possible chance of launching the station lifeboat, but when the sea where the schooner was had gone down, the roaring breakers near the shore prevented any launching.

At the height of the discussion concerning what could be done to save the men, a great shout went up, for a tugboat had been sighted, heading southward. It was the Boston tug *Underwriter,* and on a signal from the bluff, she quickly ran in as close as she dared to lower a boat, which headed for the wreck. The two survivors slid down the jibstay to the bowsprit, and dropped into the waiting boat, with a mighty roar of relief sounding up and down the Orleans shore. As the tug could not land the two exhausted men anywhere nearby, the *Underwriter* turned around and made the run back to Boston, where both men, Mate John Olsen and a sailor whose name is not now known, eventually recovered from their harrowing experience.

The circumstances of the failure of the lifesaving crew to rescue the four sailors was the subject of an investigation, but it was agreed that

The great beach at Cape Cod near Nauset Light, 1936 (photo by Edward Rowe Snow)

the conditions of wind, sea, and current prevented rescue from shore. The current was actually so strong that when the whip line was out to its full scope to the leeward, fifty stout men were unable to gain a step to windward to lighten the task of the two men pulling in the crosstrees. It was one of those unfortunate situations in which nothing could be done, but the tug *Underwriter* saved the day by rescuing the two survivors from the schooner *J. H. Eells*.

At the Nauset Coast Guard Station there begins the first of three long stretches of sand which extend southward for many miles, running parallel to the general contour of the land. The first two are known as Nauset Beach and the third Monomoy Beach, but they are confusing to almost everyone except the Cape Codders of long acquaintance. If one should venture down to the end of Nauset Beach, he would be at the entrance to Nauset Harbor. He can look across at the continuation of Nauset Beach, also called Orleans Beach. South of Nauset Harbor, Nauset Beach is in two towns, Orleans and Chatham.

I called to pay my respects at the Nauset Coast Guard Station, and then started out across the beach to visit the Cape Cod house of Henry Beston, whose book called *Outermost House* proves a delightful reading

Crew at Nauset Coast Guard Station (photo by Edward Rowe Snow)

experience. Mr. Beston had talked with me the winter before in Hingham where I was lecturing, offering me the key to his Fo'castle, which he built on the sand cliffs south of the Nauset Coast Guard Station. I had accepted his offer, but neglected at the time to obtain the key.

Being so near to the Fo'castle, I was eager to visit the house. After a sandy trudge through the dunes, I reached the Beston residence and walked around the building. The ample window space, the books on the shelves, the door step made from an old hatch, the pump which worked in the coldest weather, and the small brick fireplace, all were remembered as I attempted to peer into the Fo'castle on Nauset Beach. Then I started back to the Nauset Coast Guard Station for my hike down Doane Road. I had made my pilgrimage to what was to me a place of special significance, where Henry Beston, a modern Thoreau, had spent a year's communion with nature interpreting for all of us what Cape Cod can mean to a man away from civilization.

I stopped at the graveyard in North Eastham to search for the stone of the man who made the fastest trip of all time in a sailing vessel between San Francisco and Boston. His name was Captain Freeman Hatch.

On Saturday, March 12, 1853, the clipper ship *Contest* left San Francisco, bound for the East Coast, and was followed twenty-four hours later by Captain Freeman Hatch aboard the *Northern Light*. The race of the century had begun. The two ships were about the same size and build, although the *Northern Light* was very sharp on the bottom. Both the *Northern Light* and the *Contest* reached the Equator in the same length of time, fourteen days, but on April 20, off Cape Horn, the captain of the *Contest* saw a faint outline against the sky, which told him the *Northern Light* was catching up to him. The next day the ships were together, and the excitement of the crews aboard both clipper ships was at the highest level. Then the *Northern Light* drew slowly away, and gradually vanished from the gaze of those aboard the *Contest*, who did not see her again during the race. In the late evening hours of May 28, 1853, the *Northern Light* sighted the gleam of Boston Light, and arrived at Boston seventy-six days and six hours from the time she sailed out of San Francisco. It was the fastest time ever made between the two ports by a sailing vessel!

Finally I found the object of my search, the tomb of Captain Freeman Hatch. The inscription informed me that Captain Hatch, who was born in 1820 and died in 1889, had accomplished a feat "won by no other mortal before or since."

Continuing my journey, I reached the center of Eastham. Three hundred and two years before, also in April, seven Pilgrims had stood together near the same location to plan the town which is now Eastham. They were Governor Thomas Prince, John Doane, Nicholas Snow, Josias Cook, Richard Higgins, John Smalley, and Edward Bangs. The famous Prince pear tree stood on Governor Prince's old farm in Eastham, but had vanished by 1849, when Thoreau made his hike on the Cape. Deacon John Doane, another of the first seven men of Eastham, lived to be 107 years old, and was rocked in a cradle as a baby during his last few years. Edward Bangs was a member of the early guards who protected Eastham from the Indians.

I am particularly grateful to Thoreau for his indirect reference to my ancestor Nicholas Snow in the Eastham settlement of April 1644, for he says that some of the "most respectable of the inhabitants of Plymouth removed to Eastham."

The Reverend Enoch Pratt's *History of Eastham, Wellfleet, and Orleans* tells us that Nicholas Snow was "a man of considerable distinction," having one share in the division of 1623. He was a deputy, a selectman for seven years, and town clerk for sixteen years.

Nauset was incorporated in 1646, the name was changed to Eastham in 1651, and twenty-three years later Mayomoyick, Payomet, and Satucket were brought within the limits of the town. I wanted to visit Millennium Grove, the scene of great religious activity in the nineteenth century, so I hiked along the Eastham highway until I came to Massasoit Road, which I followed until reaching the triangular junction of Massasoit Road, Campground Road, and Herring Brook Road. The meeting place of the spiritual leaders of a century ago was just ahead, off the highway to the westward. The history of the movement is of interest.

When the Methodists came to Cape Cod around 1795, their method of worship appealed to the people at the tip end of the Cape around Provincetown. The Quakers had arrived on Cape Cod to become active at Sandwich, the Mormons were later to organize in Dennis and also Provincetown, but the Methodists, possibly the largest religious group on the Cape, had their beginnings at Provincetown before showing their great strength at Eastham. It all began when Captain William Humbert went ashore around 1793 to preach to the men of Provincetown. They liked his message. Two years later a meeting house for Methodists was erected. The first load of lumber for the church was burned on High Pole Hill by those of other faiths, and the preacher was burned in effigy as well, but the determined group posted guards day and night when the second load of lumber arrived, and the church building was completed successfully.

But it was really at Eastham that the Methodists attracted the attention of the rest of America. Eighteen twenty-eight was their first big year in Eastham, where they bought ten acres of land and named it Millennium Grove. At the height of activity no less than 5,000 persons listened to the sermons preached in Millennium Grove, with more than a hundred ministers who worked in relays to minister to the impatient throngs.

A century ago the people were willing to endure much more for their religious convictions than they are today, it seems. Would you journey from 100 to 500 miles on foot, in old wagons, or on horseback, to the Millennium Grove in Eastham for a week's religious conference, knowing that when you arrived at your destination you would have to sleep with hundreds of others in a great tent on a bed of straw, with a single curtain to separate the men from the women; knowing that all the food you could have was what you brought with you; and knowing that in the morning you would have to stand in a long line, not for stockings, or bread, as has recently been done, but for water, the only source of which was a single spring which led to a well? I wonder.

Nevertheless the services were of great importance to those who attended, and when at nighttime scores of lanterns flickered among the trees it was an inspiring sight. But the trying times of the Civil War arrived and the Millennium Grove activities ended forever. Although the grove is abandoned today, summer camp meetings are still held in several other locations on Cape Cod.

I wandered over to what was left of the Millennium Grove, and was able to find the remains of the old well which did such good service for the thousands who gathered there every morning for water, but the area is being more or less overrun by the small scrub oaks. I opened my Thoreau to find his reference to the Millennium Grove activities, which were in full swing at the time he was visiting Cape Cod.

> *This was the Eastham famous of late years for its camp-meetings, held in a grove near by, to which thousands flock from all parts of the Bay. We conjectured that the reason for the perhaps unusual, if not unhealthful development of the religious sentiment here, was the fact that a large portion of the population are women whose husbands and sons are either abroad on the sea, or else drowned, and there is nobody*

but they and the ministers left behind. . . . We saw one singularly mas-
culine woman, however, in a house on this very plain. . . . It was
enough to see the vertebrae and sinews of her neck, and her set jaws
of iron, which would have bitten a board-nail in two in their ordinary
action,—braced against the world, talking like a man-of-war's-man
in petticoats, or as if shouting to you through a breaker. . . . This
woman told us that the camp-meetings were not held the previous
summer for fear of introducing the cholera, and that they would have
been held earlier this summer, but the rye was so backward that straw
would not have been ready for them; for they lie in straw.

Thoreau goes on to tell us that a man is appointed to clear out the
pump a week beforehand, "while the ministers are clearing their
throats," and then Thoreau suggests that the latter do not always
deliver as pure a stream as the former.

I saw the heaps of clam-shells left under the tables, where they had
feasted in previous summers, and supposed, of course, that that was
the work of the unconverted, or the backsliders and scoffers. It looked
as if a camp-meeting must be a singular combination of a prayer-
meeting and a picnic.

Leaving the old Millennium Grove campgrounds, I hiked down
Camp Ground Road until I came out on the bay side of Eastham. Eventually I reached the town landing at the end of Kingsbury Beach Road.

I still had a long hike ahead for my next objective, known as First
Encounter Beach. It was there in 1620 that the *Mayflower* Pilgrims,
among whom was Stephen Hopkins, resisted an attack by a band of
hostile Indians. I turned to the right at Samoset Road, and after a walk
of a little more than a mile, reached the tablet which marks the spot.

The engagement occurred while the *Mayflower* was at anchor in
Provincetown Harbor. The expedition of fifteen men had camped on the
Eastham shore while trying to find a permanent location for their settlement. One of their number wandered a short distance from camp, when
suddenly he came running back followed by war whoops and a shower
of arrows coming from the woods. It was the colonists' first encounter
with the red men, and they set up their arquebuses and fired them off in
the general direction of the place they believed the Indians were gathered. After a few rounds, nothing more was heard from the Indians. We

should realize that the hostility of the Indians was not the Pilgrims' fault, but came about because of a certain Captain Thomas Hunt, who had landed at Cape Cod in 1614. Hunt tricked several Indians to go aboard his vessel, where he captured them and brought the poor red men across to Europe, so the Indians had reasons to mistrust the white men.

While standing there on the shore, I was reminded of Enoch Pratt's reference to the adventures of Captain Matthew H. Mayo and Captain Winslow L. Knowles near this beach during the War of 1812. In 1814 they sailed from Eastham to Boston with a load of rye, which they sold in Boston, where they purchased a larger vessel for their return journey. Then, loaded with supplies for their families and others, they sailed for Eastham. Reaching the Gurnet Light, they fell in with a "pink-stern" schooner of sixty tons, which started firing at them. After two shots the Eastham men hove to, and Captain Mayo threw his valuable spyglass over the side that it might not fall into the hands of the British.

The two captains were taken aboard the schooner and brought to the British man-of-war *Spencer*. Captain Knowles agreed to go to Boston, where he could get $300 for his ransom money, but upon his arrival in Boston his friends and a certain American naval officer advised him to give up the idea.

Captain Mayo, placed aboard the schooner which had captured him, was then ordered to pilot the schooner around Cape Cod. Mayo was accompanied by twenty-three British marines and sailors from the *Spencer* who kept a sharp watch over him. One night a gale began to blow, and Captain Mayo was ordered to find shelter from the storm. He headed for Billingsgate, where he anchored in the lee of the island.

Going forward unobserved with his penknife, he sawed through all except a few strands of the hawser, which parted shortly afterwards. The schooner began to drift away. Captain Mayo suggested to the British officers that they should seek a harbor to leeward, ten miles distant. It was his intention to recapture the vessel if possible. The schooner grounded, but Mayo allayed the fears of the others by telling them the vessel would soon drift off the flats of Eastham, where they had struck. He advised them to go below so that the townspeople might not see them and become suspicious. After they had all gone below, he gave one of the sailors a gimlet with which he could bore into a keg of West India rum, and the sailors soon became intoxicated. Meanwhile Mayo had thrown overboard all the arms on deck except two brass pistols, which he concealed under his jacket.

The tide was going out, and the schooner soon heeled over to such an alarming extent that even the drunken British sailors realized that something was wrong. Appearing on deck, they were quickly subdued by Captain Mayo armed with his two brass pistols. He then jumped over the side and waded through waist-deep water to the Eastham shore, where there was quite a crowd on the beach. Telling them of the situation, Mayo was pleased to obtain the complete cooperation of the Eastham militia, who after going out to the stranded schooner at dead low water, ordered the British sailors to leave the vessel, and marched them all up to the public house of Thomas Crosby. From this place they were taken the next morning to the barn of George Collins, where a guard was placed over them. In some unexplained way the Britishers escaped, stole a whaleboat, and within a short time were back aboard the man-of-war *Spencer*.

The deputy marshall now appeared to demand Mayo's captured schooner, which originally had been taken from Duxbury by the British. It was agreed, however, that Captain Mayo should be paid $200 for his daring efforts in getting it back. Commander Richard Raggett of the *Spencer* then sent ashore a demand for $1,200, agreeing that if it were paid he would not destroy the saltworks, the town buildings, and the vessels of Eastham. A hasty council was held, the outcome of which was the decision to pay the money and secure immunity from harm. The $1,200 was paid, and the British left Eastham alone for the rest of the war.

On my return from First Encounter Beach, I passed by the Prince Hurd House on Samoset Road, formerly known as the public house of Thomas Crosby, where Captain Mayo's captured British sailors were marched the first night after their capture. Continuing to the center of Eastham, I obtained lodgings for the night.

The next morning I ate a typical Cape Cod breakfast (the details of which I shall allow the reader to guess) and then prepared for my eight-mile walk through Orleans and out to the Orleans Coast Guard Station on Nauset Beach. Hiking right down the railroad track across Governor Prince (or Prence or Prance) Road and through Boatmeadow Bog, I arrived at Orleans. Then I headed due east to Beach Road, which I followed until I reached the Atlantic.

Walking south along the shore toward the Orleans Coast Guard Station, I began to consider the Cape and its beaches and former islands from a geological viewpoint. It seems reasonable to assume that the Cape at one time continued right out to Nantucket Island. Also it is possible that

George's Bank and the Great South Shoal were at one time islands. It is of definite record that Captain Joseph Wharf played ball on George's about 150 years ago, and 125 years ago Cape Codders would see long strings of gulls sitting on the dry sandbars at the same location. When Bartholomew Gosnold doubled Cape Cod in 1602, he encountered breakers twelve leagues to the south of Provincetown Harbor, naming them Tucker's Terror.

Tucker's Terror was off Orleans and gave warning to the mariner that he was approaching Isle Nauset. As far as we can tell today, the north side of Isle Nauset was in Eastham near Nauset Light. Probably the island extended at least eight miles out into the ocean. Another island apparently extended an equal distance to the eastward of Chatham in the days of Bartholomew Gosnold, but has, like its companion, Isle Nauset, been washed away for many years.

<hr />

The "Three Sisters of Nauset" lighthouses were reunited in the 1980s after being purchased by the National Park Service. Today the restored towers can be visited at a site on Eastham's Cable Road, accessible by a walking trail from

Nauset Light today (photo by Jeremy D'Entremont)

the parking area at Nauset Light Beach. Nauset Lighthouse was moved 336 feet away from the eroding bluff in 1996, and the keeper's house was later moved. The Nauset Light Preservation Society maintains the tower and holds open houses on selected dates in summer. Visit the society's Web site at www.nausetlight.org for further information.

Henry Beston died in 1968, and his Outermost House, which had been declared a literary landmark in 1964, fell victim to the great blizzard of February 1978.

It is said that as the clipper *Northern Light* was passing the *Contest* during the race described by Snow, Captain Freeman Hatch sent a message to the captain of the *Contest* informing him that he felt he "had to depart from their side since he could no longer restrain his horse." The *Northern Light* met its end in 1862 when it sank after a collision with the French brig *Nouveau St. Jacques*.

Rampant erosion and the rising sea level continue to claim acres of real estate on Cape Cod each year. The average erosion rate on the Atlantic side of the Cape is around 3.8 feet per year, and it is generally accepted that in a few thousand years—maybe sooner—Cape Cod will cease to exist.

CHAPTER 5

The Shipwrecks and
History of the Town of Orleans

Finally I reached the Orleans Coast Guard Station on Little Pochet Island. After meeting the men on duty, I told them of my plan to hike the four miles southward so that I would be in the vicinity of the wreck of the *Calvin B. Orcutt*.

The disaster which befell the four-masted schooner *Calvin B. Orcutt* has never been written up fully, although it has been half a century since the unfortunate craft, hailing from Manasquan, New Jersey, went to her doom in the great snowstorm of December 23, 1896. So many conflicting stories have been recorded, and so many different dates given, that I decided to gain access to the official records before telling the story of the *Orcutt*. Most of those who were actively in charge that bitter night have passed away, and time has removed much of the hard feeling which developed because of what happened off the great Nauset Beach. Many unfounded charges of cowardice and thoughtlessness were carelessly hurled as an aftermath of the disaster.

On December 22, 1896, the *Calvin B. Orcutt* sailed without cargo from Portland, Maine, bound for Norfolk, Virginia. It began to snow the next day, a heavy, smothering snow which alternated with sleet as the afternoon wore on, and changed into a howling blizzard before nightfall. We shall never be certain just what happened aboard the *Orcutt* as she made her passage down the coast. We do know that around 3:30 that afternoon Jonathan Eldridge of North Chatham, while standing at Bevan's Point, Chatham Harbor, sighted a four-masted schooner apparently just coming to anchor off the outside beach north of the harbor entrance.

Head to the wind, the vessel slowly dropped astern, as though a long scope of chain was being veered. Then her anchors seemed to catch her, and Eldridge could see her pitching and straining crazily in the great breakers then rolling ashore. Only two sails were set, the mizzen and two-reefed spanker, and the mizzen was being settled away while the startled Eldridge watched. Then the snow shut down so hard that further view of the schooner was impossible.

Fred W. Nickerson and two other men joined Eldridge. When the snow let up for a moment, Nickerson looked across to see the schooner with her spanker set. One by one the townspeople gathered, and the group soon consisted of eleven good and strong men of Chatham. Nickerson, a former lifesaver who had served five seasons as seventh man at the Chatham Life-Saving Station, realized that the schooner could not possibly last the night in her desperate position.

The men decided that the afternoon patrolman from the Orleans crew had already returned to his station, approximately four and a quarter miles to the northward of the wrecked schooner, and Nickerson said it was doubtful if he could have been near the schooner at the time she hit the bar. Therefore, declared Nickerson, they should launch the old pilot boat then on the shore and attempt to row across to the Outer Beach. If they would row with him, he promised to reach the Orleans Station himself. The trip around by land was much too far and out of the question.

"It may be the means of saving the lives of the crew of the schooner," he shouted to the others above the roar of the storm. "What do you say? Let's try it!"

But there was no response from the other ten men. They had no stomach for rowing across the bay just at dusk to be stranded all night on Orleans Beach, and not one would volunteer to go with him. Nickerson then obtained a half-hearted promise from the others that they would all meet again at Bevan's Point at 7:30 and if the gale had gone down would row across to the beach.

Nickerson was not through trying, however, and determined to reach the Chatham telegraph office three miles away. Starting out with a companion, he arrived at the office at about 6:00 that night. He asked the operator there to send a message to Highland Light, the nearest station which had wires to the various life-saving stations along the Cape Cod shore. Unfortunately, the report came back that the telephone line was down between there and the Orleans Station. Two weeks before, the changing currents across Chatham Harbor had broken the communication between Chatham and the Orleans Life-Saving Station, so with the breaking of the Highland Light-Orleans line, the Orleans Station was isolated from the rest of the Cape.

Nickerson thought rapidly. Wasn't there some other way which he could use? Then the idea struck him—Superintendent Benjamin C. Sparrow lived at East Orleans, and Nickerson knew there was a telephone between Sparrow's home and the Orleans Life-Saving Station. Getting in touch with Miss Amelia Snow, the operator at the Orleans railroad Depot, he asked her to send a messenger through the deep drifts in an effort to reach Sparrow's home. Nickerson, believing that someone would soon arrive at the district superintendent's house, called up the Chatham Life-Saving Station to talk with Keeper Hezekiah Doane.

Back in Orleans, Miss Amelia Snow was trying desperately to get some one to take the message over to Superintendent Sparrow's home, but there were no volunteers. A local livery stable owner flatly refused to allow any of his horses to leave the stable on such a night, with the blizzard then pushing the snow in such a terrific fashion that the drifts were then six and seven feet deep. A boy offered to take the message through the drifts to the Cape Cod district superintendent's house, but said that someone would have to pay him five dollars before he would move from the station. As there was no one with authority to advance him that sum, and no one else cared to risk the five dollars, nothing was done about it. The local expressman, then awaiting the arrival of the down-Cape train, already two hours late because of the storm, said that he would go when the train arrived and his Christmas rush business was taken care of for the day.

Shipwreck news always travels like lightning, and by 10:00 that night practically every alert person in Orleans knew of the situation. Shortly before that time Henry K. Cummings, a young merchant of Orleans, learned the particulars and volunteered to start out for East Orleans with the message. Arming himself with a powerful lantern, he set out for the Cape Cod district superintendent's home. An hour later, after bucking through drifts which at times taxed every ounce of strength he could muster, Cummings was banging on the door of Benjamin Sparrow's residence.

"Ship ashore, sir," Cummings cried to the startled man who came to the door. "It looks bad and we can't rouse the Orleans Station, for all the lines are down."

Grasping the situation at once, Sparrow rushed to the private phone which connected his home and the Orleans Life-Saving Station. Keeper James H. Charles answered his ring almost immediately.

"Jim," said the superintendent, "there's a vessel in trouble, but we don't know too much about it. I'm afraid it's rather a wild-goose chase, for we don't know where the vessel is, and don't even know that she's ashore, though I can't see how she could help being in trouble by now. It's somewhere south of your station, probably in line with Bevan's Corner at Chatham."

"We'll get ready at once, sir," came the reply of Captain Charles, "just as soon as my north patrolman gets in. He won't be back until midnight."

"Well, by that time, I'll be at your station," replied Captain Sparrow as he hung up. He telephoned five of his nearest neighbors who gave halfhearted offers to help. Dressing warmly and putting on his high boots, Sparrow set out for the Orleans Station. The snow, however, was much deeper than he had believed, and he was soon floundering in the drifts. Finally reaching the outer beach, he set out through the half-slush, half-sand composition just above the reach of the waves to make better time, but it was not until 1:00 in the morning that he arrived at the Orleans Life-Saving Station. His eyes were half closed by the blinding sand and snow, and they smarted badly. The only person at the station was Mrs. Charles, as every man had gone to the wreck.

"Captain waited for you until 12:20," Mrs. Charles told him as the tired superintendent sat down for a brief respite, "and then he said he had to go out."

When Captain Charles and his seven men left the station at 12:20, they shoveled for some time to get the drifted snow away from the boatroom doors. Soon the horse was pulling the beach apparatus along the inside road to the south, for the tide was then rising outside and a high surf was pushing its way right up over the bank and around the sand dunes. It was a trying experience. The previous high tide had saturated the snow, and the wheels of the beach cart clogged and stuck time after time. Strung out ahead at right angles to the line of progress, the surfmen were engaged in trampling down the snow, shoveling through the higher drifts, and making sure of the road. When the thick snow squalls struck and whitened everything, they would all get lost for a few minutes, finding each other when the sudden squalls let up. Every few minutes one of the surfmen would go over to the outside beach to make sure the wreck was not there. Around 2:00 the exhausted horse showed signs of collapsing, so all hands grabbed the wheels to help push the cart through the sand. Then a strange light appeared and vanished, high in the heavens. It was the moon, trying to break out from behind the storm clouds. Again and again it lighted up the scene as the snowstorm waned and the squalls came less frequently. Finally, the full light of the moon shone down upon that drama of exhausted men and a tired horse, all pulling the beach apparatus through the wet, sticky drifts of Nauset Beach.

"There she is," suddenly shouted Captain Charles, and there was the wreck, showing in the moonlight about a half mile down the beach. It was then 2:25 A.M., and they were four and a quarter miles south of their Orleans Station.

The cart was halted on the beach abreast of the schooner, which lay half a mile offshore, with her head pointed to the northeast, seemingly held by her dragging anchors. The four masts were still standing, but the hull was submerged. Between the rollers which swept her from stem to stern, the Orleans lifesavers could make out the gaffs and booms, with the lower sails apparently snugly furled between them, all except the spanker, which was two-reefed and standing.

It was a difficult situation. First the surfmen lighted the cart torches to attract the attention of anyone who might be alive on the doomed vessel. The moon then began to dart in and out of new cloud formations, but there was enough light to scan the entire part of the schooner above water for possible survivors. The outlines of the spars and rigging revealed not even one clinging form, and there was no response whatever from the four masts. But to avoid all possible chance of criticism later, and to make doubly sure for himself, Keeper Charles prepared to aim his Lyle gun and fire into the rigging. In a short time the ebbing tide would allow him to set up the apparatus on the beach.

Suddenly, an immense breaker crashed over the *Calvin B. Orcutt*, splitting the spanker from boom to gaff. It was the beginning of the end. The foremast soon sagged out of line, and the *Orcutt* started southward and shoreward. Keeper Charles decided to try a line into her rigging, and ran toward the cart. Before he was halfway, the foremast crashed into the sea, and the other masts began to topple. At this dramatic moment, Superintendent Sparrow, terribly exhausted and cut by the sand and storm, reached the scene of the disaster. The second district head had noticed something dark in the port fore rigging as the foremast began to fall, but even as the mast dropped into the sea, there was no sign of life from the dark object in the rigging.

A Lyle gun was now set up and a number four shot was fired 400 yards into the rigging of the mastless vessel. No one appeared to take advantage of the line, so then and there it was decided that all hands had been drowned hours before. The shot was ordered hauled back ashore, but the mass of wreckage refused to yield and during a shift on the wreck, the line was tauted and snapped. No attempt was made to send any other lines aboard, as it was almost certain that there was no living person aboard. The *Orcutt* began to break up shortly afterwards, and her wreckage soon covered the beach far and near. The surfmen searched the wreckage diligently for miles until daybreak, but no bodies were found then or later on Nauset Beach. Masses of debris from the schooner literally filled every foot of space that morning. Outside planking, spars, timbers, deck beams, and cabin fragments came up on the beach along with the topgallant forecastle and the upper half of the bow, with parts of the windlass still attached. Several of the cabin doors and other pieces of light woodwork were picked up that same morning in the cut-through below Chatham Lights by residents of Chatham, so it is probable that they were carried there by the flood tide some time between 11:00 and 2:00 A.M. As none of the inside cabin work ever came in on the beach at that location, it would seem that the vessel had been entirely swept out and left a gutted shell, stripped clean long before the surfmen arrived at the scene. Thus it would appear that the schooner was disemboweled out of range of any Lyle gun apparatus, and that all hands perished far from any possible aid. Otherwise bodies and inner cabin works would have come ashore on the Orleans part of Nauset Beach.

The surfmen at Chatham Station had been busy throughout the night. It was a physical impossibility to reach the Outer Beach during the storm, but an alert double patrol was active along the Chatham shore. At 10:40 the south patrol reported from the halfway house that he had found in the surf a yawl belonging to a schooner. Keeper Doane then rang up the north patrol, who said there was no wreckage. Therefore

Doane started out along the southern patrol, taking with him a heaving line and stick to bring ashore anything which might be seen in the surf. All hands went with him. A half-mile from the station they came across some light wreckage out in the surf. The keeper swung his line to haul in a broken quarterboard, which read CALVIN B. OR—. The rest of the last name was broken off.

By daylight the storm was over, and everyone who could, crossed over to the scene of disaster. Keeper Hezekiah Doane and his crew from the Chatham station arrived on the Outer Beach about 8:00 A.M., and after surveying the wreckage and finding that there was nothing they could do, returned to their station. The Number Seven surfman from Orleans had injured his leg, so was resting in a barn on the Orleans Beach. It was then that the complete name of the schooner was made out, when a large fragment of the stern came ashore with the words CALVIN B. ORCUTT, MANASQUAN, N.J.

Captain Sparrow had stayed on the scene until 4:30, when he left to hike back to his Orleans residence. He never fully recovered from the effects of his strenuous ordeal that December night on Nauset Beach, for his eyes bothered him for the rest of his life.

At 8:00 the Orleans surfmen decided to return to their station, as the Number Seven man had sufficiently recovered the use of his injured leg to limp along the beach. The tide was then out, and they pulled the heavy beach apparatus along the hard-packed sand to reach their station about 9:00.

Within the next month five heavily sanded bodies were found, not one of them near the wreckage on the Outer Beach. On December 24 a body washed ashore at the south point of the harbor entrance, and another a mile below the Chatham Station. January 9, 1897, the remains of Albert Dubblark of Germany, the engineer, came ashore at the same place. Eight days later the body of the captain of the *Orcutt*, Edgar Pierce, was found floating near another dead sailor on the beach near Monomoy Light.

It seems strange that the life-saving service should have received adverse criticism, for the lifesavers had done everything within their power to help the doomed schooner, but she had been too far out in the dangerous seas to launch a surfboat even if the surfmen had reached the scene earlier.

Indeed, praise should be given those who tried in vain to save the crew, for it is harder to do everything possible and still fail to accomplish your objective than it is to succeed and receive praise. As it is the effort that makes the hero, there were several heroes during that wintry blizzard half a century ago. Fred Nickerson, Henry K. Cummings, Superintendent Sparrow, Keeper Charles and his entire crew, and Keeper Doane and all his surfmen deserve the credit rightfully due them for their efforts.

Cummings, though noted for his shipwreck pictures, never made a photograph of the *Orcutt*, as she went to pieces before he reached the scene.

Some time later the lifesavers were again vindicated, when the boat davits and bow were found by wreckers on the end of the most northerly projection of the Outer Chatham Bars, fully 1,000 yards from the shore, far out of the reach of any Lyle gun. Captain Benjamin Mallowes, the agent of the underwriters, later declared that the *Orcutt* pounded bottom at 8:00 that night and filled with water. Then the hatches washed away, and the inside of the cabin went, together with every member of the crew. Naturally, if the crew had still been on board, alive or dead, at the final breakup of the schooner, it is reasonable to expect that one or more of their bodies would have come ashore with the wreckage on Nauset Beach. Instead the five bodies all came ashore on the Chatham and Monomoy beaches. In the opinion of Lieutenant Frank H. Newcomb of the United States Revenue Cutter Service at Boston, if all the life-saving crews in the country had been on Orleans Beach that night nothing could have been done to save the doomed crew of the unlucky four-masted schooner.

The most ancient Cape Cod marine disaster of all times was the shipwreck of the *Sparrowhawk* at Old Harbor. In December 1626 the ship *Sparrowhawk*, loaded with passengers from England to Virginia, went ashore in the night at what was then called Monomoyick. The captain ran the craft up on the flats directly before a small harbor. A tribe of Indians, the Nausets, approached the stranded mariners, suggesting that they could send a message to Governor Bradford in Plymouth. This pleased the white men aboard the *Sparrowhawk*, who watched the Indian runners as they began their long journey over the forest trails to Plymouth. Governor Bradford responded at once, landing near the bottom of the bay at Namskeket Creek, whence he hiked overland to visit the other Englishmen, bringing with him corn, oakum, and spikes. The shipwrecked men repaired their ship and were about to leave the harbor when a great storm came up and so wrecked the vessel that it became unfit for further use. The entire party aboard the *Sparrowhawk* was thus forced to spend the winter with the Pilgrims, leaving for the South in the spring.

Two hundred and thirty-seven years later, on May 6, 1863, Solomon Linnell and Alfred Rogers of Orleans, walking at a location traditionally known as Old Ship Harbor, discovered a wreck in the mud approximately due east of the Sipson Islands. A recent storm had washed away a high sea beach, which evidently had been over the mud for countless generations effectively concealing the bones of the *Sparrowhawk*. Digging and scraping around the wreck, the two men exposed many oaken timbers which were sound and clean and located the keel and sternpost a short distance away. Hundreds of persons visited the wreck within the next few weeks, each taking away his own bit of wooden souvenir. To prevent the total disappearance of the wreck of this ancient hulk, it was decided to move its remains to Pilgrim Hall in Plymouth, where it is today. While excavating the mud around the vessel, quantities of beef and mutton, bones, leather soles, shoes, an opium pipe, and a metal box were discovered, which were also taken to Pilgrim Hall in Plymouth. Shebnah Rich tells us that old Deacon Doane and his sons and grandsons had cut hay and piled their stacks here for generations, never realizing that an ocean relic was beneath their feet.

Another visitor from Europe, almost three centuries later, came up out of the ocean during the summer of 1918, when the First World War was brought closer to America's shores. On Sunday, July 21, 1918, a German U-boat surfaced twelve miles northeast of the Orleans Coast Guard Station to shell a tug and sink three of four barges in tow. At the time the man in the Orleans tower reported to Captain Robert F. Pierce that there was heavy gun firing in the vicinity. Pierce ordered the surfboat made ready, and then telephoned Superintendent George W. Bowley at Provincetown for instructions. It was an unheard of situation in American history. Should the surfboat be launched to save lives at the scene of the sinkings, or should the surfboat be kept ashore until the submarine menace had passed?

Superintendent Bowley, in good American fashion, ordered the surfboat to proceed to the scene of gun firing, where Pierce was to place himself and his crew in readiness to save lives. Launching his surfboat, Captain Pierce arrived in time to see the German submarine standing by on the surface of the water. One loaded barge had already gone down, the other three were on their beam-ends in the water, while the tug was on fire. Lifeboats from the four barges and the tug were pulling away from the sinking and burning vessels.

Captain Pierce discovered that several of the crew of the tugboat, *Perth Amboy*, had been wounded by gunfire from the submarine, so he removed them to the surfboat and started back to the station. Meanwhile the U-boat slowly submerged. Then the other lifeboats followed the surfboat, and a short time later all had landed without further excitement at the Orleans Station, where a special train took the wounded men up to Boston.

When interviewed, Captain Pierce admitted the situation had not been a pleasant one. "It looked rather hard to be sent twelve miles offshore in a small surfboat to a German submarine firing heavy guns on a tow of barges, but orders from the superintendent must be executed and I had no excuse," were his words. One hundred and forty-seven shots were counted, at least one of which landed on United States soil at Orleans. Aviators from the local Chatham Naval Air Base were up in Provincetown at a baseball game, although there is a persistent rumor that one plane actually took off and dropped a monkey wrench on the deck of the U-boat, which submerged shortly afterwards.

My friend, Walter Walsh Eldridge, otherwise known as "Good Walter," who enjoys calling me "Professor," was at the scene of the U-boat attack within a short time after Captain Pierce's surfboat left the scene. The U-boat had disappeared, so Good Walter and his associates went aboard the smoldering tug.

"We got off a few chairs from the *Perth Amboy*," said Walter. "A short time afterwards a big steamer came by loaded with passengers. We were half expecting to see it blown up, but I guess the U-boat was pretty far away by that time. I knew there was a mess out there when I heard the firing, so we started out to see what we could salvage."

There is a real mooncusser for you. He knew there might be great danger when he went, but it was in his blood to be out there retrieving what he could before the sea claimed it. Yes, there is something that gets in your system about this mooncussing salvage business, and it finds you doing strange things. I shall never forget a usually calm and dignified lady, dressed in her everyday finery, who waded out to the wreck of the excursion boat *Romance*, ruining her shoes and stockings, to come out of the pilothouse of the *Romance* yanking and pulling at an old broken-down chair. She would have been insulted if a second-hand dealer had suggested she purchase it. Well, I guess we all have a little of that feeling in our bones, for I have tugged and pulled along the shore many articles and pieces of wood I should never have thought of twice but for the fact they had washed up on the beach. Incidentally, Captain Jim Tapley of the *Perth Amboy* later brought his tug to port.

Striking inland, I approached the main highway at a point just above a little settlement which identified itself as the Church of the Holy Spirit. I walked across to the parish house and was admitted by the Reverend Richard Bowland Kimball, who was sitting in front of the pleasant fireplace. His secretary, Miss Lois Ritchie, was at the time conferring with him about his new book, *The Story of a Church*. An atmosphere of peace and serenity prompted me to ask the good man how he had happened to establish this particular Episcopal church when and where he did.

"Well," said the Reverend Mr. Kimball, "it all started some years ago, when my wife and I were living in New York. She was the editor of a religious magazine. I was growing tired of the city life, and we decided to move down here to Cape Cod. It was the middle of winter, too, but the change has made us as happy as larks ever since. She converted me to the faith, for at the time I was not a churchgoer. Although we were happy at first, we needed a church to attend on Sundays. The nearest Episcopal church to the north is at Provincetown, and in the other direction one must travel to Barnstable. Both are more than twenty miles away.

"Therefore it was apparent that something would have to be done at home. Gradually the Christian people of the neighborhood for miles around came to meet in Orleans every Sunday, people of all denominations, but laymen, of course. We met at Camp Mayflower. Our numbers grew and finally we decided to build a church.

"The ground was broken in July 1935, and a month later we held our first services. The little church held fifty people. From this beginning the church has been enlarged, the parish house has been erected, our crafts shop has come into being, and we have classes in metal working. We specialize in aluminum. There is a church gift shop where we sell our materials. Our rectory is an old barn, torn down and rebuilt. Our heavy beams come from the old Chequisit Inn, which was wrecked some years ago by an Atlantic storm. An old wrecker sold us the lumber. The man who built Eastham's church, Frank Brooks, although at the time seventy-five years old, was the head carpenter. He knew about beaming.

"A man was selected from our group to become the minister, and I was the one chosen. Bishop Sherrill gave me special permission to study at home and come to Boston for monthly reports. Finally, after my years of study, he journeyed down here to Orleans and ordained me in 1938.

"Thus you see the usual procedure was changed. First we had our congregation, next our church, and finally the minister. I love the Episcopal church because I was converted to it, and I love Cape Cod for the same reason," said the Reverend Mr. Kimball. "Come on out into the church itself."

We walked around the auditorium and my eye caught a circular window. "That glass came from up in Boston, where it was in the old Saint John's Episcopal Church at Jamaica Plain, torn down over a century ago." Everywhere in the auditorium were evidences of the care and handiwork of the group.

Then we walked out of doors across to the rectory. It was a delightful experience, stepping into the home of the Kimballs. The wide floor planking of the living room gave the furniture a special setting which enhanced its beauty. The minister led me out toward the kitchen. Here was an unusual room, suggesting a ship at sea.

"Here is a surprise for you, Mr. Snow," said the rector. "You are now standing in the old galley of the *Orissa*, wrecked on these shores about one hundred years ago. They hauled the galley up the bank and over here by oxen, and we now live in it!" But my host was not finished with his surprises. "Wait until my wife shows you some goat's milk," he said.

"Why, haven't you ever tasted goat's milk?" asked Florence Kimball, who was busy preparing the noontime meal. "Well, you must try it now," and she poured me out a generous amount of real goat's milk. "You know, this has it all over cow's milk in every way." I drank it quickly, not knowing what to expect, but there was no apparent difference, and I told her so. "Well," she said, "there actually is no comparison. I've already converted Lois Ritchie, our secretary." And thus it was that I took my first drink—of goat's milk.

On my way out I noticed the unfinished fountain of Saint Francis, which the church members had begun for the pets. "We should have that completed this year," said my host and guide. We shook hands and I crossed the lawn to head southward. It had been a remarkable experience, meeting this good man and his wife at their establishment of God on the Orleans road. I would not soon forget it. I made my way back to Orleans, where I went at once to the store of Henry K. Cummings. Mr. Cummings is a fine example of Cape Cod integrity and resourcefulness. He is the man who braved the storm to get word to Captain Benjamin

Sparrow the night the *Calvin Orcutt* was lost back in 1896. Today, half a century later, he is hale, hearty, and still in business, continuing to run the oldest dry goods store in all Cape Cod, an establishment started by his father, J. H. Cummings, back in 1861.

"What about that night you took the message to Superintendent Sparrow?" I asked, "Was he still up?"

"I should say not," he answered and went on to tell me that when the door was opened a great amount of snow blew in on Captain Sparrow, who had answered Cumming's knock in his nightshirt. But he was game, and went out into the storm to reach the Orleans Life-Saving Station shortly after midnight.

I asked Cummings about his pictures, the photographs taken under all kinds of conditions, which have made him one of Cape Cod's greatest wreck photographers.

"Well," he mused, "the strangest wreck I have ever photographed was the *Charles A. Campbell*, which was wrecked twice in the same part of Cape Cod! Then I remember especially the *Katie Barrett*, the *Jason*, the *Lily*, and the *Kate Harding*. But the *Jason* was the most picturesque wreck, and I made the only photograph taken the morning after she hit

The Charles Campbell, *wrecked twice at Cape Cod (photo by Henry K. Cummings)*

A lifeboat returning from the wreck of the Jason, *December 1893 (photo by John R. Smith)*

the bar. There were plenty of pictures taken later on, but I always felt proud of my getting ahead of the other photographers." After talking quite a while with Henry Cummings I bade him farewell and set out for the main highway.

It was a mile to Rock Harbor, where the British fought the Cape Codders during the War of 1812. Commodore Raggett had demanded tribute from the various Cape Cod towns, but Orleans refused to pay. When as a result Raggett began a bombardment of Orleans, he was chagrined to discover his cannon balls dropping harmlessly into the marshes and flats off the town. The British battleships drew too much water to get in close enough to reach Orleans itself. In attempting to sail nearer shore, the frigate *New Castle* ran aground, so the captain sent in several barges, which burned two Orleans vessels lying on the mud flats.

British sailors captured two other craft, the *Betsy* and the *Camel*, which were afloat. Later a Yankee pilot escaped in the *Betsy* by running her ashore at Yarmouth, but the *Camel* was not recaptured by the Americans. British landing parties had met opposition from the men of Orleans, who in the battle which followed killed several of the Englishmen and sent the rest back to their boats. Sixty years later a tardy Congress remembered this Battle of Rock Harbor by rewarding the militiamen who fought that day "or their widows" with 160 acres of public lands.

Leaving Rock Harbor, I headed down Main Street, where I thought over my next move. Should I turn to the right and head for Brewster, five miles away, or should my next destination be the famous cottage of Captain John Kenrick near the North Chatham line? If I chose Brewster, then the rest of my journey would be Dennis, Yarmouth, Barnstable, and Sandwich until I reached the Cape Cod Canal. The other route would lead to the drama and excitement of Chatham's shipwreck history. Deciding to save Chatham for the last, I began my journey to Brewster.

The remains of the hull of the *Sparrowhawk* are still on display today at the Pilgrim Hall Museum in Plymouth. They are the only surviving remains of a seventeenth-century transatlantic vessel.

The German U-boat's 1918 assault on the *Perth Amboy* and the barges can be considered the only assault on American soil during the war, as at least one of the shells landed on the beach. It was the first enemy shell to strike the American mainland since the War of 1812.

CHAPTER 6

Brewster, the Town of Deepwater Shipmasters

I was anxious to visit Albert Crosby's Tawasentha mansion, located about half a mile or so up Crosby Lane. Built in 1888, it soon became a Cape landmark. The great castle-like house almost completely encloses the older residence of Crosby's grandfather, and the two houses are now joined together. The cupola of the newer building is visible high above the original residence. Crosby made his money during the gold rush days, after which he married and moved to Chicago, where he built the Crosby Opera House. Finally returning to the land of his birth, he built the Tawasentha mansion around his grandfather's old home.

The queer, rambling building became a showplace, for to grace its walls Crosby brought paintings worth $100,000, including beautiful creations by Millet and El Greco. Many noted men and women visited Crosby at his Cape Cod palace, among them Minnie Maddern Fiske and Joseph Jefferson. Some years after his death, the house and its furnishings were auctioned off, because none of the remaining members of his family had any further interest in Tawasentha.

After rambling around this curious structure for an hour, I returned to the main road and headed for the Lower Mill Pond, north of the Upper Mill Pond. My objective was the large Indian Prayer Rock, which is found on the eastern side of Lower Mill Pond. After some time spent in locating the boulder, I climbed to the top and sat down, my feet dangling over the split in the rock which divides it. It was exciting to be at the place where the ancient Wampanoags, the warriors of King Philip's tribe, conducted many of their ceremonials. I pretended that I could hear the sound of war drums and the chanting of the braves as they settled tribal difficulties and made their plans for the future.

My thoughts then turned to the Cape Cod sea captains of later days. Brewster was the town famous for its many master mariners, for well over 100 sea captains hailed from there. In proportion to its population, Brewster had more deepwater shipmasters than any other location in the country. In 1930 a list was made of ninety-nine captains from Brewster who had sailed the seven seas. Elijah Cobb should be placed close to the top of that impressive honor roll, but there are many others whose deeds and daring brought everlasting fame to this town at the inside elbow of the Cape.

For example, there was Captain James S. Dillingham, homeward bound aboard the clipper *White Squall* during the thrilling days at the outbreak of the Civil War. Sighting another American vessel, the steamer *Tuscaloosa*, he was hailed and asked for the name of his ship. Captain Dillingham, scenting danger, shouted, "The *White Squall*," and received an order to heave to as a row of gunports opened up in the side of the *Tuscaloosa*. Getting out from under the lee of the Confederate *Tuscaloosa*, Captain Dillingham ignored the orders and sailed away. In spite of all the *Tuscaloosa* could do, Dillingham completely eluded his enemy and was not hit once by the shots of the Confederate steamer. Sailing proudly into New York Harbor, Dillingham later received a special purse of almost $1,400 as a reward for his daring.

Later in the same war Captain Dillingham was actually overhauled by the same Confederate steamer *Tuscaloosa*, but this time the wind failed him and he was captured. The two captains had many a good talk over their varying fortunes of war, as they sat in the Confederate's cabin, and the Southern master presented Dillingham with a receipt for $1,500 for the latter's navigating instruments. The draft was honored in full after the war.

Then there was the giant Jeremiah Mayo, the six-foot-five Brewster lad who captained the French-owned brig *Salem* and took her in and out of the British blockade. Later he was captured by the British off Baltimore. Mayo's real claim to fame was his part in an episode which might have had far-reaching consequences. Late one night, a month after Waterloo, he was at Havre aboard the brig *Sally*. A high officer close to Napoleon asked Mayo if he were interested in sailing Napoleon to neutral America. Greatly excited by this suggestion, he gave his consent at once. Napoleon never came, however, for the British grabbed the Little Corporal as he planned to go aboard the *Sally* and sent him to Saint Helena instead. Captain Mayo cooled his heels for several days before he was told that Napoleon had been captured, and then he sailed the *Sally* home, naturally disappointed at losing his great chance. But Captain Mayo talked about what might have happened for the rest of his life. He died in 1867 at the age of eighty-one.

Another well-known Brewster sea captain was twenty-six-year-old Captain J. Henry Sears, who took over the clipper *Titan* in Liverpool Harbor to carry troops and ammunition to the Crimea. Two years later the *Titan* sprang a leak when she ran into a full gale off Liverpool, and had to have her mizzen and main masts cut away to right her. Rerigged, she made a voyage to Melbourne with a thousand passengers and a heavy cargo. From Melbourne, Sears sailed to the Chincha Islands for a load of guano for Queenstown, but the old leak opened up off Cape Horn and Captain Sears was in serious trouble. Finally he resorted to the desperate measure of abandoning ship 1,100 miles off Brazil. All hands took to the boats, and after terrible suffering and hardships were picked up and landed at Pernambuco. Some time later Sears returned to Boston, where he spent the remainder of his active life in the shipping business.

The most spectacular of all stories concerning Brewster sea captains is that of Captain Elijah Cobb, whose father died at sea when Elijah was six years of age, making it necessary for the boy to go to work. Seven years later he embarked from Orleans for Boston, where he found the great town exciting, especially the vessels tied up at the piers. Engaging passage as a cook on a ship bound for Surinam, he continued at sea until he was twenty-four, when he returned home to be married. At the height of the Reign of Terror in France, Cobb sailed for Cadiz aboard the brig *Jane*. Off Gibraltar he was captured by the French and brought into that port as a prisoner. The French prize master took over his papers so that Cobb could not prove that he was sailing for Cadiz. Meanwhile his cargo was removed. He wrote to the American representative in Paris for help, and was told to bide his time. Six weeks later he was informed that all was well as he was to be paid in full for his stolen cargo and also receive demurrage charges. But more trouble developed when it was decreed that no money could be taken out of France. Cobb then arranged with an agent for the latter to deliver to Cobb government bills of exchange for which he would receive payment by the French agent in

Hamburg. After vainly waiting a month, Cobb sent the *Jane* home and made plans to go to Paris to fight his case.

Cobb then had two copies of his claims made, and after much bother, was allowed to take the government coach to that city. He had already sent the first copy of his claims to Paris, but on his own arrival was informed the copy was not to be found. He pulled out his second copy, and the next morning was told that, too, had either been lost or burned.

Desperate and discouraged, Cobb was told by a Frenchman that his only hope was Robespierre himself. Cobb wrote a request for an audience with the French leader and within an hour he had his reply—Robespierre would see him. The next morning at 10:00 Robespierre and Captain Elijah Cobb of the United States had a long conference, at the conclusion of which Cobb went at once to the office where he had already been rebuffed. Captain Cobb immediately received his bills of exchange and profuse apologies as well, and then went out in person to see the Reign of Terror. For three weeks he walked unmolested around the city of Paris, and in that time he saw more than one thousand persons guillotined. Among them was Robespierre himself!

The death of Robespierre cut the face value of Cobb's exchange bills to one-half their former price, but later he was fortunate enough to receive full payment.

Back in Boston, his ability to deal with the French sent him on another cruise to that country, where he again became entangled in a situation which involved flour, silver ingots, silver crowns, and Spanish doubloons. By strapping the silver and gold in money belts around his body and that of a steward, he successfully eluded the watchful eyes of eight French officials. Returning to Boston, he discovered that his wife had become financially involved in a Cape Cod farm, so he stayed home with her on the farm for a year to straighten things out. He sailed in 1799 for Europe.

His next assignment was landing rum in Ireland, actually forbidden by law, but Captain Elijah Cobb, after unusual proceedings, was told that the only way he could sell his rum was to bid for his own ship at auction. He acquired it in this strange manner for five shillings. Then he was told to sail out by the pilot boat and heave overboard eight hogsheads of rum, for which he received 264 English guineas thrown up on deck in a small sack. He then sailed to Hamburg, where he sold the rest of the cargo. Cobb remained in Hamburg, sending the *Monsoon* home by David Nickerson.

While Cobb was in Hamburg there was trouble at home. His brother died and his wife became ill. When he returned to America, he took a brief rest, and then sailed again to Hamburg where he discovered the port blockaded. Momentarily delayed by the British, Cobb found a canal from Lubeck to Hamburg, so that he was able to discharge his cargo after all.

In 1807 he got around the famous British Orders in Council preventing his trading with Napoleon by paying the proper parties two ounces of gold. In 1812 his vessel was taken from him on the high seas when war started. Cobb later reached Brewster to become town moderator. While holding this position, it was his embarrassing duty to hand over $4,000 to the British admiral who then agreed not to burn Dennis. He became a major in the militia during his enforced stay ashore, but again went to sea at the war's end to start trading with Prince's Island in the Gulf of Guinea.

Returning to Cape Cod in 1819, Cobb never left America again. Kittredge tells us that his quarterdeck voice might be heard for years afterwards in town meetings, at the local Lyceum, and at Boston's State House where he was Senator. His death at eighty-one brought to an end the life of one of the most colorful sea captains which Brewster or any other town on Cape Cod has ever had, Elijah Cobb, the Yankee skipper.

There is the incredible story of John Higgins of Brewster. A member of the crew of Captain Winslow Knowles from the same town, he sailed from Boston aboard the *Albatross*. Higgins changed ships at San Francisco, signing on the steamer *Monumental City*, bound for Sydney, which was wrecked on the Australian coast. He shipped out once more only to be wrecked again, this time in the Caroline Islands, and it is believed that he was the only one saved.

A native tribe living on the island adopted him as one of their own, and he married the chief's daughter. Higgins taught the tribe Christianity and many of civilization's better advantages, the tribe accepting practically all his suggestions and plans. Passing whalers, finding Higgins's methods of trading for cocoa oil, swine, and other local commodities suitable for their purposes, patronized Higgins' tribe. In this manner a Brewster whaling captain, Charles Freeman by name, came upon Higgins at his little Christian kingdom in the Caroline Islands. After spending a week with the former Cape Codder he took back several letters to Higgins' relatives. Higgins himself never did see the streets of his native village again, for some years later a tribe from another island invaded the Higgins settlement and in the fracas Higgins was killed.

The relationship between the town of Brewster and Pitcairn's Island is twofold at least, for not only did Captain Josiah N. Knowles of Brewster have some thrilling adventures there, but Miss Clara Freeman of Brewster became the first white woman ever to go ashore at that Pacific island. Carteret named the island for Pitcairn, who discovered it, while Nordoff, Hall, and the movies have done their share in spreading the fame of Pitcairn's Island all over the United States. It was with particular interest that I examined the source material in the Brewster Library which linked that town and the Pacific island so far away.

I first studied the journal of Captain Knowles who left San Francisco on February 9, 1858, as master of the clipper ship *Wild Wave*. Knowles lost a man overboard six days out and, owing to the speed of twelve knots which the vessel was making, Knowles could not get the ship around in time to save him. Then, at 1:00 in the morning of March 5, with the *Wild Wave* making thirteen knots, the lookout reported breakers under the lee, and in "less than five minutes," to quote Captain Knowles, "the good ship was on a coral reef, full of water, and the sea breaking all over her."

A terrible time followed. Eventually Captain Knowles found that he had hit the island of Oeno, twenty miles off its proper position on the chart! Two tents were pitched on the beach, and Knowles consulted with his mate, Mr. Bartlett, on the plan of action. It was agreed that the two men should sail in one of their boats for Pitcairn's Island, where they might borrow a vessel from the descendants of the *Bounty* mutineers.

Leaving the others in charge of the second mate, Captain Knowles took the ship's gold, $18,000 in specie, and then with his first mate and five sailors, set sail for Pitcairn in the longboat. As they sailed away, three hearty cheers came out to them from the others left on the island. The weather soon grew stormy and they had some narrow escapes, but they raised Pitcairn's Island a few days after the storm went down. On reaching shore, they hiked overland to find the settlement deserted, and notices posted in several of the buildings that all inhabitants had moved to Norfolk Island. Knowles and the men could not hide their disappointment, for combined with their having had no rest for fifty-six hours, this further strain was too much to bear. Several broke down and wept bitterly. Captain Knowles buried the gold and he and the mate slept over it each night of their stay on the island.

Captain Knowles decided to make the best of it, and read *Jane Eyre*, hunted goats, and dreamed of his wife in Brewster. Finally he could stand the idleness no longer, and decided to construct a substantial vessel in which the group could sail to Tahiti. After weeks of toil, they launched a thirty-foot craft on July 23. Three of the sailors decided to remain on the island rather than risk the uncertainty of a 3,000-mile sea voyage. Heavily provisioned with goat's meat, live chickens, oranges, pork, and water, the newly christened *John Adams*, with $18,000 in gold stored below decks, started for Tahiti. Their enforced stay on the island, together with the new vessel's unusual motion, soon made them all seasick. But the speed of the craft was seen in the entry for July 25, when they made in the "last twenty-four hours, one hundred and twenty-seven miles."

On their arrival at Tahiti, Captain Knowles felt that the natives did not appear to be very friendly and he decided to push on for the Sandwich or Hawaiian Islands, almost 3,000 miles away. As they rounded the point of land at Nukahiva, one of the Marquesas group, there was the American man-of-war *Vandalia* anchored in the harbor, so the longer trip became unnecessary. I shall let Captain Knowles continue.

> *We anchored within a few rods of her and were hailed. We gave them in response an account of ourselves, stating our ship's name and nationality. The captain sent his boat off with his compliments and a request for us to come aboard. In the boat was a sailor who had been with me a year before, who at once recognized me. I put on my best clothes, consisting of a ragged coat, a shirt and pants all dilapidated, and went on board, taking my gold. The ship proved to be the U.S. Sloop-of-war* Vandalia *which had reached here the day before and was about to leave. No American ship had been here for nearly five years. . . . I gave them an account of my adventures, and stated the whereabouts of the remainder of crew and passengers.*

The next day, after selling his vessel to a missionary at Nukahiva for $250, Captain Knowles sailed with the *Vandalia* for Tahiti, where he booked passage on a French frigate then leaving for Honolulu. From Honolulu he sailed on September 15 for San Francisco. Coming into San Francisco Harbor, he thought that the inhabitants were celebrating because of his arrival, but found later that they were demonstrating because of the successful laying of the Atlantic cable. The next day

Knowles learned by mail that his wife had a daughter seven months old. He left San Francisco, arriving on September 28 in New York, where for the first time he was able to telegraph to his wife, down in Brewster, who long before had given him up for dead. Captain Knowles never forgot his telegram from home—a two-word reply from his happy wife at Brewster down on Cape Cod. "All well," was the conservative answer she sent.

On October 31 Captain Knowles again saw his wife, who was weak from uncertainty and shock, but as Captain Knowles writes, "baby well and hearty." His mother was also in poor health because of the anxiety. "The meeting with my family," continues Knowles, "was quite affecting; such a meeting seldom takes place. Everyone had long since given me up as lost."

In the meantime, the *Vandalia* picked up the other survivors of the shipwreck of that fast American clipper ship, the *Wild Wave*, wrecked on a coral reef in the Pacific Ocean, and they were landed in the United States.

Turning my attention to other documents in the Brewster Public Library, I found a series of letters written to Miss Clara Freeman at Brewster from Pitcairn's Island. I plunged into the reading of a delightful journal of events which occurred after the visit of Miss Freeman. Clara went ashore with her father at Pitcairn's Island in 1883 while sailing with him through the Southern Pacific. They discovered that the Pitcairn natives who had left the island at the time of Captain Knowles' visit there in 1858 had returned. While on the island, Clara met Rosa Young, the granddaughter of Edward Young of the *Bounty* mutineers. As young girls will do when they are brought together by unusual circumstances, Rosa and Clara became good friends. Clara learned that she was the first white girl ever to come ashore at Pitcairn's Island. It was a great event in the lives of both girls. After many delightful days the visit came to an end, and Clara and Rosa knew they probably would never meet again. And they never did. But before sailing away from Pitcairn's Island forever, they pledged that they would write long letters as the next best thing to seeing each other again.

In due time Clara Freeman returned to her home at Brewster, where she wrote a letter to Rosa, and was agreeably surprised to receive a long journal from Rosa even before her letter could have crossed to Pitcairn's Island. For many months Rosa recorded perhaps everything of interest which happened at Pitcairn's Island, probably many items which the moving picture writers who dramatized the *Mutiny on the Bounty* would have been hungry to read. And all the time these items were preserved in a small Cape Cod library in the town of Brewster, Massachusetts.

Rosa was amazingly naive and frank in her letters. Mentioning a chaplain aboard a man-of-war which visited Pitcairn's, she felt that she would like to go aboard and meet him. Perhaps his rough manner surprised her, possibly he wasn't actually an ordained man of God, but she returned from her visit strangely upset at the peculiar activities of the so-called chaplain. "I certainly thought," said Rosa Young in her letter, "that a more unchaplain-looking man was hard to find, and if words and manner are an index to a man's character, he certainly did not seem rightly fitted for a sacred office." The final blow to Rosa's ideals was dealt when she was leaving the ship, and the chaplain told her he was going to sing a song called "The Girl I Left Behind Me."

Another incident which Rosa tells about is the call of a trading schooner on board of which were two Tahitian women "said to be wives of the captain." The flashing earrings of one of the women and the very large hat she wore attracted the attention of the observing girl. All the group came to church on Sunday, where Rosa inspected them at leisure. When they left the island, one of them squirmed and wiggled when carried to the boat, so the other woman, "fearful lest anyone should take her up, kept at a safe distance and waded right into the water; then seemingly without effort, she stepped right over the side of the boat and into it without any trouble, dragging about three yards of dripping wet garments after her."

The last item of this unusual group of letters which I shall include concerns the mysterious death of Mrs. Elizabeth Young's first husband in the waters off Pitcairn's Island many years ago.

> . . . *Did anyone ever tell you, Clara, how her first husband met his death? Long ago when the little colony was young there was a day when the men of that time went out in their canoes to fish. The old people used to say for a fact that Matt Quintal's canoe—Matt was Mama's first husband—usually carried two persons, but on that particular day three or four attempts were made for two men to go in the canoe, but each time it was overturned, so that Matt was obliged to go alone. When it was time for the fishermen to return, his boat was observed to be resting on the water.*

Matt Quintal was never seen again. Nordoff and Hall do not give the same account of Matt Quintal's death that little Rosa Young does. Incidentally, Captain Josiah N. Knowles of Brewster had returned to Pitcairn's Island in 1873, where he met Rosa Young. He referred to her then as "the belle of the island."

Reading there in the library, I learned that Brewster was not set off from Harwich until 1803. Before then it was known as the North Parish of Harwich, and when the time for a vote on separation drew near, there was much bitterness. Thoreau said that when they named the new town they called it Brewster, "so named after William Brewster, for fear he would be forgotten else."

There are many locations all along the Cape which claim to be the real refuge of the Lost Dauphin of France. The legend goes that the young Dauphin was taken away from France during the times of the French Revolution by an American sea captain. Many in Brewster believe that it was Captain David Nickerson who was given the infant on the streets of Paris. A heavily veiled woman handed him the baby and vanished, after telling Nickerson the child's name was Rene Rousseau. Captain Nickerson then returned to America and brought the boy up as any other Cape Cod lad of his day by making a sailor of him. When twenty-five years old, young Captain Rene Rousseau was drowned at sea. In the Brewster graveyard, however, on the family tomb of Captain David Nickerson, is the name of Rene Rousseau, who may have been the Lost Dauphin of France.

The hour was getting late, and my next port of call was Dennis. After bidding the librarian farewell, I shouldered my belongings and headed westward. Before long I reached the junction of the GAR Highway and Depot Road. Continuing along the main highway I passed Schoolhouse Pond on my left, and a few minutes later came to Poverty Lane. About 500 feet ahead was a junction of three roads, the GAR Highway, Briar Lane, and Setucket Road. I chose the main highway, which I knew continued for several miles before it reached the road leading to the tower on Scargo Hill.

Albert Crosby's Tawasentha mansion, built for his wife, Matilda, played many roles over the years—as a school for the arts, as the Gold Coast Restaurant and Hotel, and finally as a summer camp for overweight girls. The property eventually was left to neglect and vandalism. The Friends of Crosby Mansion now work for the ongoing restoration of the mansion, which today is located within Nickerson State Park. The house is sometimes opened for "Brewster in Bloom" weekend, which usually takes place on the last weekend in April or the first weekend in May.

Brewster sea captain J. Henry Sears was also the first president of the Cape Cod Pilgrim Memorial Association and had a great deal to do with the establishment of Provincetown's Pilgrim Monument.

Sadly, the young wife of Captain Josiah N. Knowles died soon after his return to Brewster. Knowles went on to marry again and to captain several other clippers, including the *Expounder*, the *Charger*, and the *Glory of the Seas*. In 1864, while he was captain of the *Charger*, Knowles was indicted in San Francisco for manslaughter for not picking up a sailor who had fallen overboard. The evidence showed that a rescue had been impossible. This story was covered for the *San Francisco Daily Morning Call* by a young reporter named Samuel Langhorne Clemens.

CHAPTER 7

Dennis and Yarmouth

Dennis was named for the Reverend Josiah Dennis, of whom it was said that his sons were all daughters. He settled in what was then part of Yarmouth in 1725, and for the next thirty-eight years preached the gospel to the people of his community there. About thirty years after his death, when the time came for the people of his district to incorporate as a town in 1794, they honored the memory of their beloved preacher by calling the new district Dennis. There was no controversy about the separation here, for as far back as the Revolution the eastern and western parishes of Yarmouth had carried on their business as separate areas. Today Dennis has developed into five communities, known as Dennis, Dennisport, East Dennis, South Dennis, and West Dennis.

Well over 120 vessels hailed from Dennis in the days before the Civil War, but today the four harbors or ports cater mostly to activities which include pleasure boating, fishing, and lobstering.

I was eager to climb Scargo Hill and visit the tower I had seen so often from the air. The tower was easy enough to locate for Scargo Hill is the highest elevation in the vicinity. After passing through East Dennis, I turned left on Scargo Hill Road and was soon climbing. The hill and the tower were at my right all the way up, until I turned off on a path which finally came out at the top of my objective, Scargo Hill Tower.

Sitting down near the tower, I pulled an old poem from my pocket which I had copied in the library of the American Antiquarian Society in Worcester several years ago. Written in 1922 for *Cape Cod Magazine* by an unknown poet, the poem tells of the Indian Princess Scargo, the beloved daughter of Sagam, chieftain of the Nobscusset Indians. Scargo's mother had died when the girl was born, so her father decided to keep the thought of death ever from Scargo's mind.

A gift of live fish from a neighboring tribe made the little Indian princess very happy, and the fish were placed in a small pool near her home. But a summer without rain dried up the ponds and all the fish died except a few which she had placed in a bowl. Although she was never told of their death, Scargo instinctively knew what had happened, and was very sad. Growing weaker and weaker grieving for the loss of her pets, the Indian princess wasted away. Finally her father told her he would build a mighty fishpond, one that would never dry up, one which would be as wide as an arrow's flight. Greatly cheered, Scargo recovered her health to officiate at the shooting of the arrow, which would decide the pond's size. Let the unknown poet continue the story:

> *Scargo watched the arrow's falling*
> *Placed a shell on either side,*
> *Cheated some on east and west lines*
> *Got it longer than 'twas wide.*

Week after week the willing Indians worked in the hot sun and the chilling rain for their Indian princess. Finally, in the autumn of the year, the lake was completed. A great pile of sand, reaching high into the heavens, was made by the excavations from the lake. Thus were formed Scargo Hill and Scargo Lake, according to our unknown poet, for the rains of October filled the lake to brimming, and Scargo Hill was soon covered with trees and foliage. The happy princess tenderly placed the fish which she had saved in the great Indian-made lake.

> *Now she placed them in the pond,*
> *Watched them as they swam away,*
> *There they are, or their descendants*
> *Swimming to this very day.*
> *And on quiet summer evenings,*
> *At the far side of the lake,*
> *Calling gently, "Scargo, Scargo!"*
> *Then the echoes will awake.*

Where the shadows lie the deepest
Loving couples often pause.
They are listening to the echoes,
'Tis the grumbling of the squaws.

As I sat there alone at the top of Scargo Hill, it was easy to believe the poem I had just read. I could imagine I heard the echoes of the squaws' grumblings, and the wind, gently rustling the trees, added to the illusion.

The tower is not as high as one might suppose, rising twenty-eight feet into the air. Built by Henry Ellis's father, James Allen Ellis, it was finished at the expense of two former residents of Cape Cod, Charles and Frank Tobey, then of Chicago. Originally they had erected a wooden tower, which was connected with a nearby hotel. The stone tower was built around 1912.

As I slowly made my way down Scargo Hill, my thoughts were about the Indian princess and her people. Half an hour later I was standing by a small granite marker, which identifies a burial ground of the Nobscusset Indians, to which Princess Scargo belonged. As the Indians did not mark their graves, I shall never know if the princess lies buried there.

Next I hiked over to the more modern Dennis Cemetery, where I spent the next three hours. A trip to Cape Cod should include a visit to this cemetery if you can possibly spare the time. In fact, Jack Frost suggests that only a cartoonist like Dahl of the *Boston Herald* could have cut many of the interesting stones to be found here. Eleanor Early, Dean Tarbell, and Jeremiah Digges all speak of Dennis and the graves, so if you still fail to stop at Dennis to visit the many unusual gravestones, it should be your own responsibility.

I shall mention only a few of the tombstones. Jonathan and Uriah Howes, of Dennis, are commemorated in this cemetery. They were lost at sea in the October gale of 1841, in which the *Bride of Dennis* and other craft were wrecked. Another stone is that of Daniel Howes, on which we read:

Cut off in a tremendous gale
A watery grave appeared in all its form
And in a few minutes he was gone.

The single white stone with the two urns is in memory of the two sea captains who never returned to Dennis, Captain Barnabas Crowell, who died while in Sumatra, and Captain Nathan Crowell, who died at sea after sailing from Liverpool, England. On one of the stones I read this statement:

> *It is well to believe that those that we love,*
> *If we miss them below, we shall meet them above.*

A rather ghastly tombstone is that of Joseph Hall, who in 1787 died in the sixty-fourth year of his life. The imaginative stonecutter of Dennis has depicted a skull fastening his upper teeth into one of the cross-bones usually found adorning pirate flags. And then there is the major who, thanks to the stonecutter, is depicted watching "over his own Grave." Major Micah Chapman is evidently dressed in full uniform regalia, for on the tombstone he is seen in wig, waistcoat, buttons, and blouse. Obed Howes, one of a long line of Howes all buried in Dennis, has a statement on his tombstone which makes us pause and think.

> *Reason was his guiding ☆*
> *That one truth was clear,*
> *Whatever is, is right.*

A variation of the usual epitaph involving the occupant of the grave and the person who reads the inscription follows:

> *Stop, my friends, and drop a tear,*
> *Think of the dust that slumbers here,*
> *And when you read the fate of me,*
> *Think of the glass that runs for thee.*

The last two inscriptions quoted above brought me to the end of my visit in the Dennis Cemetery, so I walked toward the center of town again. Three other locations in Dennis awaited me, the Shiverick Shipyard site, the Dennis Playhouse, and the largest mural painting in the world.

To reach the shipyard I headed down Highway No. 6, the GAR Highway, until I came to the place where Bridge Street and East West Dennis Road meet. Turning up Bridge Street toward the north, I crossed Sesuit Creek and reached Sesuit Neck. Sesuit Harbor was off to the right, and there before me was a small commemorative boulder which told of Cape

Cod's contribution to shipbuilding. Of all the Cape Cod locations where ships were built, none was more famous than the Shiverick Shipyard.

Asa Shiverick, born in Falmouth, moved to East Dennis to learn the shipbuilding trade in Jeremiah Crowell's yard, and when he had mastered it, built vessels for himself. Asa Shiverick, Junior, was born in Dennis in 1816, and went to both Boston and Maine to learn all he could about shipbuilding. Then he returned to East Dennis in 1837, just before the clipper ship era began. His father had never built ships, although he had turned out many brigs and schooners, but when he retired shortly afterwards he was willing that his sons Asa, Paul, and David should attempt the construction of larger vessels. Christopher Hall and Prince Crowell backed the Shiverick boys financially, and in 1850 the shipyard began to build big vessels, ships which, according to Henry C. Kittredge, "would have done credit to any yard in the country." The rest of the story is known to all lovers of the clipper ship, the most beautiful thing ever made by the hand of man. The *Revenue, Hippogriffe, Belle of the West, Kit Carson, Wild Hunter, Webfoot, Christopher Hall,* and *Ellen Sears* were all full-rigged ships or barks, and the *Belle of the West* attracted attention because of her graceful lines wherever she went. She and the *Wild Hunter* probably were the best known of all the Shiverick clipper ships.

The depression hit the Shiverick yards as it did the East Boston shipyards and others, but Cape Cod's brief moment of shipbuilding glory had been a reality. Asa Shiverick moved to Woods Hole, and the yard became a guano plant. Even the plant closed later, and for many years Sesuit Neck lived only in the memory of those who had seen the clippers of Cape Cod launched there.

In 1847, Captain Joshua Sears sailed the old squarebowed *Burmah* to the East Indies, where his adventures were many. On the first trip his cargo was ice, and he managed to beat the ship *Geneva* by sixteen days. On his return journey, in spite of the fact that the chronometer went wrong and the ship hit a heavy gale, he was able to pass the bark *Isabelle Blythe,* which had left Calcutta a week earlier. The storm left the *Burmah* in poor condition, and at one time Captain Sears despaired of ever getting her home. When he finally sighted the welcome gleam of Highland Light, Sears tells us in his log that the *Burmah* was leaking 200 strokes an hour! But she made the port of Boston, and after being overhauled and refitted, Captain Sears took her out to Madras, covering 14,000 miles in 108 days.

The *Orissa*, whose famed galley is now part of the Episcopal church parsonage in Orleans, was Captain Joshua Sears's next ship. This time his wife sailed with him. The couple made Calcutta trips in the next five years between 1849 and 1854, and Mrs. Sears enjoyed most of her experiences, but said she never could get used to the big snakes which swam in the Bay of Bengal.

The *Orissa* was ripped by a great typhoon in 1853, and left in a sorry condition. "I never saw a ship in such a state as she was in about decks before in my life," was the comment of her captain. Sears brought the damaged *Orissa* into Hong Kong, where she was made ready for sea again. Several years later the ship *Orissa* went to her doom off the great beach at Cape Cod.

It is said that Venice held for many years the honor of having the world's largest mural, designed and painted by the great Tintoretto in the late sixteenth century. In 1930, however, Venice lost that honor when Rockwell Kent and Joe Mielzener painted the mural in the Cape Cinema at Dennis. There in the painting is the bull jumping over the moon, Lovers Lane in the Milky Way, horses in the sea, a brilliant comet, and many other colorful flying figures.

Dennis has another theater, the Cape Playhouse, which came into being because of a California botany teacher's dream of establishing himself as a playwright. After traveling across the country to Provincetown, Raymond Moore opened a studio there. When he had written and produced several plays, he decided to look for a larger playhouse. Buying land in Dennis, he purchased the old Nobscusset Meeting House and remodeled it into a playhouse, moving his headquarters there in 1927. Many outstanding actors and moving picture stars have graced the stage of the Cape Playhouse, including Bette Davis, Gregory Peck, Fred Stone, Grant Mitchell, Taylor Holmes, and Gertrude Lawrence.

I had visited both the theater and the playhouse before. Neither was open that April day, so I walked around the area for a half hour and then started for the place where the old salt works used to be.

I looked in vain for a souvenir from the saltworks of Dennis, but found nothing that I could prove was part of the old structure, although I hunted diligently around the area where the Dennis saltworks once stood. Finally I contented myself for the moment by reading what available notes I had brought on Cape Cod salt manufacture.

In 1776, when it became almost impossible to obtain salt because of the British blockade of Cape Cod, Captain John Sears of Dennis built a

Edward Rowe Snow autographing his lighthouse book for Gertrude Lawrence at Hyannis Airport (photo by Richard Kelsey)

wooden trough 100 long and 10 feet wide, pumped sea water up into the trough, and by the end of the first year actually accumulated eight bushels of good salt. When it rained he covered over the salt troughs with boards. It was slow work, but the good man was encouraged by the General Court's bounty of three shillings per bushel on all salt. This bounty started other men experimenting also. One of them, Nathaniel Freeman of Harwich, brought out the idea of a windmill to pump the saltwater up into the troughs. The plan was successful, and by 1802 there were 136 separate saltworks at Cape Cod. By this time Reuben Sears of Harwich had invented a rolling roof to cover and uncover the troughs or vats, as they were called. Hattil Kelly of the same town devised a system whereby two vats at a time were covered. The greatest advance in salt making came with Loring Crocker's Common Fields Saltworks at Barnstable. Crocker built water reservoirs which automatically fed the various vats. Three of the seven vats he called the first, second, and third water rooms. The next three were the pickle rooms, and the last, the salt room. Epsom Salts and Glauber Salts were both by-products of the process. Prices per bushel went as high as 82 cents, and at one time the sum of $2 million was invested in Cape Cod saltworks. Outside competition, unfortunately for the Cape's industry, ruined the trade, and one by one the saltworks were given up and their lumber sold for building purposes elsewhere.

My next destination was the town of Yarmouth. As I went along I could see acre after acre of cranberry bogs scattered far and near. One of the largest cranberry bogs in the world is located between two ponds in this region, but I was unable to identify which particular bog it was. Hiking along the road, I wondered who was the first man to commercialize cranberries. Of course, I had heard the old story about the Plymouth colony men in 1677 sending 10 heavy barrels of cranberries across the sea to their King Charles, along with 3,000 codfish and 2 hogsheads of samp. I had also read Eleanor Early's statement that in those days they were called crane berries. Charles, according to Eleanor, after tasting one, told Nell Gwynn that the cranes could have them. That didn't prevent me from wishing I had some just then on a plate with some turkey, for it had been over four hours since I had eaten.

I am not going to suggest who the first cranberry expert was. But the first successful cranberry grower was Henry Hall of Dennis, who began his cultivation of cranberries on Cape Cod in 1816. Others whose names should be included among the pioneers in the business are Zebina H. Small, Alvan Cahoon, Cyrus Cahoon, and Nathaniel Robbins of Harwich. In 1847 Captain Abiathar Doane of Harwich decided to lay out his bog with close-set vines, and almost at once his yield sprang ahead of other bogs in the vicinity. The great expansion in cranberry growing came shortly before the Civil War, when good prices and unusual profits were recorded.

About that time Nathan Smith came back from the California gold fields looking for some way to add to the small revenue which his farm afforded him, and spent quite a little money developing cranberry bogs in the vicinity of Barnstable. When the boys came back from the war, unemployed and restless, many of them took up cranberry growing. Thousands of acres of useless swampland were made into cranberry bogs and cultivated with success. By 1875 Smith had half a hundred pickers working for him, and because of the disruption of the schedule caused by the need for children to pick cranberries, the schools changed their calendars beginning around the third week in August for a five-week term, after which the young people were given a vacation until cranberry picking was over.

When harvest time arrived at the cranberry bogs, women left their dusting and ironing—everyone from the smallest youngster able to scramble around to the most aged and tottering grandfather did what he could to harvest the crop. Teams went around the various villages and farms to pick up the willing workers early in the morning, and returned them to their homes after sundown, tired and hungry.

Methods have changed, of course, for early in the industry's history there were no wooden scoops or automatic pickers. Stalls of white cloth were wrapped around the fingers and heavy mitts pulled over the hands to prevent the scratching from the vines. The aprons were curious combinations of oilcloth and blue denim, the oilcloth to keep the knees from getting wet when the bog was soggy. Long lines, similar to those used at a track meet, were stretched from one end of the bog to another, and races were held to see which persons would be champions of their particular bog. Lunch at noon, with tea from bottles, was followed by work again until sunset. At the end of the season a Cranberry Dance would be the highlight of the social activities. Those days are all gone forever, and the pickers now do their work with wooden scoops, a method monotonous but effective.

When Abel D. Makepeace decided that West Barnstable would be the center of his cranberry bog activities, men not only from every part of the Cape, but even from Finland, Portugal, and the Azores came to help work the bogs. The Portuguese and Finn newcomers arrived at just the right time to buy up the property belonging to the old Cape families, many of whom were dying out. It was several years before the new foreign strain had been assimilated, but by the outbreak of World War II the Cape was settling down again to a united community life, the goal of all towns on Cape Cod.

Dean Tarbell informs us that it was not until 1845, when white sugar became plentiful and cranberries could be sweetened properly, that this berry became so popular and profitable. By 1895 the crop on Cape Cod, probably 150,000 barrels, was worth $1 million. Barnstable County's contribution in 1930 of 400,000 barrels brought $6 million, while the 1945 Cape Cod cranberries packed in 470,000 barrels brought $8,460,000 to their growers.

Half-famished by this time, I sat down by the side of the road and opened some milk and sandwiches I had purchased. Ten minutes later

I had eaten everything. I packed all my equipage and again began my walk to Yarmouth. As I proceeded toward Yarmouth and Yarmouth-port, on my left I passed a hill which was called by the intriguing name of Black Ball Hill, while a settlement a little farther on to the right was identified as New Boston. Reaching the South Yarmouth Road, I went along to the boundary line between Dennis and Yarmouth, and ten minutes later came to the junction of Follins Pond Road and the GAR Highway. Soon I was in the center of Yarmouth.

The event connected with Yarmouth which interested me more than any other was the voyage of one of her sons, Captain Asa Eldridge, when he took the clipper ship *Red Jacket* across the ocean on her record trip. The *Red Jacket* was designed by Samuel Pook and built by George Thomas, in Rockland, Maine, where both my mother and father were born and where my great-grandfather Israel Snow had started the Snow Shipyards many years before. And so for several reasons I was interested in Dennis and its famous sea captain.

When the *Red Jacket* reached New York, she appeared to all who saw her as a clipper of strikingly beautiful lines, with sharp ends and a long, flat floor. Her length was 251 feet and she registered 2,305 tons. Seacomb and Taylor of Boston, her original owners, invited Captain Asa Eldridge to become master of the *Red Jacket*, and he accepted with pride.

On January 10, 1854, Captain Eldridge sailed the *Red Jacket* out of New York Harbor. Every day of the trip to Liverpool it stormed, but by the time the *Red Jacket* came sailing up the Mersey River to Liverpool, greeted by the roar of cheering thousands lining the sides of the channel, she had made a record for sailing ships which still stands today. The time was thirteen days, one hour, and twenty-five minutes from dock to dock. On the ninth day she had logged 413 miles, a distance exceeded only by three other sailing vessels. When the *Red Jacket* neared the dock, the captain gave a command and the sails came fluttering down as the wind spilled out. Captain Eldridge brought his great clipper into the wind and slid her against the pier to the astonishment and wonder of the captains and crews of puffing tugs which surrounded her. No less an authority than Henry C. Kittredge tells us that "not one shipmaster in a hundred would have dared to try it."

Captain Eldridge's sailing journey of thirteen days across the Atlantic brought the acclaim of the people of every nation. The *Red Jacket* was sold almost immediately upon her arrival in Liverpool. After a glorious career which lasted until the close of the Civil War, the *Red Jacket* was sent to the Cape Verde Islands to be converted into a coal hulk.

Captain Eldridge's final moments were more spectacular. About two years later he was master of the Collins steamship *Pacific*, which never made port, having sunk at sea. There are those who believe, says Dean Tarbell, that he crowded her boilers too hard, wishing to make another record, but we shall never know. No one, however, will ever take away from Yarmouth the glory of her Captain Eldridge's Atlantic crossing record of thirteen days.

This *Red Jacket* ended her days as a coal hulk and Captain Eldridge was lost at sea, but the name again attracted momentary attention to the Cape years later. An Indian by the name of Red Jacket living at Mashpee was crossing the street one day in 1933, hurrying home for a supper of baked beans. An automobile struck and killed him.

Yarmouth is also associated in my mind with a colonial ship wrecked off Thacher's Island. The island was called Thacher's Island because Anthony Thacher and his wife were the only survivors of the ship, which went on the rocks there during the first great hurricane of 1635. All their children were drowned. Thacher established himself at Marblehead, where he stayed for four years. When their new baby, John, was a year old, they started out for Yarmouth, bringing with them a cradle coverlet of red broadcloth salvaged from the wreck. The Thachers prospered and multiplied at Cape Cod, and there is a tradition that every Thacher baby since that time has been christened wearing that same broadcloth coverlet.

I passed down the main street in Yarmouth, which has almost a mile of beautiful elms, planted by Amos Otis during the middle part of the last century. Otis is famous also for his genealogical research. It was Jeremiah Digges who rescued from oblivion Otis' statement about the Crocker family, whose genealogy Otis investigated so intensively that he finally became worn out from his efforts. Otis said that he brought his research to an end "not because my subject is exhausted, but because I am."

Reaching the last of the row of elm trees, I thought again of Yarmouth's place in the shipping history of the world. It was a Yarmouth man, Captain Ebenezer Sears, who first rounded the Cape of Good Hope with an American vessel.

Two Cape Cod captains, famed for their sailing prowess, raced their clippers around Cape Horn in 1853. They were Captain Frederick Howes of Yarmouth and Captain Moses Howes of North Dennis. Captain Moses Howes sailed from Boston for San Francisco aboard the *Competitor* on March 27, 1853, while Captain Fred Howes left Boston a day later on the *Climax*. Moses was reckless and split the *Competitor's* stem off Cape Horn, thus losing the lead he had piled up. Fred, on the other hand, was cautious and arrived off Cape Horn in such perfect condition that he had every reason to expect to reach San Francisco before his rival. But Moses repaired the damage to his ship, overtook the *Climax*, and arrived one day before Captain Fred. Thus the race ended in a tie, both reaching port in 115 days. The race accomplished something else, however, for Captain Frederick Howes had equipped the *Climax* with the new Howes double topsail, his invention. It worked so well that he put it on the market, and it was soon adopted by almost every new vessel. It was the race of 1853 which brought the Howes double topsail into such prominence.

There is another story about an erstwhile resident of Yarmouth—that of the Reverend Stephen Bacheler, the minister there for a short time in 1637. His first two wives had died in England, and his third passed away in Portsmouth, New Hampshire. At the age of eighty-one Bacheler became interested in the wife of his neighbor and was excommunicated. About seven years later he remarried, but marital trouble started at once, as his wife presented "vehement suspicion of incontinency." He then sailed for England after hiking from Kittery, Maine, to Boston. She was punished for her association with one George Rodgers, and both she and George Rodgers were stripped down and given thirty-nine lashes each.

Mary Bacheler then was forced to wear the letter "A." Thus she was possibly the original for the character Hester Prynne in Hawthorne's book *The Scarlet Letter*. On October 18, 1656, she applied for divorce, alleging that her husband had gone to England several years before and married again.

The final episode in this strange drama occurred in London, where the Reverend Stephen Bacheler passed from this world when he was about a hundred, his English wife at his bedside.

The stone tower on Scargo Hill still stands, affording those who climb its thirty-eight steps a view from 160 feet above sea level that on clear days extends all the way to Provincetown.

The "Jack Frost" Snow mentions in this chapter was an artist who published *A Cape Cod Sketchbook* in 1939. In the 1950s he also originated the idea of the "Yankee Homecoming" celebration, designed to showcase New England traditions. The concept spread from Cape Cod to Newburyport, Massachusetts, where Yankee Homecoming Week remains a yearly highlight.

The renowned Captain Joshua Sears was prone to seasickness and even confessed that he hoped to go to a place where he would "never see a ship again." Not only did his wife and daughter accompany him on some voyages, but also his daughter's pony, which she rode around the deck.

Rockwell Kent's 6,400-square-foot mural in the Cape Cinema is a modernistic concept of the heavens that, according to the artist, was "designed to make people think." The mural survives in the still-operating 1930 cinema.

The cranberry is one of only three fruits, along with the blueberry and the Concord grape, that originated on American soil. Massachusetts has fallen to second in cranberry production—with about 2 million barrels (100 pounds per barrel) yearly—behind Wisconsin.

Anthony Thacher (sometimes spelled Thatcher) is considered a founding father of Yarmouth, where he served as town treasurer, teacher, and selectman. An out-of-the-way boulder in Yarmouthport bears a plaque identifying the site where Thacher lived and died.

CHAPTER 8

The Shire Town of Barnstable

As I was to come back again to Yarmouth after reaching the Cape Cod Canal, I did not turn south and visit South Yarmouth and Bass River at that time. Instead I continued along Highway Number 6, also known as the GAR Highway, leaving Yarmouthport at a point directly to the south of Hallett's Mill Pond. I was then in Cummaquid, one of the many sections of the great town of Barnstable. Approaching the Cummaquid Post Office, I knew that nearby was the grave of Iyanough, the Indian sachem of Cape Cod.

When we recall the help which Iyanough gave the Pilgrims at the time when young Billington lost himself on Cape Cod, it is hard to understand how it happened that Captain Myles Standish was responsible for Iyanough's death some years later. In 1623 Massasoit told the Pilgrims that an Indian conspiracy against them was in the making, so Standish decided to settle it in his own way, and rushed over to Weymouth, where he killed four Indians outright and then hanged another. This sudden outburst of Myles Standish terrified all the Cape Indians, and when two more red men were killed, Iyanough fled into the swamplands there, where he contracted a fatal illness and died. Prince, in writing of the incident, says that the people of Plymouth heard that the sachems of Nauset and Pamet had joined the conspiracy. Prince then says that "among others, who fell victims to their fears, was Aspinet, the sachem of Nauset, and Iyanough, the courteous sachem of Cummaquid." Iyanough was buried on a hill nearby.

Two hundred and forty years later, at the time David Davis and Patrick Hughs were plowing a field in Cummaquid, they overturned a brass kettle under which they found a skeleton in a sitting position. The kettle had been placed over the skull, and a stone pestle, bow and arrow, and other implements were nearby. They rest today, skeleton and all, in Pilgrim Hall, Plymouth, and the small monument to Iyanough's memory was placed at Cummaquid near the post office in 1894. I would like to know what Iyanough's thoughts of the Pilgrims were as he lay on his deathbed in 1623.

I had already visited the marker on a previous occasion, so I asked Miss Edith Davis, whose father was in the field when the skeleton was uncovered, if I might wander out to the stone marking the location.

"Yes," she said, "but the field hasn't been cut." Then she gave me directions for finding the monument, but I was so sure of the spot that I paid little attention to them, and ten minutes later stood again in the little post office.

"I'm sorry, Miss Davis, but I couldn't find the stone," I apologized.

"Well, you should have listened more carefully," she admonished, and then gave me very definite directions. "Go straight back through the field and up the hill. Walk along the crest of the hill to the left and then turn right again at the end of the clearing." I followed her directions

Sandy Neck Light, September 7, 1897

carefully and found the monument almost completely buried by masses of sumac trees, golden rod, and brambles. I stood at the spot where Iyanough's bones had been buried for more than two and a quarter centuries and read the inscription:

> *On this spot was buried the Sachem Iyanough, the*
> *friend and entertainer of the Pilgrims, July 1621.*

Returning to the main highway and continuing on my way, I soon could see Sandy Neck Light, across Barnstable Harbor, standing out against sea and sky. This pleasant view recalled to my mind Samuel B. H. Parker's excellent review of the sea captains of Barnstable in Donald Trayser's volume. He mentions the various types of Cape Cod's seafaring population—the deep-sea fishermen, the shore fishermen, the offshore captains, and the coasting captains, who have been more or less neglected in Cape Cod histories and guidebooks. When he was sixteen, Parker frequently was asked by marine reporter Aurin Crocker to go out in his catboat *Gypsy* and ascertain the names of the vessels, their captains, the ports of hail, and their destinations.

One day a vessel which was anchored in back of Point Gammon went ashore on Dog Fish Bar at high tide; all hands got off safely, but the vessel became a wreck and was condemned. After acquiring the ownership, Parker hired two schooners, the *Luella N. Nickerson* and the *Madgie*, to go after the wreck, putting Captain Handy aboard the *Madgie* and Captain Carlton Nickerson in charge of the *Nickerson*. On their way out to Dog Fish Bar, the mainsail suddenly jibed to port, knocking Joshua Chase of Hyannis into the water. Then followed an unusual show of seamanship. Captain Handy continued on his course, realizing that Nickerson, following in the other schooner, knew what had happened. Captain Nickerson threw over his wheel to bear away from the man in the water, who thought both schooners were deserting him, and commenced yelling and gesticulating with his hands. Nickerson luffed to and came directly for him, and a moment later the frightened man was taken aboard. Joshua Chase learned that day that a schooner captain wastes no time in vain maneuvers when a life is at stake.

We are told in the pages of the *New England Gazetteer* for 1839 that there were nearly a thousand widows in Barnstable County whose husbands had perished at sea. What of those poor women, their happy families broken forever, who lived on through the bitter years which followed? No book could be written with enough pages to cover the sorrows which the sea gave those families.

Many other women preferred to dare the dangers of the sea with their husbands. In the memoirs of Charles R. Flint we read that his wife was left alone in the cabin of an American bark off Colon with 500 workmen aboard. Looking out of her cabin, she saw to her consternation that the workmen were starting a mutiny against the crew, but instead of being panic-stricken, she reached out and took the signal halyards off the mizzen pin band, bending on and hoisting from inside of the cabin the signal "Mutiny Aboard." An American flagship lying nearby came and subdued the mutiny just as the workmen were entering her cabin.

Imogene Peak's father kept Point Gammon Light. School for her meant a walk of six miles each way. One of nine Peak children at the light, she said later that the walk of twelve miles daily with other children of the family was beautiful in spring, summer, and fall, but lonely in the winter.

The little school which Imogene Peak attended was not the only one in the town. Barnstable Academy, first of its type, was established there in 1839. Among its early teachers was Benjamin Drew, who went on to greater fame in St. Paul, where a school now bears his name. He later wrote a poem entitled "Bartholomew Gosnold's Vision," explaining how Cape Cod was named. Signor Monti of Palermo taught Italian in Barnstable and became a character in Longfellow's *Tales of a Wayside Inn*. The Hyannis Village Seminary opened in 1849.

Years later plans were made for a Cape Cod State Teachers College, and on November 1, 1894, Hyannis was chosen for the site. A new school building with a grammar school for the normal school pupils to teach in was then erected in Hyannis, but on the evening of January 24, 1896, the new building burned to the ground. Another building was voted, and on September 9, 1897, the Hyannis Normal School opened for its first term, with many competent teachers graduating to take positions all over New England as the years went by.

On July 1, 1942, the Massachusetts Maritime Academy moved into the same building with the Hyannis State Teachers College, to become known as the Shore Base of the former institution. Captain Robert M. Gray was appointed superintendent of the school. Later the Teachers College moved away. With the establishment of the Shore Base, the enrollment at the Academy gradually increased from 116 to 275 men.

Considerable new equipment for machine shops and also additional equipment for seamanship training has been installed. A very important addition is the 110-foot submarine chaser, acquired in April 1946, in which students take short cruises.

That Barnstable is a township of considerable size is apparent to anyone who attempts to cover it on foot. Actually there are seven precincts of Barnstable. Barnstable itself is at the northeast, West Barnstable at the north, Hyannis at the southeast, Marston Mills to the southwest of West Barnstable, Centerville at the central south, Osterville, wedged against Centerville to the southwest, and finally Cotuit, at the extreme southwest. The precinct known as Barnstable also takes in Sandy Neck Light and Cummaquid, and there are other districts which make up parts of the other precincts, such as Craigville in the Centerville precinct and Pondsville and Newton in the Marston Mills area. High Ground is part of Cotuit.

Now that you have figured that out (or have you?), we may as well go along with mathematician Donald Trayser and absorb some more interesting statistics. I am sorry that I cannot share the average person's enthusiasm for statistics as a method of proving almost anything he wishes; regardless of that I hereby offer two statistical statements. Barnstable stands first in the county as far as area is concerned, for taking the towns in alphabetical order, Barnstable has 62.74 square miles, Bourne 41.54, Brewster 25.16, Chatham 16.31, Dennis 21.90, Eastham 14.60, Falmouth 45.72, Harwich 22.41, Mashpee 25.96, Orleans 14.19, Provincetown 8.75, Sandwich 43.62, Truro 21.60, Wellfleet 20.82, and Yarmouth 25.53. Secondly, the towns of Massachusetts are listed by area with only Plymouth at 103.20 square miles and Middleboro at 72.96, larger than Barnstable.

As a relief from statistics I turned to a whaling story, the terrible experience of the men of the *Essex*.

The story of the *Essex* disaster will probably be told as long as descendants of whalers live on Cape Cod. Two Barnstable boys, Seth Weeks and William Wright, shipped aboard the whaler *Essex,* which in 1819 sailed out of Nantucket with Captain George Pollard, bound for the whaling waters of the Pacific. A year later, on November 20, 1820, her boats once more went out after whales, and a gigantic bull sperm whale charged the ship itself, crashing headlong into the *Essex* just forward of the forechains. It was a terrific blow, but the whale swung around and again headed for the *Essex*, hitting her the second time just under the

Destruction of the Essex *by a whale*

cathead, demolishing the bow completely. Satisfied with the destruction, the whale then swam away. The *Essex* soon filled and rolled over on her side, the victim in the only recorded instance of a whale charging and wrecking a whale ship.

The astonished whalers out in their individual whaleboats rowed to the rescue of the stunned members of the crew still aboard the sinking vessel. Working rapidly, the crew members cut away the masts and debris, and were thankful to find that the *Essex* was able to come back to an even keel, although she was waterlogged and actually a floating hulk. They soon made plans to leave her, however, realizing that slow starvation faced them at sea. After two days spent stocking provisions, Captain Pollard chose three longboats in which to sail for land, the coast of South America some two thousand miles away.

On December 20, after trying experiences in which the food ran so short they ate the barnacles off the boats, Captain Pollard landed at Ducie's Island, a barren bit of land inhabited only by birds and shellfish, where they were fortunate enough to find a spring of water. Resting for a week, they stocked up with fresh drinking water and set out again, leaving the two Barnstable sailors and an Englishman, all three of whom chose to stay on the island rather than to trust the uncertainties of the voyage.

The three boats kept on, but in a January storm First Mate Chase's longboat lost the other two. Left alone on the sea, their strength failing, the men weakened one by one. Finally a sailor named Isaac Cole went mad, dying later. The awful decision was made to eat his remains. The meat of Cole's body kept the others alive for ten days, and then the survivors watched each other. Another sailor weakened and sank to the bottom of the boat. The two remaining survivors eyed him hungrily, but he still lived. Then, on February 18, Chase saw the brig *Indian* coming to their aid, and they were picked up and landed at Valparaiso, Chile, February 25, 1821.

The other two boats stayed together for two weeks after parting from Chase's longboat. When Charles Shorter died, they divided his remains among them. Two others succumbed; both were eaten. In a heavy sea January 28 the boats separated and one was never heard from again.

Captain Pollard, in charge of the remaining longboat, was forced to another terrible decision on February 1. He ordered the men to draw lots for survival. Owen Coffin, cabin boy, was the unfortunate one in the draw. His executioner was then chosen; poor Charles Ramsdell had to kill his friend by shooting him, after which Coffin's body was divided. Another man died and the two survivors, Pollard and Ramsdell, lived on him for twelve days more. On February 23, Captain Zimri Coffin, a Nantucket whaler aboard the *Dauphin*, sighted the longboat of the *Essex*, rescued the two survivors, and landed them later at Valparaiso. Thus, of the seventeen who left Ducie's Island, only five were saved.

Later the English ship *Surrey* was sent into Ducie's Island to find the three men still alive. While wandering around the island, they had discovered eight skeletons in a cave, with the name of a ship, the *Elizabeth*, carved on a tree.

After returning to America, nothing more was heard of William Wright of Barnstable, but the career of Seth Weeks is well known, for he actually continued to go whaling after his terrible experience. In 1879 he retired to live at his home in West Barnstable, and in 1884 he moved to Osterville, where he died three years later, the last survivor from the whaler *Essex*.

I finally reached Barnstable County Courthouse and was fortunate enough to find Superior Court Clerk Don Trayser in his office. Donald G. Trayser, who in 1939 brought out a fine 500-page book about Barnstable, told me of the early beginnings of this community, which many believe is the most important town on Cape Cod. The trouble which eventually led to the settlement of Barnstable began in England, when

John Lothrop of Yorkshire was sent to prison for standing by his convictions. Getting out of jail, Lothrop sailed for Boston in 1634 aboard the *Griffin*. He settled at Scituate, Massachusetts, but later moved to Barnstable, where he could be free from opposition.

Lothrop and his followers settled down beside the Great Marshes and began a town which has had many important distinctions. Barnstable is the shire town or seat of one of the oldest counties in the state. Its history forms many contrasts. For example, although it does not have an exceptionally good harbor, Barnstable became a flourishing maritime town. Again, although there were many outstanding Tories living in Barnstable during the Revolutionary times, the town produced the man whom many consider Massachusetts' outstanding contribution to the cause of American freedom, the great James Otis.

Without question Otis was Barnstable's greatest citizen. Born in 1725, Otis was the eldest of eleven children. He went from Barnstable to Harvard in 1739, graduating with the Class of 1743. Part of his career which I enjoy reading about is his trip to Halifax as a young lawyer to defend three men accused of piracy there. Winning his case, he received a fee said to be the largest up to that time ever paid a lawyer in the province.

But a crisis came in his life shortly afterwards. Appointed advocate general of the British Court of Vice-Admiralty, James Otis one day realized that his duties would make him prosecute a case which went against his ideals of right and justice, a case involving the Writs of Assistance, which allowed officers to search homes and business establishments without a special search warrant at any time during the day. Otis chose to oppose the British government. Thus it was that on a cold February day in 1761 a young Barnstable lawyer, standing in the council chamber of what is now the Old State House in Boston, defied the British Empire in general and five richly clad judges in particular by declaring that he would oppose "to my dying day . . . all such instruments of slavery on the one hand and villainy on the other as this Writ of Assistance is." From all accounts it was one of the most passionate pleas ever made for liberty. A half-century later John Adams called it "the most impressive . . . of any I ever heard before or since," and went on to say that "American Independence was then and there born."

We should never forget that James Otis was willing to declare himself against the politics of the British crown long before the Boston Massacre, the Tea Party, or the battles which began the Revolution, thus making him a target for the opposition. Some taunted him with the name "Traitor." When he called them liars, they determined to act. One night in 1769 Otis went into the coffee house on what is now State Street in Boston. A certain John Robinson, armed with a heavy sharp-sided cane, swung a terrible blow against Otis's head, which not only opened up his flesh in a deep cut but shattered his reason as well, for the blow cracked his skull and injured his brain. Thus America lost a great man, one who was sorely needed in the dark days to follow. Otis, it is true, lived on, but he never was the same again. He often asked that "when God Almighty. . . shall take me . . . it will be by a flash of light-ning." On May 23, 1783, as Otis left his room in the old Osgood farm-house in Andover to cross the hallway to join his friends, a bolt of lightning entered the house by way of a beam and killed him.

Many years ago, when I came into Boston on a rainy afternoon, the kindly clerk of the Bostonian Society in the Old State House, knowing that I had a deep interest in old historical pictures and photographs, would unlock the gate to the private staircase leading up into the attic floor of that building. There I would browse throughout the afternoon, until the faint tinkling of the closing bell would warn me to leave. Turn-ing out the lights one by one until only a single beam remained to guide my steps to the top of the stairs, I would prepare to leave. A forbidding picture would always be facing me as I made my way toward the door, a stern gentleman staring out from his frame in such a manner that he seemed to discourage levity forever. But I would take a deep breath, turn out the light, and hurry across to lock the door and descend the staircase. The man in the picture was Chief Justice Lemuel Shaw of Massachusetts, born in Barnstable, Cape Cod, in 1781.

The impressions of youth remain sometimes to influence mature judgment, so I was agreeably surprised years afterwards, to read that Lemuel Shaw went through a normal early life getting into trouble at Harvard for throwing snowballs, walking on the Sabbath, and keeping on his hat in the hall. On the other hand my first impressions of this great man, for such is truly his place in history, were confirmed by some of the anecdotes about him. Rufus Choate said that Shaw was ugly, but he bowed before Shaw's superior intelligence. Then an old newspaper clipping pictured him as short and stout with hardly any neck, "so that his large head seemed to be placed almost directly upon his body and sunk in his neckerchief. . . . People would involuntarily turn around and look at him as he passed in the street." One day Ben Butler, leading a big mastiff along the sidewalk, was asked where he was bound. "To the

Supreme Court," was Butler's reply, "for I am going to show my dog the Chief Justice so I can teach him to growl."

Shaw's place in history can best be understood by the fact that it took fifty-five volumes to contain all his reports, and fifty-two more for his case notes, while his opinions would fill another twenty volumes. His great powers showed influence which extends even to this day in matters pertaining to railroads, public utilities, and water power. Of him, Chafee writes that "no other state judge has so deeply influenced commercial and constitutional law throughout the nation," and Rugg is the authority for the statement that Shaw did for "common law of the country what Marshall has done for its constitutional law."

Chief Justice Lemuel Shaw passed away in 1861, but it was not until August 1916 that honor was given him in the little West Barnstable parsonage where he was born. Judge Frederick Swift, who was present on the occasion, told his friends that he had never heard such an eloquent flow of oratory as on that August day in 1916, when several distinguished men gathered there to pay tribute to the memory of Lemuel Shaw. Among the speakers were Abbott Lawrence Lowell, Samuel McCall, Arthur P. Rugg, and Richard Olney.

In the midst of our talk Superior Court Clerk Trayser became occupied with two men who planned to establish a flying service, having Hyannis as one of the principal terminals, so I sat down in the corner of the office and studied my maps of the township. A few minutes passed and Trayser arose and walked over to me.

"Would you like to see the courthouse?" he asked, and I readily assented. Soon we were exploring under the huge arches of the cellar to examine the meticulous but ponderous construction of brickwork and granite which supports the upper stories of the building. Trayser commented, "We realize how well this building is constructed when a change is necessary. We wanted to put in a drinking fountain out in the hall and found it was necessary to drill through almost two feet of solid stone to lay the necessary pipes."

After our trip through the cellar, we walked outside to examine the great pillars which adorn the facade of the Barnstable Courthouse. I tapped one and found that it seemed hollow. Most definitely it was not the giant stone column I had imagined it to be.

"No," said Trayser, "that is merely a wooden exterior, but the deceptive finish we put on fools almost everyone. The pillars of the Barnstable Courthouse are wooden imitations of the real thing." Another cherished idea of mine had to be relegated to the background. I thought of the many times I had passed the impressive-looking building, thinking of the great stone columns standing majestically in front. I had always assumed that they were stone, and now I found I was mistaken.

"Let's go up into the courtroom itself," suggested Trayser, leading the way up the back stairs. A moment later he had unlocked the door and we were inside the room where many famous trials have been held. "Here's the place where they questioned Charles F. Freeman and Nurse Jane Toppan," Trayser commented. "If you go over and sit behind that rail you'll be right where they sat."

I went over and rested a few minutes in the dock, while Trayser told the horrible story of the religious maniac who killed his own daughter, and of the nurse whose desire to watch her patients die led her to kill thirty-one victims before she was apprehended. The stories in detail appear in another section of this book.

Of the thousands who have visited the State House in Boston to view the Sacred Cod hanging there, few of them have even heard of the Sacred Cod of Cape Cod, which hangs serenely from the very center of the Barnstable Superior Courtroom. Its early history is not known to anyone of this present generation, because most of the court records were destroyed in the great fire of 1827.

Don Trayser and I looked up at the truly handsome codfish which dominates the ceiling of the court room. "You know," he said, "during the long drawn-out trials which take place in this courtroom, there are many periods when practically nothing happens, and I find myself staring up at the codfish. Quite often it seems to move. Now I don't know whether it may swing in the wind or not. After one particularly long day in court I was talking with Judge Joseph E. Warner, and he agreed with me that it did seem that the codfish moved slowly as the day wore on."

"How long is it?" I asked.

"Well, during the last session here Donald Grant appeared with a ladder and said he was going to climb up and measure the thing. He did climb up and measure it, but I don't remember now how long it was." So there was nothing remaining for me to do but to measure it again. Getting a twenty-foot ladder, for the codfish is at least twenty feet from the floor, I climbed up and measured the fish to find that it was approximately forty-four inches from head to tail. I told him that Alton Hall Blackington suggested attaching it to a weather vane, so those in court could tell which way the wind was blowing by glancing at the codfish in the ceiling.

"Have you had any unusual court cases lately?" I asked.

"At the last session we settled one which has been hanging on for several years. We call it the bed case. A man and his wife rented a cottage for a week, and during the third night of their occupancy the bed came

Edward Rowe Snow and Barnstable's Sacred Cod (photo by William Ayoub)

down with a crash, injuring both of them. The decision was that if the cottage is rented on a weekly basis the defendant or owner of the house is responsible for the condition of the bed. However, if the owner rents the house for the season, the occupants must assume the responsibility for the condition of the beds. It was an unusual case, and attracted much out-of-court comment."

Perhaps the most outstanding visit in history of a superior court justice to Barnstable was the last trip of the late Judge Nelson P. Brown in April 1942. Arriving in Barnstable on the morning train, Judge Brown was met at the station by Sheriff Lauchlan Crocker. The sheriff was dressed in all his trappings, and his regalia was truly magnificent. He wore a blue cutaway coat and trousers comparable to full evening dress, with a buff-colored vest. His tall silk hat had a handsome black rosette and silver-blue cockade, and he wore a black tie with a white shirt. Carrying his mace, he proudly escorted Judge Nelson Brown to the Barnstable County Courthouse, and then, with appropriate dignity, the judge walked through the tall pillars to preside at the bench of the superior court with the Sacred Cod peering down at the proceedings.

Without question, the high sheriff creates much of the color and pageantry of Barnstable County Court life. At every session he precedes the judge in the parade to the courthouse from the court's living quarters nearby. Watching him one day I thought of other high sheriffs, Enoch Hallet who was sent to Cuttyhunk to bring back a Tory and who was later ordered to take charge at the wreck of the *Somerset*, Shubael Gorham who had his troubles with an Indian murderer named Stevens, and Sheriff David Bursley who had in his custody a female spy. Most of us like this old-time ceremony and pomp, which gives us just a bit of the pageantry of a bygone day and age.

Referring again to the court cases, I found that in 1823 Richard Johnson of Martha's Vineyard was accused of beating a girl to death. Allegedly he had arranged a rendezvous with Mary Cuff at the foot of the many-colored Gay Head Cliffs. During an argument, it was claimed, he seized a club and struck her. Her lifeless body was later found by the keeper of the lighthouse there. John Reed, an able lawyer of the period, succeeded in winning an acquittal for his client in spite of all the circumstantial evidence.

A most interesting story is that of Eleanor H. Jones, a Boston girl who was a spy for the South during the Civil War. In 1862 she appeared mysteriously in the army of Rappahannock, where she became a pet of the Union officers. They gave her a horse and everything else she needed, calling her Major Jones. Her secret mission was to obtain all the information possible and pass it along through various channels to her Southern confederates, but after a time she was placed under observation and found to be communicating with the enemy. Arrested at Secretary Stanton's request, she was sent back to her native state of Massachusetts, where Governor Andrews granted Miss Jones's request that she be sent to Barnstable. She stayed in jail there one year. Her sentence served, Miss Jones left for New York, where a physician who formerly loved her turned her away, as he had married someone else. One day shortly afterwards she stood on his doorstep and committed suicide. She was then twenty-two!

Many happy hours were enjoyed by the law fraternity even in the courtroom because of the clever replies and retorts of various characters and dignitaries there. One day Timothy Ruggles, who combined his law practice with keeping a tavern, played a joke on the chief justice, for when the judge entered the court there was an old woman sitting in the judge's sacred chair. The judge roared out a question, demanding an explanation from the shaking old lady, who pointed a trembling finger at Ruggles, saying that it was he who directed her to sit there. Ruggles calmly explained to the judge that he thought the seat was reserved for old women!

The famous Ruggles who suggested to the woman witness that she take the judge's seat had a daughter Bathsheba. The girl married a man named Spooner, and moved to Hardwick, near Worcester. It was a December-and-May marriage, and Bathsheba, soon tiring of the choice she had made, decided to do away with her husband. After other methods failed, she threw him down a well to his death, getting a British soldier to help her in the deed.

I went up to the site of the famous Blue Tavern, a very fashionable hotel built about 1928. The Blue Tavern, which had a limited number of beautifully appointed rooms, was both exclusive and expensive. The architect had so designed it that each room looked out on Barnstable Harbor, across to Sandy Neck Light, and over to the picturesque dunes of the Outer Beach. But one night about ten years ago the hotel burned down, and it has never been rebuilt.

Should the Cape enthusiast desire to appreciate the same view across the harbor that guests at the Blue Tavern enjoyed, it is only necessary for him to become an inmate of the attractively located Barnstable County House of Correction and Jail situated on the hill up from the courthouse. The prisoners at the jail so realize their good fortune in having such a wonderful location that it is often hard to get them to leave after their sentences are over. Apparently not all the inmates feel the same way, however. In March 1946, three of the nonpaying guests slugged the guard and broke free. Later they were captured and brought back, their sentences were increased, and they were taken elsewhere to serve their time. Hardly had this excitement died down when a trusty fled the jail to head toward the mainland, but after a brief vacation he actually gave himself up at the nearest police station and seemed happy to return to the splendidly located jail on the hill, with its excellent view of the sand dunes and harbor.

In Don Trayser's Barnstable residence he showed me an odd contrivance, a queer-shaped object which rests on the floor. The contrivance was circular, about three and a half feet across, and the nearest description of it I could attempt would be to say it resembled a giant metal soup plate.

"What do you think it is?" queried Don.

"I don't know," I parried. "Do you think they used it to mix butter?" I suggested hopefully, feeling that in some mysterious way the entire metal device might rotate.

"No, you're pretty far off. It is actually a bathtub, believe it or not. The thing is just for a sponge bath, I suppose, or for soaking your feet. They made them a few years before the Civil War. You sit on the raised seat here, and pour water down the spout in back of you. The water runs down the pipe and into the dish-like hollow which forms what the old-timers called their bathtub. But there are several mistakes you could make. If you sat down on the raised seat before putting down the stability leg, over you would go, water and all. The stability leg is missing from this particular model, so you won't be able to try it."

I thought of my own tub at home, and of the way I like to run the water nearly to the top. Yes, I was glad that I had not lived in the days before the Civil War, at least not if I had to use their bathtubs.

Don Trayser showed me the first copy of the first newspaper ever published at Cape Cod, the *Nautical Intelligencer*, Volume 1, Number 1, for November 21, 1823. Its area of circulation was Falmouth, Woods Hole, and Holmes Hole. In one of the columns of that paper was an interesting observation that if the vessels which sailed by only had some particular identification banner they could be recognized from afar. In the Sturgis Library at Barnstable is a complete file of all the editions of the *Barnstable Patriot* from its very beginning in 1830 to the present time.

Deciding that I should give Don Trayser a little rest, I walked down to the Barnstable waterfront, where I imagined myself sailing out of the harbor in a Barnstable packet to Boston, where a clipper ship was waiting to transport me to distant lands.

The name of Barnstable was known all over the world in the days of sailing vessels. The town had three really great sea captains and many other outstanding ones. Her three sons who brought glory to Barnstable were Jack Percival, William Sturgis, and Josiah Richardson. The career of Captain "Mad Jack" Percival shall be told first.

On the third of April in 1779, a baby son was born to Captain and Mrs. John Percival at their home on Scorton Hill, West Barnstable. One day thirteen years later the boy, John by name, ran away to Boston after a parental scolding. He had reached the decision to head for Boston by standing on a large rock and gazing first toward Boston and then

Donald Trayser, Kenneth Van Buren, and Edward Rowe Snow examining Cape Cod's first newspaper (photo by Anna-Myrle Snow)

Provincetown. The former port drew him, and off he walked to Boston, where he shipped for foreign lands.

At Lisbon, Jack was impressed into the British Navy and placed aboard the British man-of-war *Victory*. Two years later, after serving on another vessel of the Royal Navy, Percival escaped at Madeira to go aboard the American vessel *Washington*. We next see him as a sailor on the U.S.S. *Delaware* during the war with France. He was discharged when the war ended in July, 1801. There are those mentally adventuresome souls who believe that in 1805 he was still aboard Nelson's flagship *Victory*, but in actuality Percival had been gone from the British Navy for a number of years before Trafalgar was fought.

During the War of 1812 Captain Percival accomplished a daring feat. Aboard the fishing boat *Yankee* on July 5, 1813, he sailed alongside the British tender *Eagle*. There were thirty-two volunteers under hatches aboard the *Yankee*, and at the appointed time "Mad Jack," as he was known because of his courage and daring, led them aboard the *Eagle*, where they killed two officers and overpowered the rest of the crew. The *Eagle* was then towed triumphantly into New York Harbor, where thousands gathered at the Battery to cheer the triumphant Americans.

His next claim to fame was aboard the *Peacock* as sailing master to Commander Warrington. Meeting the British frigate *Epervier* off Florida in April 1814, the *Peacock* suffered the loss of her foremast sails, necessitating the use of jibs for headsails, placing much responsibility on Mad Jack Percival as sailing master. Nevertheless the *Epervier* surrendered shortly after this, having lost twenty-two men to the *Peacock*'s two injured. For his efforts, Percival was presented with a handsome sword and promoted to the rank of lieutenant.

We next find Jack Percival in 1823, sailing the seven seas as first lieutenant aboard Commodore Hull's flagship, the *United States*. Two years later he was in command of the schooner *Dolphin*, pursuing mutineers from the American whaler *Globe*. The *Dolphin* became the first American warship to enter Owhyhee Harbor in what is now the Hawaiian Islands. Here he became involved in trouble because some of his men visited houses of unconcealed merriment along the waterfront. These were frowned upon by the American missionaries. One night Mad Jack had to put down a riot at Owhyhee almost single-handedly, although several of the authorities blamed him for starting the trouble.

Another incident occurred during his visit to the Hawaiian Islands. Captain Alfred Edwards, an American master of the ship *London*, had been wrecked on the nearby island of Paini. A native chieftain, Thunder by name, had placed a taboo on the wrecked vessel, so that no one would venture near the ship, preventing Edwards from removing his money and provisions. When he saw that a dangerous situation was arising, Edwards wrote Percival to sail over and help him out. Hiring a packet, Percival landed and removed the money, helped salvage the *London,* and then gave Edwards the bill of costs for the packet, $800. Edwards refused to pay it, so Mad Jack had the coin transferred to the *Dolphin*, removed his $800, and charged extra for his salvage work. Edwards paid the bill under protest. When he returned to Owhyee, Edwards circulated reports that Percival had stolen a mattress from his wrecked ship. That was too much for Mad Jack, who took a few sailors, and went aboard the *London* to demand an apology. It did not come. Mad Jack Percival grabbed Edwards, held him firmly, and drubbed the captain's hand with a piece of whalebone. Captain Edwards then picked up an axe and a gun rammer, but each time he swung, Percival stepped easily aside. The crew disarmed the now raging Captain Edwards. Percival, satisfied with the outcome of his visit, then left the ship.

Arriving back in the United States, Percival was confronted with a court of inquiry based on his actions in the riot at Owhyhee, but his explanations were satisfactory and his case was dismissed. Then Captain Edwards hailed him into court for personal assault, and Jack Percival did have to pay $100 for his energetic treatment of Edwards aboard the *London*. Although Edwards also tried to get back what he had paid to Percival, the government decided against him.

In 1834 Captain Percival, serving aboard the *Constitution* while it was tied up at the Charlestown Navy Yard, tried in vain to help those who wished to take the *Constitution*'s figurehead from the vessel. It was another Cape Cod man, Samuel Worthington Dewey, who did cut the figurehead of Andrew Jackson off at the neck, but we shall hear of that story later.

A legend has come down to us that Percival, while cruising around the world as commander of the U.S. frigate *Constitution*, threatened to bombard a village unless an American shipmaster imprisoned there was released. The truth of this story is quite different from the legend usually accepted.

Arriving at Cochin, China, in May 1845, Captain Percival heard that a French bishop was a prisoner of the natives and about to be executed.

He captured three Mandarins and kept them for several days, releasing them only after they had promised to plead with their king for Bishop Lefebre's life. At the time the *Constitution* actually did exchange shots with several of the small junks, but no real damage was done. Leaving the harbor before he learned how the affair came out, he was gratified later to learn that through his efforts Bishop Lefebre had been released.

While anchored in Canton Harbor, Percival heard of a great fire in Pittsburgh, and at once he took up a subscription for the people of that devastated city. One thousand nine hundred and fifty dollars was sent to them.

Later in the year the *Constitution* was "drifting along toward the port of Manila," when she found herself in the center of a large fleet of warships, and feared the worst. Perhaps war had been declared, for they had not heard from home for months, and anything might have happened. Captain Jack jumped from his berth and ordered the decks cleared for action. When daylight came, it was seen that the ships of the possible enemy were British, so the officers and crew were all placed at their stations. Match fires were lighted, the magazines opened, and Captain Percival prepared to defend the honor of the United States against the entire British China Squadron. The American flag was unfurled from the mast of the *Constitution*, and the Britishers replied with a display of the English ensign.

Then a boat was seen to leave the British admiral's ship, and shortly afterwards a young officer climbed the side of the *Constitution* to pay his respects to the American captain, who was waiting for him.

"Is it peace or war?" was Captain Jack Percival's first question.

"Why, peace, to be sure," was the astonished reply of the young British officer, after which Captain Percival took him below into the cabin. The request from Admiral Thomas Cochrane of the British China Squadron was for the loan of provisions, a request which was fulfilled at once.

It is said that Captain Jack carried a heavy oaken coffin with him on the entire cruise, and after arriving back home, used it for a watering trough for the remainder of his days. Retired in 1855, he lived in a house at Meeting House Hill, Dorchester, on a street later named for him. On September 17, 1862, he passed away, and the local Boston paper *Patriot* summed up his career effectively when it said, "He was generous, kindhearted, and a good navigator, always ready to do battles for his country and its flag." The concluding remarks were, "Thus has another old hero passed from this world." For many years the U.S.S. *Percival* has honored this Cape Cod hero.

I walked down the main highway to visit his grave, and found an attractive yellow highway marker guiding me to the place. It was here that Captain Jack was buried, Naval epaulets and all, that September day of 1862.

The second Barnstable captain to be discussed is William Sturgis. This Cape Cod shipmaster began his business career while very young by entering the counting room of the eminent Russell Sturgis. William, already well versed in the art of navigation at the age of sixteen, became a sailor in 1798 aboard the *Eliza*. This craft was one of the noted Perkins ships which went up into the northwest fur-trading area. It was not long before Sturgis became the liaison officer between the West Coast Indians and his own superior officers aboard ship, with the unofficial title of assistant trader. He soon developed a technique with the natives which paid heavy dividends, that of practicing the Golden Rule and speaking in their own language.

When Captain James Rowan anchored off Caiganee on the Northwest Coast, he found that two other Boston ships were ahead of him, the *Ulysses* and the *Despatch*, with a strange state of affairs existing. The crew of the *Ulysses* had mutinied and placed their Captain Lamb in irons! Captain Breck of the other ship dared not take action alone, so matters were at a standstill. When the *Eliza* arrived with 136 men, it was time for a showdown. Captains Rowan of the *Eliza* and Breck of the *Despatch* joined forces and announced that a board of inquiry would be held aboard the *Eliza*. Captain Lamb was escorted aboard, with the leaders of the mutineers, and a trial was held, during which Lamb agreed that he would treat his men better if they would return and serve under him. All the sailors agreed except Lamb's mates, who refused to go aboard the *Ulysses* under any conditions. As a result, eighteen-year-old William Sturgis signed aboard the mutineer vessel *Ulysses* as chief mate! Anxious about what could happen, he soon found that all hands were more than willing to have the remainder of their voyage a disciplinary success, so when they reached Canton, all was well again with Captain Lamb and his crew.

Another surprise awaited Sturgis at Canton, for there was the old *Eliza* in the harbor and Captain Rowan with a proposition for him. Would young Sturgis accept the offer of third mate aboard his old ship? Of course he would, provided there was no objection from Captain Lamb, who readily gave his consent, for there were replacements available in port. The *Eliza* returned to Boston Harbor in the spring of 1800 after a voyage of two years, with a young man who had sailed from Boston before the mast returning as third mate!

After a voyage on the *Caroline*, which he began as first mate and ended as captain because of the illness of Captain Derby, he came back with such good reports that his owners sent him out again as captain for a three-year cruise.

Then Theodore Lyman, the great Boston benefactor and merchant, decided to send Captain William Sturgis to the West Coast aboard the *Atahualpa* to load furs for the Canton trade. His return two years later resulted in great profits for all concerned, and he stayed ashore for almost a year to be with his family.

Then came the greatest adventure of Sturgis' career. In April 1809 Captain William Sturgis sailed the *Atahualpa* for Canton with 300,000 Spanish dollars to buy a return cargo. Aboard the vessel, as first mate was another Barnstable man, Daniel C. Bacon. Also on ship in case of emergency and against the owners' orders, were four cannon. Everything went according to schedule until the ship anchored in Macao Roads during a calm. Captain Sturgis sent Bacon ashore.

Suddenly one of the passengers, a Mr. Bumstead, shouted to Captain Sturgis that Chinese pirates were on their way to attack the *Atahualpa*. As Bumstead had lost his brother through pirates, he had been watching all Chinese junks suspiciously. Surely enough, Captain Sturgis trained his glass on sixteen Chinese junks which were sailing his way. Not willing to believe they actually planned to attack him, he ordered the gunner to "throw a shot across their bows, just to show how soon it will bring them about on the other tack." But the Chinese commanders aboard the junks chose to ignore the warning and kept their steady advance towards the *Atahualpa*.

Approaching the vessel, the pirates tried to get close enough to throw firebrands aboard, but the cannon of the white men kept them back. Time and again they came on; each onslaught was repulsed. In the middle of the confusion young Bacon rowed out through the fighting and climbed aboard the *Atahualpa* to join forces with Captain Sturgis, who at the time was standing over the powder barrel, grinding a cigar between his teeth and threatening to blow everyone to Kingdom Come should the battle go against them. Sturgis took advantage of a slight breeze to weigh anchor and work the *Atahualpa* up under the protection of the guns at the Portuguese forts on the shore, which soon began to fire with telling effect on the Chinese junks. The pirates reluctantly withdrew from the fighting and sailed out of range, but it had been nip and tuck for several hours. Captain Sturgis had almost carried out his threat several times to blow up the ship, for he had no intention of falling into the hands of the murderous pirates of the China Seas. His officers and crew, knowing his determination and purpose, realized that he would unquestionably have kept his word.

Later Appotesi, the leader of the Chinese pirates, returned for a brief test of strength, but this time a few well-aimed cannon shots were enough to make him decide against further activities. Two aftermaths of the struggle developed. First, James Sturgis, the captain's cousin, who was sick with jaundice all the voyage, found himself completely cured because of the battle. Secondly, Appotesi was captured shortly afterwards and taken into the custody of the Mandarins, who executed him in a charming fashion known as the death torture of the "thousand cuts." They hacked him to death with swords.

After a successful voyage Captain Sturgis appeared off Highland Light early in April 1810, and on the thirteenth of that month sailed triumphantly into Boston Harbor. Theodore Lyman, a true disciplinarian, secretly admired Sturgis's wonderful record on the trip and his successful fighting with the Chinese pirates. But would he let Sturgis know it? Never! Theodore Lyman not only reprimanded Captain William Sturgis for carrying the cannon against orders, but actually charged the sea captain freight for transporting them!

Captain William Sturgis then went into business for himself, teaming up with John Bryant in a firm which lasted more than fifty years. I shall mention an episode of his later career. One day Sturgis, whose bushy eyebrows and great strength were well known along Boston's waterfront, went aboard Captain Robert Bennet Forbes's ship as a guest of the captain. The latter, bringing up his own shaggy dog which also had long hair around his eyebrows, paraded him before the smiling Captain Sturgis, who remarked, "Yes, I recognize the likeness."

Then there was the eminent Captain Josiah Richardson of Centerville, who was the outstanding sailor of his generation on Cape Cod. Kittredge tells us that he tried his hand at all four branches of maritime activity then in vogue—European trade, passenger vessels, China voyages, and clipper ships. Going to sea as a cabin boy at eleven, at twenty-one he was master of a schooner. Later he crossed the ocean as captain of the brig *Orbit*. His voyages aboard the brig *Owhyhee* gave him a special place in my shipwreck stories, because I have a long copper spike from the *Owhyhee* on my mantelpiece at the present time. Leaving the *Owhyhee* he next took out the *Leander*, but by 1839 he was ready for larger vessels.

From a command aboard the ship *Chatham*, he took over the *Walpole*, arriving in the Straits of Sunda one August day of 1847 ninety-one days out. "The vessels that sailed before us one fortnight have not yet arrived," was his message to his wife at home.

Of course, his best-known ship was the clipper *Stag Hound*, built by Donald McKay in 1850. We do not believe that Captain Richardson was present when the workmen poured boiling oil on the frozen tallow at East Boston to send the *Stag Hound* down the ways December 7, 1850, but when he first saw her his heart gave a jump, for she was a beautiful object to behold.

On February 1, 1851 he sailed out of New York with her, lost her mainmast and three topgallant masts six days out, and still arrived in San Francisco in 108 sailing days. "The ship has yet to be built that will beat the *Stag Hound*," wrote Richardson to his employers. "I am perfectly in love with her."

Captain Josiah Richardson was given command of the *Staffordshire*, which braved tradition by carrying a white witch for a figurehead. Ready to sail for California, Richardson was slightly delayed by rumors said to have been started by the Fox sisters of upper New York State, two mediums who predicted mysterious trouble for the white witch and the passengers aboard the *Staffordshire*. Finally, on May 3, 1852, the vessel left Boston to arrive 101 days later at San Francisco, having smashed all sailing records from 50 degrees latitude South in a thirty-day run. Richardson then made another record after reaching Calcutta, for he sailed from Saugar to reach the United States in eighty-two days.

In 1853 the *Staffordshire* sailed for Europe to bring to America a shipload of immigrants. Whether Richardson took the rumors about his vessel seriously we probably shall never know, but he did write his wife a short time before sailing that "life is uncertain," and also stated that "in case of any accident" he was enclosing his account with the firm back in Boston. Without question, Richardson did not want to make the voyage which ended his career. But he sailed for America and for a time nothing unusual took place.

On December 23 a tremendous gale was blowing. In some manner the rudder-head became twisted, so the crew secured it with chains. Five days later a giant wave carried the bowsprit, foretopmast, foreyard, and everything forward overboard, and the wreckage took the temporary rudder with it. Then came the accident which was so hard to explain. Captain Josiah Richardson went aloft to examine the truss to see if it were possible or practical to rig another foreyard, and on descending fell thirty-five feet to the deck, landing on his back. Taken below, he tried to run his ship from the cabin.

The next day came heavy rain. Another steering gear was rigged, and the ship was "made all snug for the night," according to the report of First Mate Joseph Alden. At 11:50 the second mate sighted Seal Island Light, and the captain ordered the *Staffordshire* "to be wore around." Shortly afterwards the clipper ship struck Blond Rock off Sable Island, ripped out her bottom, and slid off into deep water. Then she began to settle and those who could took to the boats. However, 178 persons perished, and with them one of Cape Cod's immortal men of the sea, brave Captain Richardson. He chose to go down with his ship, saying, "Then if I am to be lost, God's will be done."

Other outstanding captains of Barnstable include Daniel C. Bacon, already mentioned; Allen Bursley, lost aboard the *Lion* at Port Patrick, Scotland; David Bursley, lost with the *Hottinger* near Blackwater Bank off Ireland; Captain Joseph W. Crocker; Captain Ira Bursley, 2nd; and Captain James Bacon Crocker, whose exploits in the China Seas were well known at the time.

From the Hyannis Precinct of Barnstable we list Captain Alvin Hallett, Captain Rodney Baxter, and the three Bearse brothers—Warren Bearse of the *Flying Scud*, Frank Bearse with his *Winged Arrow*, and Richard Bearse, captain of the *Robin Hood*. Captain Warren Bearse's *Flying Scud*, so it is claimed, once logged 449 miles in twenty-four hours, which if accepted, would constitute a world's record. Henry C. Kittredge tells us that the 449-mile logging should be "relegated to the realm of fiction, where it belongs." Then there were several other prominent sea captains including Howard Allyn, Elkanah Crowell, and John H. Frost.

A location of interest aboard many ships was the munching drawer. Aboard the *Independent* it was located in the cabin. Captain Willis L. Chase kept dried fruits, nuts, candy, and other sweets there where it was within easy reach of his daughter, Maud, who often went to sea with him.

One season Miss Clara J. Hallett went with Captain and Mrs. Horace F. Hallett of Hyannis as a guest aboard one of Captain Hallett's barges. On a fine day when they were tied up at a dock, Miss Hallett decided to make some pumpkin pies, and while they were baking, the stevedores began unloading coal. After a time there was a distinct list to the galley and the stove. The two discouraged women expected to see a golden ooze coming from the crack in the oven door, but no telltale yellow appeared, and so the women hoped that all was well. But they were disappointed. When they opened the oven door they found the pies several inches thick on one side and nearly burned shells on the other.

The packets of Cape Cod played an important part in the development of this arm of Massachusetts, and Barnstable was among the leaders in this field. One of the colorful packet men of a former century was Captain Isaac Bacon. He sailed from Barnstable one day aboard the *Somerset*, which he named for the warship wrecked in 1778. A leak started almost at once, for a rat had gnawed a hole through the planking. Bacon heeled the *Somerset* over on her port beam ends, crawled out along the starboard side to drive in a wedge which stopped the leak, and then continued the trip to Boston. One day he found out that his rival, Hutchins, had sold a load of onions for delivery in Salem, so Captain Bacon sailed into that port with his own load of onions, called on the merchant, and falsely claimed that Hutchins was his son-in-law. The Salem merchant believed him, and after examining the load, paid for the onions. Bacon sailed back to Barnstable, happy in the knowledge that he had put it over on his rival.

Though Barnstable is a large town, it is still startling to learn that during the period around 1800 the farmers on the north side were shipping corn to Boston and the residents of the south side were actually importing the same commodity from Connecticut! We must therefore conclude that it was easier to take a fifty-mile packet sail to Boston than to drive a load of corn over the sandy roads connecting the north and south sides of Barnstable during that period.

Donald Trayser told me that the packets were social institutions. The fare to and from Boston was a dollar, and meals came to twenty-five cents or less. An average run to Boston under fair winds was seven hours. If head winds prevailed or the packet ran into a dead calm, the seven hours became fifteen or even twenty. The smell aboard the packets drove the women topside most of the voyage, if the weather warranted it, but in rough seas (and they prevailed more frequently than calm weather), a woman's lot was not a happy one in the midst of the odors of the bilge, the ever-present smell of fish, and the smoke of tobacco.

There are those who say that a jug of New England rum was always on hand to cure seasickness in the early days, but around 1830 the temperance crusade eliminated that jug from the packets permanently. The packets competed with Uncle Sam in carrying the mail, and at no charge!

Returning to Barnstable's main street I hiked up to what is still called Barrel Hill. A century ago an empty barrel was hoisted aloft on the flagpole atop the hill to indicate the Boston packet was in at the pier. When it was time for the packet to sail to Boston again, a flag was raised, and the residents of Barnstable thus knew that when high tide came, the packet would sail for Boston.

Of course, other Cape towns had their own packet lines. In 1828 the *Commodore Hull* of the Yarmouth Line proved a faster packet than any in Barnstable, and for years the men of Barnstable had to swallow their pride. Finally they arranged for the building of another packet, the sloop *Mail,* which arrived at the Cape in 1837, ready for a test with the *Hull.* Sailing together, the two vessels crossed Barnstable Bar together, headed for Boston. Six hours later the *Mail* arrived at Central Wharf, three lengths ahead of the *Hull.*

As a rule, the packets did not sail to Boston in the winter. Elizabeth Munroe of Barnstable, daughter of a packet captain, said that "the last trip was usually made in November, just before Thanksgiving. How vividly I recall the happy time when my father made his last season's trip. With what eager eyes we children watched from our high attic window to catch the first glimpse of the vessel's topsail bringing to us our dear father with all his winter's treasures."

Steam packets were tried out, but proved neither practical nor successful, for they had to anchor offshore and be met by a barge. One stormy day in September 1844, Captain Sanford of the steam packet *Yacht* was fearful of bringing his packet in, so Captain John Hall, a passenger, volunteered to "take her in," and he brought the *Yacht* safely to the anchorage.

An early Hyannis packet, the sloop *Caroline,* carried passengers, mail, and freight to Nantucket. A tragic ending to her February 24, 1829, run came when the *Caroline* was caught in a heavy snowstorm. Captain James Scudder was confused because of the heavy snow and ran the packet aground near the entrance to Cotuit Harbor.

The small boat was launched and with everyone safely aboard they rowed to Sampson's Island, where the storm shut in worse than ever and the temperature dropped steadily. The eight shipwrecked people huddled together as best they could, but soon young Ebenezer Scudder, thirteen years old, died of the cold in spite of all the others could do to keep him warm. The storm went down the following afternoon, and the group looked out to see another vessel ashore, the ship *Golden Hunter* of Wellfleet.

The *Golden Hunter* appeared to be in no danger, however, so the survivors rowed out and were taken into the warm cabin, but too late for James Scudder, who died shortly afterwards. Thus Captain Scudder lost his two sons because of the shipwreck. Returning to the *Caroline*, he found her safe and sound, with all her cargo untouched, and two thousand dollars in currency still in the cabin. If he had stayed aboard, his sons would have lived through the storm. Captain Scudder never went to sea again.

The first mail service to Barnstable began in 1792, when John Thacher made a weekly round-trip horseback journey to Boston. Many were the adventures which Thacher encountered. It became his habit to carry a saw and a small axe, to use if he had to leave the beaten trail and hew out a path through the forests. Several Cape Codders complained that his pay of one dollar a day was extravagant.

During the War of 1812 the mail began to come twice a week. In 1820 another weekly trip was added, and Samuel Thacher, old John's son, received the contract for picking the mail up and carrying it along down the Cape. His pay was $68.75 for three months, and he was allowed to carry extra newspapers as well.

By 1800, stagecoaches were rumbling down the highway as far as Sandwich, and thirty years later stages between Boston and Barnstable were running on a regular schedule. At first the stages stopped overnight at Plymouth, but later the journey was made into one long, tedious day's travel. Taverns at Hyannis, West Barnstable, Sandwich, and West Sandwich on the Cape, and others in Plymouth and Scituate helped break the journey, but it still meant a terrific mental and physical effort, getting up to make the stage which left Hyannis at 2:00 A.M. and Barnstable at 3:00 A.M. to arrive in Boston in time for supper!

The railroad started running from Middleboro to Sandwich in 1848, and later, when the trains reached Hyannis, the days of the stagecoaches were numbered. Finally the coaches were used to carry people to and from the stations and were popularly known by special names such as *Black Maria*, *Old Mortality*, and *Noah's Ark*. Sam Knowles of Orleans resented references to his stage as *Noah's Ark* and when a prospective passenger appeared and asked if Knowles's vehicle was *Noah's Ark* and if he might ride, he received a spirited answer.

"Hurry and get aboard," said Sam, "All the animals are in the Ark except the jackass." The stages, of course, eventually gave way to motor vehicles.

Many arguments and compromises were necessary before the actual route the railroad would take in crossing Barnstable was chosen, for the Nantucket interests desired a short route from Hyannis to Boston, and naturally the Barnstable group wished the railroad to go through the center of their town. Finally an agreement was arrived at whereby both Hyannis and Barnstable were reached by rail. A special boat ran from Nantucket to Hyannis, and the owners stressed the short distance of twenty-seven miles as compared with the usual run of fifty miles to New Bedford.

The railroad reached Barnstable on May 8, 1854, and Hyannis on July 8 the same year. The first Nantucket steamer, the *Nebraska*, sailed from Hyannis September 28, 1854. The Nantucket-Hyannis line had a fairly prosperous career, lasting until 1872.

I returned to the courthouse a little later to continue my explorations through the many records there. Thus occupied I spent a most enjoyable afternoon reading records of trials and other eventful happenings of this Cape Cod county. I read of the night when the old county courthouse burned, October 22, 1827, well over a century ago. All the county records and all the court records were lost at that time, besides ninety-three volumes of deeds. Only one volume of deeds survived the disaster and that was accomplished by the quick thinking of Josiah Hinckley. The probate records were all saved.

On the evening of the fire two young men, Captain Joseph Bursley and Josiah Hinckley, were playing cards at nearby Crocker Tavern. At 10:45 that night the Reverend Henry Hersey discovered that the county house was in flames and gave the alarm. The two men playing cards were the first to respond, and they rushed in to save what they could. There was a gale of wind blowing, dooming the building in advance, for the fire had a good start before the Reverend Mr. Hersey discovered it. Bursley and Hinckley, forcing their way into the probate office, passed the record books out to the minister and Isaac Chipman, who in turn carried them to safety.

By this time there were about a dozen persons around the building. Hinckley then decided to try to save the records from the registry of deeds office on the second floor, but the smoke was so dense in the hall that they had to leave the building. Obtaining a ladder, Hinckley climbed up to the north window of the Registry office. As the window was fastened, Hinckley kicked it through, and the draft allowed the smoke and flames further advantage. Before the flames forced Hinckley down the ladder, he reached in and grabbed a record book on the desk, the only deed book saved.

The new courthouse was built in 1831, and is now the north or central wing of the present courthouse. Enlargements were made in 1879, 1905, and 1924. It was on my return visit that I found further details of the famous trials held in Barnstable. One of the most inhuman murderers ever tried in Barnstable County Courthouse was Jane Toppan, whose trial revealed her strange nature and stranger avocation. A registered nurse, Miss Toppan began to poison her patients in Cambridge, Massachusetts, and then moved to Bourne, where she continued her activities with astounding success. Clever enough to mix her poisons so that the investigators were completely bewildered, this woman later admitted that she had poisoned thirty-one victims in her career! Donald G. Trayser thinks that she must hold the record in this type of crime.

When they decided that she was insane and not really responsible for her crimes, this woman said, "How can I be insane? When I killed the people, I knew what I was doing. I was perfectly conscious that what I was doing was not right." Nevertheless, she was sent to the hospital for the criminally insane, where she died quietly in 1938.

In 1877 a group of Pocasset people became interested in an unusual type of religious fanaticism, which led to fatal results two years later. Charles Freeman and his wife joined the group and became sincere followers of the faith. In May 1879 Charles Freeman awoke in the middle of the night, believing that he had seen a vision of the Lord. The Lord told him, according to Freeman, to make a sacrifice, but the sacrifice Freeman was called upon to make was his little four-year-old daughter Edith. The disturbed Freeman awakened his wife, who was completely dominated by her husband.

The couple knelt in prayer in an effort to solve their problem. Freeman prayed that God would stay his hand at the last minute as He had done with Abraham over Isaac. He prayed, however, that if he had to kill his daughter, he preferred to do it at once and get it over with. Then he claimed that God ordered him to kill his daughter. Commanding his wife to hold the lamp, Freeman walked to the bed of his daughter Edith with sheath knife in hand. Bending over the girl, he gently pulled the covers down until only her nightdress covered her tiny body. Then Freeman acted. He plunged his sheath knife into his daughter's side, and the poor girl, awakening, looked at her father with the bloody knife in his hand and said, "Oh, Papa!" A moment later she was dead.

When the authorities took Freeman and his wife away from their little home at Putts Hollow, Freeman quietly told them that he had done right. When Constable Redding asked him if it were right to murder his daughter, Freeman tried to explain that Edith would rise again in three days. She was buried in a tiny coffin which read, "Little Edie—lived only 57 months. She shall surely rise again.—John vi. 39."

After a year in the Barnstable jail, Freeman was sent to an insane hospital, and his wife was released. In 1887 Freeman was allowed to leave the hospital. He went west, where, it is said, he caused no more trouble for the rest of his life.

Hiking down to Cobb's Village, I borrowed a boat, and with the owner of the craft in the stern, started rowing across to Sandy Neck Lighthouse. Although in former years the harbor had been a busy one, there seemed very little marine traffic as I neared the old lighthouse. Jumping ashore, I bade farewell to my accommodating Barnstable friend, who began the row off slightly more than a mile to the opposite shore. I was on my own again.

Approaching the lighthouse, I found a cluster of about thirty buildings and shacks to the westward of the old light, but I was anxious to meet Fred Lang, the Yankee Network radio star, who now owns the lighthouse property there.

"Ahoy, Fred," I shouted when about fifty yards away from the tower. Fred Lang himself came out to greet me.

"Well, you did make it," were his first words. "I really didn't expect you, although you said that you were coming." And Fred Lang took me inside and gave me a drink of milk to cool me off.

"So this is your place!" I said. "What do you know about it?"

"Not as much as I'd like to," was his reply. "But I have learned quite a lot. The old beach around here for many years before the lighthouse was built was pretty busy as a try yard for blackfish catchers and even for whalers. You can still see traces of their buildings. There is an old shipwreck about a quarter mile due northeast of the light. It is buried in the sand, but a few of the ribs are sticking up. Nothing can be learned as to why, when, or how it was wrecked."

Fred went on to tell me that the lighthouse had been put up in 1827 because of a terrible experience which befell the occupants of the schooner *Almira*. At the time the vessel sailed from Sandwich that year, an old mariner had warned Captain Ellis against the trip. Seeing them sail out, he went to a nearby hillside and exclaimed, "Gone out! He will never come in again." And his prediction proved correct, for the *Almira* was soon caught in the below-zero weather and floated, a frozen hulk, by Sandy Neck with no one to rescue the sailors aboard. Captain Josiah Ellis and one sailor froze to death, but Ellis's son was still alive when the *Almira* hit the Dennis shore. He recovered completely from his tragic experience.

Other sailors have been trapped in the ice of Cape Cod Bay. In 1875 the lighthouse keeper witnessed many narrow escapes when the bay froze over a good part of the winter, shutting in schooner after schooner. Then, not too many years ago, several boys were trapped on the ice floes offshore from Sandy Neck, and were rescued only after great difficulties.

"I have seen 6,000 to 10,000 wild ducks at one time along Sandy Neck," said Fred. "During the hunting season there are times when I have seen the wild deer racing down the beach to plunge into the water and swim across to Yarmouth."

"Old Clarence Chase is the harbor master of Barnstable, and he has told me many yarns of Sandy Neck and the harbor. He is surely an interesting character. Shirley Lovell is another personality who should be included. He runs a ferry boat back and forth from Barnstable to Sandy Neck Camp, which he operates in the summer. Also a lobsterman and fisherman, he has quite a busy life. You can see him come in several times daily at the fish pier in Maranspin Creek, either returning from or going out to his camp."

I had stopped at the home of Harry Baxter Ryder in Yarmouth before rowing out to Sandy Neck Light, and he told me much about its history. His sister, Mrs. Clara Ryder Collins of Everett, had suggested that I visit him. They both are the grandchildren of Thomas Baxter and his wife Lucy Hinckley Baxter, who kept Sandy Neck Light for many years. Harry Ryder still has one of the original logbooks of the lighthouse.

While at his home, Ryder had told me that his grandfather always had visitors at Sandy Neck, for he kept open house. The packet boat from Boston and Provincetown often stopped at the light. One day Baxter was crossing to Barnstable over treacherous ice and open water, pulling, pushing, and rowing the dory. Suddenly he caught his leg between the dory and the ice, causing an injury which later resulted in his death from gangrene. Lucy Hinckley Baxter then applied for and received her husband's position as keeper of Sandy Neck Light. She stayed there with her three children until they reached school age. Realizing that she would have to make plans for their schooling, she moved her family to Barnstable, and later married Lathrop Elliot of Yarmouth. "The picture she often described to us of her having to heat the whale oil in the winter months behind the kitchen stove and carry two oil butts up into the tower at midnight is one we never forgot," Harry Ryder told me at the time of my visit.

Fred told me that there were rumors that one of the keepers of those later days was more or less active with the rumrunners, but Mr. Lang would not tell me whether the keeper favored the government or the rumrunners.

Fred hiked along the beach with me toward the west when I left, for I refused his kind offer of a ride. We looked out at the fishing weirs as we walked along, where they hauled in about eighteen or twenty tuna, some of them weighing from 500 to 700 pounds. Before we parted, he told me that more than thirty years before one of the Sandy Neck families decided to have his house moved across to the mainland, and made all arrangements. Finally the barge was brought in, the house put aboard, and the family went to bed for the night, being assured that when the movers returned, they would be awakened to make plans for the trip across the harbor. But this arrangement was forgotten when the barge captain arrived at sunrise the following day, coming early to take advantage of the wind and tide. The family later awoke when the barge slid gently into the pier at Barnstable, and it is said the members of that particular family never got over the strange feeling they experienced when looking out of their windows, as they had done for years at Sandy Point, to find that the town of Barnstable had moved into their back yard!

Fred and I stopped for our final farewell, and then he sprang the question which he had been holding back all morning. "By the way, Ed, I know you wrote a book which has the names of all the shipwrecks of New England in it, so give me the answer to this question: What is the name of the shipwreck near the Sandy Neck Light?" He had me, for I had never seen or heard of the wreck before and told him so. "Well, I don't know either," said Fred Lang. "Here's a consolation for you!" and he threw me an orange. Then we parted.

The old Point Gammon Lighthouse on Great Island in Hyannis has been privately owned since the nineteenth century, but it can be seen distantly by thousands of ferry passengers and sightseers in Hyannis Harbor each year.

The Massachusetts Maritime Academy moved from Hyannis to Buzzards Bay in 1949. In 1977, the Academy became coeducational, and women now constitute about 15 percent of the student population.

The harrowing tale of the *Essex* has been most recently recounted in the pages of *In the Heart of the Sea: The Tragedy of the Whaleship Essex*, by Nathaniel Philbrick. It is generally accepted that the *Essex* story was a chief inspiration for Herman Melville's *Moby-Dick*.

Chief Justice Lemuel Shaw was once engaged to Nancy Melville, daughter of Major Thomas Melville, a leader of the Boston Tea Party and grandfather of the *Moby-Dick* author. The marriage never took place, as Nancy died in 1813. But the families would be united in 1847, when Herman Melville married Shaw's daughter Elizabeth.

Cape Cod sculptor David Lewis's statue of James Otis can be seen today outside the Barnstable County Superior Courthouse. Nearby is a sculpture of Otis's sister, Mercy Otis Warren, a writer who has been called the "First Lady of the American Revolution." Her works include the first published history of the Revolution.

Historic postcard of Point Gammon Lighthouse (from the collection of Jeremy D'Entremont)

According to Snow's measurement, Boston's Sacred Cod is longer than Barnstable's by more than a foot. Cod, the official state fish of Massachusetts, was eaten along with turkey at the first Thanksgiving.

The incident involving Mad Jack Percival, the *Constitution*, and a would-be prisoner exchange took place in 1845 at what is now Danang Harbor, Vietnam. The French bishop being held by local authorities was never released, and Old Ironsides did, in fact, bombard the village, resulting in as many as three dozen deaths.

The Sturgis Library in Barnstable is named for Captain William Sturgis, who made a bequest of his home along with $15,000 and 1,300 books for the founding of a "free library for the use of the inhabitants of the Town of Barnstable." The original part of the building dates to 1644, making it the oldest library building in the United States.

You can see the now-lanternless Sandy Neck Lighthouse distantly from Sandy Neck Beach, but you'll need to be in a boat to get good photos. The private property around the lighthouse is strictly off limits.

CHAPTER 9

Sandwich, Famous for Its Glass

I continued westward along the beach. At one point, the old bombing practice range of the government, I found several fragments of shells dropped there during the active years of World War II. An hour and a half later I was in Sandwich.

On April 3, 1637, the records at Plymouth, Massachusetts, mention ten good men of Saugus who are given liberty to "view a place to sit down and have sufficient lands for threescore families, upon the conditions propounded to them by the governor and Mr. Winslow." That place was Sandwich, and of the ten names mentioned, three families were still flourishing in Sandwich as late as 1889, those bearing the name of Freeman, Dillingham, and Tupper.

Before the year 1637 came to a close, fifty other citizens arrived on the Cape from Lynn, Saugus, Duxbury, and Plymouth, and most of the new arrivals brought their families. A Pilgrim church was set up the same year, with the Reverend William Leverich as minister. Sandwich was actually incorporated in 1639, two years after its settlement, and became the fourth town in the colony. The delay had been caused by the reluctance of the Pilgrims to accept men who were not of their own group. In 1654 a town mill was planned, followed the next year by arrangements for the raising of a church building.

Myles Standish himself laid out the town lines of Sandwich, and it is quite probable that there were some exciting discussions as to where the lines should go. I recall Hubbard's remarks about the Plymouth captain, that as "a little chimney is soon on fire, so was the Plymouth Captain, a man of very small stature yet of a very hot and angry temper."

The Reverend Mr. Chamberlain tells us that the settlement of Sandwich was preceded by a storm, that of August 1635, and followed by an earthquake, that of June 1, 1638. The storm is well known, for it was the first recorded New England hurricane. The earthquake was felt in Sandwich between 1:00 and 2:00 in the afternoon, and according to those who were there, it started as a low murmur of distant sound, which grew louder and clearer until they could all hear what seemed to be thunder rumbling far away. Then, two or three minutes later, it increased in sharpness and in volume until it resembled the rattling of fiercely driven carriages proceeding over granite pavements. Shortly afterwards the earth began to tremble beneath them, and many inhabitants of Sandwich ran toward the gathering place where they all huddled together, terribly frightened by this first great earthquake ever recorded in New England history. The shaking continued until no one could stand erect unless he took hold of posts or fences.

Inside the houses there was great alarm also, for the foundations shook and it was feared that the buildings would come down, but the damage was confined to the top-heavy fieldstone chimneys, which fell with a loud crash.

Four minutes the earthquake lasted; then half an hour later another quake of less severity occurred. For the next twenty days earthly disturbances of little importance were experienced. The farmers always claimed that the weather for several years after the earthquake was cool and unseasonable.

Without question the only way of travel in the early days of Sandwich was by horseback and boat, since there were no wagons on Cape Cod for many years after the first settlement. Even as late as 1687, Judge Samuel Sewall journeyed from Boston to Sandwich on horseback along the sandy beach. Many a good Sandwich citizen trudged on foot all the way to Plymouth with a sack of corn to be ground, while the old Indian trails were probably used for bringing cattle into town. What a pioneering enterprise it must have been for the new settlers arriving at Sandwich, with the women on pillions mounted on horseback, and the menfolk and youngsters hiking along the Indian trail or following the high-tide mark across the sand toward their destination.

The buildings in Sandwich before the year 1700 were usually set north and south, with the front facing south to take advantage of the winter sun and also to tell the seventeenth-century Sandwich resident when noon arrived, for there were few timepieces. The poorer type of homes were all small, usually consisting of one room with a fireplace. An oven in the back of the fireplace was often built out-of-doors. Sometimes these early homes were built into the side of a bank to provide warmth and fireplace security, as well as to save windows and furniture.

Timber was cut in the woods and sawed by hand, so that the cost of a building was merely the labor in putting it up. The floor was placed on sleepers below the sill, which was allowed to project into the room for seats and as a shelf on which driftwood could be piled. Sill beams were bored with two parallel rows of holes six inches apart, into which sharpened poles were set, with the upper end of the pole entering the plate above. The space between these poles was filled with stones and clay to make walls which were firm. The roof was thatched with "creek stuff" or thatch.

No plastered houses existed before 1700, but the clay made the dwellings livable. Fireplaces were the most important part of the residence. Often eight feet wide, four feet deep, and almost six feet high, they were made so that a tall housewife could walk right into her oven in the corner without stooping. There was a hook on each andiron to hold the spit, on which the meat was roasted. The narrow mantelpiece of wood ran the entire length of the fireplace, and the hearthstones were taken from the nearby field. No glass windows existed, although oiled paper was often used to let the light in the houses. The old Sandwich meetinghouse was rather small, resembling a thatched barn in appearance. It had oiled paper windows and wooden shutters. Used for all public activities, it soon showed the effects of time, but it was not until 1756 that the second meetinghouse was erected on the same spot. The new building had galleries and doors on three sides, and the pews were square, with seats on hinges. The deacon sat directly under the pulpit, while the men and women in the choir sat apart from each other.

When it was found that the boys and girls were becoming unruly, Mordecai Ellis and Joshua Fish were appointed to "take care of the young people who are very often rude." That they did their work well is evidenced by what happened in 1767 when two young girls were fined for laughing in meeting. They petitioned the town for the remittance of their fine, however, and evidently showed a truly penitent spirit, for the petition was granted.

Judge Samuel Sewall, interested in the erection of the Sandwich meetinghouse, wrote to carpenter Edward Milton on September 26, 1687, asking Milton to build a "convenient, comfortable meetinghouse for the natives of Sandwich." He guaranteed that Milton would be paid, saying, "Now if it may in any way forward the work, I do engage that upon the finishing of the work, you shall not miss of your pay."

Many of the Irish who left their homeland around 1690 went to Cape Cod from Boston. Those who arrived in Sandwich a few years later were from the north of Ireland, and two families, Higgins and Kelly, became well known all over Cape Cod.

Chamberlain paints a vivid picture of Sandwich during the seventeenth century:

> We will make it . . . a yellow, hazy autumn day, when the golden rod bends graciously towards the late grasses and the Cape sky has put on its cool robe of liquid blue . . . Houses there are among the hills and scattered at long intervals, from Sagamore hill to Scorton. Yet everybody likes to live near the mill, the market, and the meeting. Perhaps we hear the rumble of the mill-wheel at the pond and know that the stream below is swift running over the old stones, as it ran for the amaze and joy of all the children of the town. We see the cattle are on Town neck, lazy and busy. The meeting-house has, for us, some rather singular embellishments. There is a wolf's head nailed up in plain sight, for all to see it. Wolves have troubled the fathers of this town not a little. They have thought to build a palisade wall from Scusset bluffs to Buzzards Bay, but on having had it proved to them that this wall will keep in more wolves than it will keep out, they have given up the plan. And here is coming along just now a squad of Mashpee Indians with a wolf's head among them, bareheaded, blanketed—one long heavy gun in the crowd, with plenty of bows and arrows, and a squaw with a papoose in a basket on her back, who has joined these hunters to share their good luck in a little white man's firewater, after they are paid the £2 this wolf's head calls for out of the town treasury, which is never overfull. They have had better luck than Benjamin Bodfish on the north side of Scorton hill, when he struck at a wolf in his trap with a rotten club, and the wolf sprang at him, broken trap and all, so that only a swift dodge saves him a whole skin, or enables him ever to eat another dinner. The selectmen and hunters will keep at these wolves and have their hands full to boot, until the

last Sandwich wolf is laid on the town hall steps, and your selectman pay the last bounty in 1838. But in 1654 the Old Colony will bag nineteen wolves; in 1655 thirty-one; nine in Barnstable; in 1690, thirteen; in 1691, nineteen.

There are also some curious machines we see near the meetinghouse door. They are the stocks and whipping post; very useful furniture, our fathers thought, to hinder men from stealing chickens or their neighbors' provisions, to keep a scold's tongue quiet, or a lazy fellow from the work-house, or a mean man from beating his wife; and besides there is no county jail to send them to and pay their board out of the county tax. . . . It gives us a good look into our forefathers' larders, as well as court matters, that one hungry thief took from a house, venison, beef, butter, cheese, bread and tobacco, value, 12d, and was whipped at the post with 28s costs. This very week down Plymouth road came armed men, going down the Cape to look for some shipwrecked pirates; a family going the same way to settle. . . . And here comes two Puritan maidens' red cheeks, russet hands, good, wholesome, healthy girls, who helped their father in the late harvest; with a red hood over the blonde hair, and were it colder, a red cloak of good honest wool homespun. . . . They are not laughing, and all the men are afield—they are demure, self-contained, reticent, as Pilgrim maidens are. Sweet sleep and a happy future to them both.

The story of the poor Acadians who were taken from their homes in Nova Scotia is well known because of Longfellow's *Evangeline*, but few are aware that these same Acadian refugees actually arrived at Cape Cod in their search for new homes. On July 20, 1756, seven two-masted sailboats reached Cape Cod, loaded with the homeless Nova Scotians. These unfortunate people, men, women, and children, only recently having left Rhode Island, arrived at the Manomet trading post at Aptucxet. Desiring to go to Boston, the Acadians asked for permission to carry their craft overland to Massachusetts Bay, evidently fearing the long water journey around Cape Cod itself in their canoe-like craft.

But the Cape Cod authorities decided that the Acadians should not be allowed to go to Boston, and ninety Acadians were then separated into small groups and distributed around the towns of Barnstable County. Thus Cape Cod shared in this disgraceful treatment of the Nova Scotians. Acadian families were broken up, their children bound out in service until they lost their identity entirely and disappeared from the records. A few years later the General Court made the decision that "the canoes left at Sandwich by the French neutrals, who deserted from the southern government, shall be sold," and this item is the last mention of the Acadians in local Sandwich history. We shall never be able to explain to future Americans why these aliens, doomed for the most part to live and die among those of other faiths, should have been treated so shamelessly.

Another unfortunate incident involving miscarriage of justice concerned Captain Matthew Fuller's servant Robert. Captain Matthew Fuller of Scorton in West Barnstable died in 1678, and after his funeral the loyal Scotch servant Robert was wrongly accused of having stolen the jewels of his master. The honest Scot, terribly upset by this charge, wandered away into the woods, where he died of grief and starvation. Later the jewels were discovered and Robert was vindicated. When Robert's body was found, the snowdrifts prevented burial anywhere except on the northeast side of Scorton Hill. In 1889 two rough stones marked the final resting place of Robert, Captain Fuller's servant, whose honor meant more to him than his life.

While we of the twentieth century are anxious to call our present way of life the best, there is much to say for the old days when the people of Sandwich lived their simple and peaceful existence. Of course they had their troubles and also their hard work—the Indians were too near and the doctors usually too far. Long tedious hours were spent candle making and cloth making, spinning and knitting. Nevertheless, if we had dropped into a typical Sandwich home near Thanksgiving time around 1725, we would have found the family eating the last meal of the day, perhaps, with the children standing around waiting for their turn at the festive board. Out in the barn hung an ox for winter meat, and there, too, were the cows which had been brought out of the woods in the fall. Fish and wild game abounded. These typical Sandwich residents had prayers morning and evening, plenty of exercise, and enough sleep in the cold, barnlike quarters overhead.

After supper, with the dishes put away and everything snugly in place, the entire family gathered around the roaring fire, the center of interest, to spend the evening. The father and his grown sons discussed plans for the morrow's work, while the mother and daughter worked on their knitting. Mother sat in her low chair in the chimney corner on the right, her husband, his leather jacket around his shoulders, was in his favorite chair, while the other older people were seated comfortably around the room. The youngsters of the family were on a high-backed bench, squirming and active, in the other chimney corner. On evenings such as this, countless tales were told up and down Cape Cod—stories of shipwrecks at sea, pirate's gold, witches and ghosts, and battles with the Indians. And then, after the last story was over, the family prepared for the rigors of the upper rooms, where it was almost as cold as out of doors, but there was plenty of fresh air to bring out the glow of the youngsters' rosy cheeks. When morning arrived they all came down to dress by the warmth of the fire. Yes, we have our comforts—the auto, the radio, the telephone, and countless other inventions which have made life easier for us all. I cannot help thinking, however, that the balance is not completely in favor of what we call our modern generation.

Cape Cod has always emphasized education. In 1787 the Reverend Jonathan Burr became pastor at Sandwich. He was deeply interested in having a substantial place of learning located within the borders of the town. Because of his intense interest, Sandwich Academy was founded in 1804 and proved to be a center of learning for the entire Cape for many years. Housed in a long, narrow building, the academy had a main room into which one came through a short entry. On the left of the classroom was a large box, atop of which, four feet in the air, sat the monitor. On the right was the master's platform, not quite as high, with three steps leading to it. There was a main aisle through the center of the room, with two rows of seats on each side. Another row of seats was attached to the walls on each side of the room, each seat holding one pupil. The central seats held two pupils each. The desks were not on a level, but the floor gradually rose toward the back of the room, where the pupils had to climb into the back seats from the main aisle below. Evidently it was a very large room or else the master was deaf, for one of the former pupils later said he remembered that "a boy in the southwest corner could talk all the morning with his neighbors and not disturb the master." Apples were also eaten in that same corner unseen by the teacher.

At the far end of the main center aisle, there was a door which opened into a room much smaller than the boys' room, where the girls studied.

The first master of Sandwich Academy was the Reverend Mr. Burr himself, who had private pupils many years before he began the Academy. Students came from as far away as the West Indies to this seat of learning, and there were many boys who came from the South to study at the academy. On the windowsill of the Reverend Mr. Burr's old home for years after his death were seen the initials W. W. They stood for William Wainwright, a distinguished bishop of the Episcopal Diocese of New York. Unfortunately, with the passing of the good preacher who founded the school, the academy fell into decadence, and finally closed its doors. For many years it remained a Sandwich landmark, its library filled with ancient books covered with cobwebs, its desks and seats unused and forgotten. Today a dwelling stands where once the Reverend Jonathan Burr began the successful Sandwich Academy.

By the early eighteenth century there were actually eight grain mills in running operation in different parts of the original Sandwich. They were at East Sandwich, Spring Hill, Sandwich proper, Scusset, Herring River, Monument, Pocasset, and Cataumet. Of the eight locations, three are still in Sandwich, while Bourne claims the other five. In addition to this activity, there were three tanneries, where the cattle hides were put in vats and tanned into leather. Then the leather was taken to the village cobblers and made into shoes for the families of Sandwich. All the eight mills and their millers, all the three tanneries and their tanners, vanished years ago, as has that world-famous industry started in 1824 by Jabez Dame under the direction of Deming Jarves, the making of Sandwich glass.

Although it was not until July 4, 1825, that active steps were taken in this remarkable industry, Dame arrived in Sandwich in 1824 with plans for the making of flint glass, as it was called. A large, well-built factory was erected, and by 1854, $500,000 worth of capital was tied up in the glassmaking enterprise. Railroads, cement factories, a lumbering empire on the Cape, cargo vessels, and company stores all indicated what a going concern the Boston & Sandwich Glass Company actually was. For ten years a steamer plied its way between Sandwich and Boston, carrying freight and passengers.

Many think that it was the Sandwich sand which attracted Dame and Jarves, but this was not the case, as the sand actually had to be brought in from Florida, New Jersey, and elsewhere. Cape Cod sand simply was not suitable. The factory was established at Sandwich because of the plentiful forests close at hand, forests which would feed the hungry furnaces for the energetic glassblowers.

And what glassblowers there were at Sandwich! The first to arrive were giants, huskies who thought nothing of doing a day's work of tremendous proportions. The most interesting glassblower was Gaffer Bonique, whom many suspected was actually the Lost Dauphin of France. Another celebrity was Rice Harris, who was brought over here from England for a six-month period at a cost of $5,000.

Sandwich made the first pressed glass and the first lace glass in America. A quarter-century after its start, the business was turning out 100,000 pounds of glass a week, the 500 skilled artificers making many beautiful pieces. In 1841 Deming Jarves presented the great Daniel Webster with the largest piece of flint glass ever made, and later Grover Cleveland was the recipient of a fifty-piece set of beautiful cut glass.

The exquisite shades of various colors had much to do with the popularity of Sandwich glass. Golden Ruby, Jade Green, and Opalescent were three beautiful tones on which the artisans of Sandwich rightfully prided themselves. The secret formula which produced the colored glass was lost when the industry crashed years later.

The basket banks, which had an 1830 dime sealed inside, proved a popular item. White dolphin candlesticks, goblets, witch balls, lamp shades, and scores upon scores of other ornamental glass articles were the result of the efforts of these gifted men of Sandwich.

A crisis in the business came, unfortunately, in 1887. The workers organized into a union, and decided to strike on the first important issue which developed. When glassblower Nicholas Black received his pay with eighty-seven cents missing from his wages, the company refused to give him the extra money, and the union struck because of the company's refusal. The heads of the firm warned the men that if they were still away from work on New Year's Day, 1888, the fires would be allowed to go out—forever. The men stayed out, the fires died, and the plant closed down for all time.

But today, all is not Sandwich glass that is so represented, for present-day manufacturers know how to duplicate this ancient glass. In fact, none but the experts can really tell the reproduction from the original. Enormous quantities of glass were also made elsewhere, some of which can be distinguished from Sandwich glass only with difficulty.

I walked down by the railroad station to visit the last remaining building identified in any way with the old industry, and then walked over to the museum, where many of the workmen's tools are still preserved.

There was so much in the Sandwich Museum to see that I reserved an entire day for the visit. After inspecting the tools of the glassblowers, I was particularly interested in looking at various articles which originally belonged to actor Joe Jefferson. The famous trout basket was prominently displayed, as was his wig mold, his well-known beer stein, and the flowerpot which was part of the scenery in his play *The Rivals*. When this great American thespian died in Florida in 1905 at the age of seventy-six, his will revealed that he had bequeathed to Grover Cleveland his "best Kentucky reel."

A baby carriage for twins is another exhibit which recalls the past. The little vehicle looks more like a small stagecoach than a carriage in which crying infants were once transported about the streets of Sandwich.

The glass collection, of course, is probably one of the best of its kind in the world. On exhibition are several unusual glass oddities turned out by the inspector, Christopher Muldoon, whose duty it was to test every batch of glass, and he usually made some peculiarly shaped object at the time, which he later gave to his friends. These pieces are very valuable today.

Edward Rowe Snow and Isabel Minot at Sandwich, with twin baby carriage

While I was in the museum at Sandwich, I learned of the benevolence of the Sandwich Glassworks manager, George Washington Lafayette Fessenden, who never let a wounded Civil War veteran who was in need of a job pass by the plant without hiring him. The Fourth of July was a red-letter day for every Sandwich boy who knew Mr. Fessenden, because new shiny half-dollars to be used in buying firecrackers were his holiday present to each youngster.

Other exhibits in the Sandwich Historical Society Museum include an old flintlock musket and a collection of Indian arrowheads. The flintlock musket was the famous one which shot a big bad wolf of another day—in fact, of the year 1675. The Indian arrowheads were collected from nearby Indian mounds and shell heaps.

Gustavus Franklin Swift, the meat packer, was born in Sandwich in 1839. He showed early promise as a businessman. Before he was fifteen years old, he was purchasing hens from his grandmother at forty cents each, and selling them for a small profit. His next venture was to buy a heifer from a neighbor, kill it, dress the carcass, and sell the meat. By the time he was eighteen, he was buying steers in Brighton and delivering the meat to his customers at Cape Cod. Selling his product from door to door, he built up enough capital to open a meat market in the village of East-ham, and then established another market in West Sandwich. A short time later he had transferred his headquarters to Barnstable, and he was soon selling his Cape Cod cattle to become a regular cattle dealer with the other meat men. Then he moved off Cape Cod to set up headquarters at Lancaster. In 1872 he enlarged the field of operations by forming a partnership with James Hathaway of Boston. Establishing branches in Buffalo and Albany, he moved to Chicago in 1875. Two years later Gustavus Swift inaugurated the system of sending dressed beef eastward, building refrigerator cars for that purpose. By 1930 the business which this Sandwich-born meat packer began grossed around $1.4 billion.

Another well-known man who was born in Sandwich is Thornton W. Burgess, whose animal stories of Peter Rabbit, Grandma Otter, Sammy Jay, Jerry Muskrat, and other active creatures of the forest, meadow, and briar patch have given happiness to millions of people, both young and old. Burgess was born on School Street, Sandwich, in 1874, but moved at an early age to nearby Jarvis Street, where he spent the greater part of his childhood before his family moved to Boston.

I felt I must visit the original briar patches of the stories, located at Spring Hill behind the Chipman place. Following a wooded road, I soon came upon the briars where Peter Rabbit and all his famous animal friends and enemies lived and cavorted. Nearby are said to be found the original Wide Marsh and Green Forest of Burgess fame.

Thornton Burgess lost his wife when his son was quite young, so he created for the boy the many characters and stories of the animal friends he has immortalized for all schoolchildren. Dean Tarbell pays Burgess a high compliment by saying that this Sandwich-born writer could easily be the children's candidate for president of the United States, at bedtime, or any other time.

Once there was a girl of Sandwich named Hannah Rebecca Crowell. She attracted the eye of a young Brewster lad, who at the time was going to sea, and he began writing letters to her from afar. In his letters he mentioned his high ideals, his vow against swearing, and his daily prayers. As she received the letters, arriving at intervals after their long journeys from far distant lands, Hannah made the decision that young William H. Burgess was the man for her, and was ready with her answer when he finally reached her Sandwich home. These two young people then became engaged. William Burgess made ready for another voyage, this time as mate aboard Captain Bangs Hallett's *Herbert*. All during the trip Captain Hallett watched his mate as Burgess carried out the captain's orders. Upon arriving back in Boston, Captain Bangs Hallett sprang his surprise—he was going on a vacation and wanted Burgess to take command of the *Herbert*.

Portraits of Hannah Rebecca Burgess and Captain William Burgess, with other memorabilia (courtesy of the Sandwich Historical Society and Glass Museum)

Captain William H. Burgess sailed out of Boston Harbor on the *Herbert* September 17, 1851, and arrived at Sand Heads off Calcutta in 119 days. His letters to Hannah reached the girl while she was preparing her hope chest, and they continued to speak of prayer, God, and, of course, his love for her. After sailing from India on February 5, 1852, Burgess came into Boston Harbor on July 17, writing in the log that he had been mate of the *Herbert* for eighteen months and master ten. "I now resign her to her former and able commander, Bangs Hallett, Esq., wishing her pleasant and successful voyages."

Hannah and William were married and spent their honeymoon in Boston. At the time, the new clipper ship *Whirlwind* was building on the ways at Medford, Massachusetts, and William took his happy bride out to see the progress of the vessel. One day William and Hannah ate dinner at Brigham's Saloon, where she declined to order the green turtle soup. Hannah decided that the soup was too close to the color of muddy water, and ordered pie instead.

In her diary of nearly 100 years ago Hannah writes, "I am happy in the love of my husband, yet one thing grieves me; he does not carry out those principles he once professed to sustain. In his letters written to me at sea, he appeared to enjoy sweet communion with his God. Oh, that he might again experience this happy feeling!"

A short time later the clipper ship *Whirlwind* slid down the ways at her Medford yard, and by 1853 Captain Burgess had been out to San Francisco and back. However, it was a lonely life at home for Hannah, who dearly loved her husband, and she asked if she might go along on the next voyage. He decided in her favor, and she sailed with him for San Francisco in February 1854. Captain Burgess then found himself constantly subjected to his wife's campaign to make a better man of him. After working on his vocabulary for three months, she recorded that his swearing was not so frequent. She also noticed that her husband was fond of planning work "for others to do," but admitted that his patience was improving. "I think he stands it well," she said, "considering his disposition."

The voyage proved to be a disappointing one, for head winds and calm spells were frequent. Rounding Cape Horn, the *Whirlwind* eventually reached and passed Juan Fernandez Island off Chile to cross the equator 102 days out. Hannah writes wistfully in her diary, "We have had a long passage, but I hope may not be beat by all the ships." Twenty-two days later Captain Burgess makes an entry in his wife's journal, "Bad luck attends us well, 124 days at sea."

Finally arriving at San Francisco 129 days from Boston, the *Whirlwind* had actually beaten Paul Curtis's *Queen of the Seas* by a week! This made Mrs. Burgess very happy. The trip back to Boston was more or less uneventful, and Captain Burgess then made arrangements to take Hannah along on his newest acquisition, the clipper ship *Challenger*.

From Boston to San Francisco and then down to the Chincha Islands for guano was the route of the *Challenger*. Unfortunately Captain Burgess fell ill at the Chincha Islands while loading the vessel and took to his berth. He rapidly weakened, and the frantic young wife hurriedly held a consultation with the first mate, Henry Winsor, to discuss their situation. Winsor could take the sun, but refused to accept responsibility for working out the ship's position. Hannah, an expert navigator in her own right, for her husband had taught her well, agreed to make all the calculations. Under this unusual arrangement, the *Challenger*'s bow was headed for the nearest port, Valparaiso. Hannah prayed by the side of her sick husband day after day, and read passages to him from the Bible. She stayed close by him in those last fleeting hours of his life, and watched his strength slowly leave his body. Twenty days out and less than forty-eight hours from port, Captain William Burgess died in Hannah's arms, December 11, 1856.

In those days it was customary to bury the dead at sea, but Hannah could not bear the thought. Her will prevailed, and her husband's remains were brought into port aboard the *Challenger*. Hannah then arranged for the body to be sent home aboard the ship *Harriet Irving*, taking passage herself on the same vessel. Eventually the unhappy woman reached her home with her husband's coffin, and after the funeral, had the body interred in the West Sandwich Cemetery. Hannah Burgess lived for the rest of her life in Sandwich.

The Bible from which Hannah read to her dying husband had a strange history. When Hannah left the ship, she presented the Bible, with an appropriate inscription, to the mulatto steward, David Graves, who had been faithful to the last. Graves, for the next six years, kept the book constantly with him, but in a shipwreck and the subsequent looting by Chinese pirates he lost it.

After the pirates had sailed away from the wreck, a sailor named Dennison from another vessel went aboard and found the Bible, evidently abandoned by the Chinese pirates as not worthy of their consideration. Noticing the inscription, Dennison decided to send the book to Richard Henry Dana, author of *Two Years before the Mast*, with the suggestion that Dana might forward it to Mrs. Burgess. In due time the Bible arrived in West Sandwich, and Mrs. Burgess kept it for the rest of her life. This same Bible now rests in the rooms of the Sandwich Historical Society, along with many pictures and the extremely interesting diary of Hannah Burgess.

Although the people of Sandwich knew her as Hannah, I have discovered in the diary that her husband called her by her middle name of Rebecca. Hannah Rebecca Burgess died in 1917 at eighty-two.

The Sandwich Historical Society Museum described by Snow is now known as the Sandwich Glass Museum, open spring through fall. According to curator Nezka Pfeifer, "Not all of the items described are still on exhibit, as the museum has changed its displays often over the course of the last sixty years." But the following items are still on view: glassmaking tools; chairs from the stage set of Joseph Jefferson's play *The Rivals* and a wood block carved with Jefferson's portrait (used to print posters for his performances); the baby stagecoach made for a set of twins; and much of the beautiful pressed glassware that helped make the town famous.

Actor Joe Jefferson owned a summer home in Bourne called the Crow's Nest, and spent much time hunting and fishing with President Grover Cleveland. Jefferson brought a windmill to Bourne from the Netherlands.

Swift and Company, founded by Gustavus Swift, continues to operate today from headquarters in Colorado.

The nonprofit Thornton W. Burgess Society, founded to "inspire reverence for wildlife and concern for the natural environment," carries on the work of author and naturalist Burgess (1874–1965). The society operates the Thornton W. Burgess Museum in Sandwich village and the Green Briar Nature Center and Jam Kitchen in East Sandwich.

The 1854 log of the *Whirlwind*, written in by both Hannah Rebecca Burgess and Captain William Howes Burgess, is now in the collection of the Bourne Historical Society.

CHAPTER 10

Bourne, the Canal, and Mashpee

My hike to Bourne was accomplished without incident, and I headed at once for the Cape Cod Canal, where I chose a comfortable spot near the edge of the waterway. A huge freighter passed under the Sagamore Bridge and headed south just as I opened my notes on Bourne.

Actually one of the newer Cape Cod communities, Bourne was not a separate town until 1884, so the history of Sandwich, from which Bourne was created, is the history of Bourne except for the last two-thirds of a century.

Too much cannot be said of the great Richard Bourne, the most outstanding Indian missionary of Cape Cod, for although the town of Bourne was not named after him it should have been. At one time every Indian from Middleboro to Provincetown seemed to be under his guidance. Bourne began his labors about 1658, and worked hard and faithfully to the end of his life. His lands lay along the Manomet River southward to Buzzards Bay and his rights included the privilege of having 12,000 herring a year. Not only Eliot, but Cotton as well participated in Bourne's ordination at Mashpee. When Bourne reported to Major Gookin on September 1, 1674, he listed twenty-two places where the praying Indians met, and said that their attendance totaled about 500 Indians. One hundred and forty-two could read Indian and Eliot's Indian Bible, seventy-two were able to write as well, and nine Indians could read English. By 1685 these praying Indians increased in numbers to 1,014, six hundred of whom were under Bourne's direct control. He became an advisor in spiritual and also civil activities, for both whites and savages took his counsel in land deals. Long after Bourne's death he was held in such high regard by the Indians that when one of his descendants was stricken with a dread sickness and all white doctors had failed to save the child, the Indians came with their native remedies and the little one recovered.

We can best appreciate what Richard Bourne meant to Cape Cod and its Indians by quoting from the words of antiquarian Amos Otis, who said that

> *Richard Bourne, by his unremitted labors for seventeen years, made friends of a sufficient number of Indians, naturally hostile to the English, to turn the scales in Plymouth County and give the preponderance to the whites. . . . Bourne did more, by the moral power which he exerted, to defend the old colony, than Bradford did at the head of his army. Laurel wreaths shade the brows of military heroes, their names are enshrined in a bright halo of glory, while the man who has done as good service for his country, by moral means, sinks into comparative insignificance and is too often forgotten.*

A most interesting boulder known as Great Rock is located about a mile to the southeast of Bourne Village, and it was toward this prehistoric stone that I directed my weary steps. Finally I reached it, and as I was too tired to make an attempt to scale its heights, I sat down against the rock to recall the old Indian legend about this 400-ton boulder. It seems that the giant Indian Mashope came by this section of the Cape many, many moons ago, with several boulders in his apron. He was on his way to erect a causeway between Hyannis and Nantucket. As he stepped along, walking only on the higher hills and upland roads, a woodland chickadee spied Mashope taking his giant steps. When the chickadee noticed that the strange creature was carrying huge boulders in his apron as if they were pebbles, the little bird could not restrain its merriment and so burst out into a hearty chickadee laugh.

Unfortunately for the bridge to Nantucket, Mashope became enraged at the chickadee's merriment, and picking out a small boulder weighing not more than fifty tons, hurled it at the merry chickadee, who flew easily away unharmed. But the enraged giant, not watching where he was going, stepped into Bourne Pond, which made him stumble and drop his great bundle of boulders. They fell helter-skelter everywhere around what is now Bourne, and the largest boulder of them all has been called Great Rock. The humiliated giant never returned to finish his causeway.

Geologically speaking, the rocks of Bourne were brought here by the glaciers during the ice age, and are believed to have originated from a far-off part of the White Mountains or other similar ranges. It may surprise some to learn that the ponds of Cape Cod, about 270 in number, were formed by the same force, the glacier. Dean Tarbell tells us that huge blocks of ice were left in depressions of land from a retreating glacier. Covered with earthy waste by streams from later glaciers, the blocks finally melted and the land over them collapsed. This process, which took thousands of years, formed what many geologists call kettle holes.

Earth accumulations left in front of these same glaciers are responsible for the high ridge running from Bourne to Falmouth, marked by the fire towers, and the relatively lofty heights of Pine Hill's 306-foot summit, as well as six other peaks more than 200 feet high. A similar ridge runs from Bourne to Orleans. All the territory to the southward of the two ridges is what geologists might call an outwash plain.

The peaks were used from earliest times for signaling, first by fires, and later by semaphores. Some of the more important hills used for this purpose were Signal Hill in Bourne, Shoot-Fly Hill in Barnstable, Scargo Hill in Dennis, Pine Hill in Falmouth, Corn Hill in Truro, and, of course, the heights of Manomet at Plymouth. Incidentally, Shoot-Fly Hill was so named because hunters used to shoot ducks on the fly from the top of the hill.

Naturally I was eager to reach Signal Hill, for in my imagination I wanted to go back to the days when ship arrivals were signaled up to Boston. When I reached the top, I was impressed by the similarity between the pines of Montana and the pines of Cape Cod, but, of course, after seeing the great stretch of ocean in the distance the illusion passed. The huge boulders around the hill recalled the Indian giant Mashope again, and I half expected to see him striding back from his unsuccessful attempt to bridge the Cape and Nantucket Island. Legends hold Mashope responsible for much in New England, for it was also he who allegedly formed Nantucket in the first place by emptying the ashes from his pipe into the sea.

After a few hours more atop Signal Hill, I examined my notes for my next destination. It was Gray Gables, where Grover Cleveland stayed many summers. Ninety minutes later I had reached his old home.

President Grover Cleveland lived at Bourne from 1891 to 1904. His dwelling at Gray Gables was located between Buzzard's Bay Station and Monument Beach, and became the Gray Gables Inn after his death. Without question, he was one of Cape Cod's more important fishermen, and when he went out fishing with actor Joe Jefferson and *Century Magazine* Editor Richard Watson Gilder, certain sporting rules were strictly adhered to. The hour rule did not allow a boat to leave an anchorage for one hour, no matter how poor the luck was going. Another rule dictated that one might interrupt good talking by fishing, but under no condition could he interrupt good fishing by talking.

As I sat down in front of the Gray Gables Inn, I thought of all the interesting stories which have been related about President Cleveland. Alice Austin Ryder, author of *Lands of Sippican,* told me the president went fishing one windless day when the rain was steadily falling. Sitting in the boat with Editor Gilder, Cleveland suddenly realized that a train which he must take had already left Provincetown and was even then thundering along through Eastham. Gilder became uneasy, also aware that the president should stop fishing and go ashore to dress. Finally, in spite of his position, the captain decided to speak.

"We must pull anchor, Mr. Cleveland, or you'll lose your train!"

But the good man decided to put his line over once more. Then, when the last wiggling fish had been caught, he realized only too well the task confronting him. A short time later the captain had him ashore, and President Cleveland hustled home as fast as the dignity of his position allowed. Quickly he threw off his fishing clothes, but right in the midst of his changing, before he could take off his soaking wet shoes, came the whistle of the Cape train. He realized then that he could not change his shoes and make connections. His traveling clothes on, he left his home to run for the train, which had been held at Tremont Station for him. According to his story three days later when he returned, he had not been able to take off his wet shoes all that first night, for he knew he couldn't get them on in the morning if he did. One can imagine the president of the United States sleeping the whole night while traveling to Washington—with his wet fishing boots on!

There is also a good story about President Cleveland the day after the birth of his son Richard. The President was approached by Joseph Jefferson in the presence of Dr. Bryant, Mrs. Cleveland's physician. Jefferson warmly congratulated the president, and then asked him a question.

"What was the weight of your new son, Mr. President?"

"My boy Richard tipped the scales at fifteen pounds," was the proud reply.

Dr. Bryant overheard the remark, and said to the President, "Why, Mr. Cleveland, you are mistaken. I weighed the child, and he was a ten-pound baby!"

This official statement did not bother Grover Cleveland in the slightest. "Doctor Bryant, regardless of your position in the birth of my child Richard, I must state that what I have said is the truth. The boy weighed fifteen pounds. I should know, for I weighed him on the same scales that Joe and I use when we go fishing!"

Another story concerns the night when President Cleveland was lost in a heavy rain far from home and decided to take his chances with a lonely house he came across located in a clearing. Knocking on the door, he saw a light go on, the window open, and a head peer out.

"What do you want?" shouted an irate voice.

"This is the president," said Cleveland. "I'm lost, and I'd like to stay here tonight."

"Go ahead," came the answer, "Stay there!" and the window shut again with an air of finality, the light going out immediately afterwards. President Cleveland never revealed whether he stayed there outside the house in the pouring rain or not.

Joseph Jefferson, one of America's great actors, was buried in the Bay View Cemetery at Sandwich in 1905. When I made my pilgrimage to his grave, I recalled some of the stories about this best-loved character actor of his generation. Perhaps Jefferson's greatest part was that of Rip Van Winkle, although he was also famous for his portrayal of Bob Acres. The reason for his burial in the Sandwich cemetery is a strange one if the story which is told is true. When Jefferson wished to purchase a house in Sandwich, the townspeople, it is said, disliked the idea of an actor's buying property where they lived. As a result he could not buy the house he planned on. Before he left Sandwich to go south for the winter, he did purchase a lot in the cemetery, an act which brought no objections from the people of Sandwich. And to this lot in 1905 was brought the body of America's great actor. At that time his words were remembered, "They're not anxious that I should live in Sandwich, but I'll stay there yet." And he did.

Another famous American lived at Bourne, in Pocasset. His name was Leonard Wood. Born in Winchester, New Hampshire, in 1860, Leonard

Wood came to Cape Cod when he was seven years old. From his home at Pocasset, built by his father in 1875, he left Cape Cod to attend Harvard Medical School, but returned whenever the opportunity presented itself to go fishing and boating with his father.

One day they were out sailing in Buzzard's Bay when another boat came along, cutting directly across their bow. This necessitated some clever maneuvering on the part of the Wood family.

"Dad," cried the indignant young man, "we have the right of way."

"Yes, son, I know," was the reply, "but I'd rather forego my rights in the field of navigation than spend the night out here with my mouth full of seaweed and salt water."

It is said that Leonard Wood was the only Cape Codder who ever ran for president, since President Cleveland is regarded as a summer visitor. Leonard Wood was an Indian fighter in the Southwest, and afterwards served with the Rough Riders in the Spanish War. Then he was sent to Cuba as administrator and later carried out the same thankless task in the Philippines. Dying in 1927, General Leonard Wood was buried in Arlington National Cemetery at Washington.

I hiked along the beach until I reached the canal and followed the road by its side. Finally I could see ahead of me the replica of the famous Aptucxet Trading Post, which was built by the Pilgrims back in 1627. This trading post was a vital part of the Pilgrim economy, and Bradford tells us of it in his *Plymouth Plantation*:

> That they might ye better take all convenient opportunitie to follow their trade, both to maintaine themselves, and to disingage them of those great sumes which they stood charged with, and bound for, they resolved to build a smale pinass at Manamet, a place 20. mile from ye plantation, standing on the sea to ye southward of them, unto which, by an other creeke on this side, they could carry their goods, within four or five miles, and then transport them over land to their vessell; and so avoyd the compasing of Cap-Codd, and those deangerous shoulds, and so make any vioage to ye southward in much shorter time, and with farr less danger. Also for ye saftie of thir vessell & goods, they builte a house their, and kept some servants, who also planted corne, and reared some swine, and were allwayes reedy to goe out with ye barke when ther was occasion. All which tooke good effecte, and turned to their profite.

One can readily understand why this trading post at Aptucxet was so necessary. The Pilgrims had been steadily falling behind in their financial obligations to the Merchant Adventurers, who in some cases were charging the Plymouth residents as high as 50 percent on their loans. In the year 1626 the Pilgrim fathers assembled to discuss what was to happen, for they could not possibly continue to go behind financially. They still had to transport to America the rest of their brethren in Leyden. It was therefore decided that all obligations and trade controls would have to be taken over by the leaders of the colony for a period of six years so that suitable arrangements could be made with the London Company for their supplies of beaver, other furs, lumber, and sassafras. This arrangement was agreed upon in what was actually the first business contract ever written and signed in America. When Isaac Allerton was sent to England, he obtained the right to establish three trading posts in America, one of which was the Aptucxet Post on the southern bank of the Manomet River.

It is interesting to read from a Dutch source regarding this Cape Cod trading post. Isaack de Rasiere, who, according to Bradford, visited Aptucxet and was announced by trumpets, reported in Holland about his activities in America. He states in part:

> *Coming out of the river Nassau, you sail east and by north about fourteen leagues, along the coast, a half mile from shore, and you then come to Frenchman's Point, at a small river where those of Patucxet have a house made of hewn oak planks, called Aptucxet, where they kept two men, winter and summer, in order to maintain the trade and possession. Where also they have built a shallop, in order to go and look after the trade in sewan, in Sloup's Bay and thereabouts, because they are afraid to pass Cape Mallabaer, and in order to avoid the length of the way; which I have prevented for this year by selling them fifty fathoms of sewan, because the seeking after sewan by them is prejudicial to us, inasmuch as they would, by so doing, discover the trade in furs; which if they were to find out, it would be a great trouble for us to maintain. . . . From Aptucxet the English can come in six hours, through the woods, passing several little rivulets of fresh water, to New Plymouth, the principal place in the county Patucxet.*

Sewan is also known as wampum. Many articles were handled at this first Pilgrim trading post. In the pamphlet "The Aptucxet Trading Post," by Percival Hall Lombard, I found that the principal goods used in trading were wampum; the furs of beaver, otter, mink, and muskrat; beads; corn; hatchets; and knives. In addition to the above, the Pilgrims dealt in trading cloths, coats, sugar, linen cloth, cotton, tobacco, lumber, shoes, hose, and perpetuanes, which Lombard calls the rayon of early days. Guns, powder, shot, and firewater were strictly forbidden under heavy penalty, although all were sold and bartered by the usual number of unscrupulous persons who always seem to attach themselves to every community.

Beaver and otter furs were the real commodity of trade. In 1643 no less than 12,530 pounds of beaver and 1,160 pounds of otter furs left for England, and as each beaver pelt, which averaged in weight 5 pounds, brought about $25, the Pilgrims were doing well.

Little is known about the history of the trading post itself. Bradford tells us of the great hurricane of 1635, and mentions that the hurricane "caused the sea to swell . . . above twenty foote, right up and downe, and made many of the Indeans to climb into trees for their saftie; it tooke of the borded rofe of a house which belonged to this plantation at Manamet, and floted it to another place, the posts still standing in the ground . . ."

The Dutch traded here for many years with the Pilgrims. Around 1660, or thirty-three years after the establishment of the trading post, it appears that the people of Plymouth, with all their debts paid off, decided to sell the company's property at Aptucxet and relinquish their monopoly. Whether the building was torn down or burned by the Indians, or whether it collapsed from want of attention probably will never be known.

Almost two centuries elapsed. Then, in 1850, William S. Russell of Plymouth, who had known of the trading post, set out to find the site, and stumbled across two cellar pits. Two years later he and Dr. John Bachelder uncovered the eastern wall of the western pit, finding a knife blade and a hoe. In October 1926, the Bourne Historical Society undertook complete excavation of the site. To the amazement of the two men digging, Percival Hall Lombard and Nathan Bourne Hartford, they were able to uncover practically all of the foundation walls of the structure. Lombard and Hartford unearthed many interesting relics, which include Apostle spoon bowls; fragments of Dutch slipware; a riding spur, stirrup, and buckle of iron; a latten-ware candlestick; window glass; and plaster fragments.

An exact copy of the building, as far as was possible, was then erected over the original foundation of the old Pilgrim Aptucxet Trading Post of 1627. Thus, because of the diligent work of Percival Lombard, Nathan Hartford, and others, people are now able to walk into the old Pilgrim Trading Post as it was three centuries ago.

Going back to the canal a short distance away, I studied the material I had brought along about this pleasant artificial waterway. In 1623 the intrepid Captain Myles Standish rowed up the Scusset River and crossed the thirty-foot-high sand ridge which lay between the source of that stream and the Manomet River. By following the Manomet River to the bay, he was able to meet Dutch trading vessels, saving in this way a journey around the Cape. Thus it was the Plymouth captain who really was the first to take advantage of the route, which today is a waterway still used for the purposes the Pilgrims had in mind—safety, economy, and expediency.

Charles F. Swift, writing in 1897, said that the establishment of a trail through the Manomet Valley back in 1627 first started men thinking that this route was the ideal location for a Cape Cod Canal. Samuel Sewall tells us in his diary that he was visiting Thomas Smith of Sandwich in 1676, and on October 26 of that year, rode out with Thomas Smith to view the place "which some had thought to cut, for to make a passage from the south sea to the north. He said it was about a mile and a half between the utmost flowing of the two seas in Herring River and Scusset."

Henry C. Kittredge informs us that the same Thomas Smith was still agitating for a canal twenty years later. We do know that in 1698 a committee which included Smith was appointed to "view a place for a passage to be cut through the land in Sandwich, from Barnstable Bay into Manomet Bay, for vessels to pass through and from the western parts of the country." Although nothing definite was accomplished at that time, the project was not forgotten, for in 1736 the Reverend Mr. Thomas Prince mentions the fact that a canal had been discussed on the Cape for forty years.

The effective blockade which British vessels placed around the Cape during the Revolution brought renewed agitation for the canal. On May 1, 1776, the council voted to cut the canal, and appointed James Bowdoin, William Seaver, and others to visit Sandwich and determine the practicability of the location. A government engineer was hired, Thomas Machin, who proposed an elaborate canal with locks and bridges, which would cost the equivalent of $160,000. On June 10, 1776, George Washington wrote to James Bowdoin in Boston requesting that Machin be released for wartime purposes. This ended canal plans for that period.

Between the close of the Revolution and the beginning of the War of 1812, there were two distinct projects for Cape Cod canals. James Winthrop continued the activity at Sandwich, while around the elbow of the Cape another group in 1804 actually dug a canal practically on the boundary line of Orleans and Eastham. It was almost the same place where the great Cyprian Southack, master of the *Province Galley,* went through with a whaleboat in 1717. Funds were needed to finance the project, and the legislature was petitioned for permission to conduct a lottery. However, because this canal did not eliminate the dangerous shoals off the Cape, the lottery was never approved and the canal soon filled up and was forgotten. An active person can still trace the route through what was formerly called Jeremy's Dream or Jeremiah's Gutter. Jeremiah, whose last name is not known, was a seventeenth-century Cape Codder who also had an island named for him.

James Winthrop reported in 1791 that a canal was possible and practical in Sandwich, and everyone in Massachusetts, it seems, agreed with him although no one cared to start the enterprise. Again, during the War of 1812, the strategic advantage of such a canal was demonstrated, but the end of the war came and the years went by without action of any sort. Various people of importance were connected with plans for the canal. Loammi Baldwin, Major Perault, and Senator Lloyd were among those who were active between 1818 and 1830, but their efforts came to naught. Kittredge suggests that the long period of canal inactivity from 1830 to 1861 resulted from Boston's preoccupation with larger ships and long voyages to foreign countries. The coasters and the smaller vessels were forgotten completely. Railroads also began to cut into the coasters' business.

Early in 1861 New England realized that the days of the clipper ships were doomed by John Ericsson's invention of the screw propeller. With the doom of the clippers, Boston again became interested in coastwise travel and the canal. Henry Mitchell, an expert on tides and the coast, was authorized to visit Sandwich, but the Civil War prevented any action, and by the time Appomattox Court House was the scene of Lee's surrender Mitchell's fine report was thought of no more.

In 1870 the Cape Cod Canal Company was formed. The organization of the company is about all that ever was accomplished, except that in

1878 a civil engineer named Clemens Herschel defended the company's existence in a booklet entitled "The Cape Cod Ship Canal."

Henry M. Whitney received a new charter in 1880 for a company which he and his associates formed. The new group was called the Cape Cod Ship Canal Company. For the first time since Samuel Sewall had mentioned a passage to be cut in Sandwich, definite action resulted. Several hundred Italians were brought to Sandwich from New York City and put to work with pick and shovel digging the canal. Many stories have come down to the present day describing the impact on the townspeople of the nearly four hundred laborers when they visited town or chanced to move in a group along the road. There were tales of the Italians terrorizing the entire Cape, but probably there was some attempt at exaggeration. It was only a decade or two after Garibaldi's activities in Italy, so people mentioned Cape Cod's Neapolitan Revolution. The company went out of business shortly afterwards, and it is believed that all of the Italians returned to New York, and the Cape Codders spent their days and nights in peace and quietness again.

In 1883, an interesting comment was made by Shebnah Rich, who hoped that "the Cape Cod Canal will not have to wait as long after the survey as did the Suez Canal, first surveyed and undertaken by Necho, King of Egypt . . . two thousand years before the Portuguese De Gama, in 1497, discovered the Cape of Good Hope."

In that year of 1883 another company, taking the same name as Whitney's defunct group, announced its plans for the canal. Frederick A. Lockwood soon became the leader. Trouble began early. Locked in litigation with the railroad, the new company also had two rival canal men to consider, Alfred Fox of Montreal and Gerard C. Tobey of Wareham. Although Tobey fared well with the people of Massachusetts, Fox's Canadian nationality gave him little hope of success. But as Lockwood already had a charter and was first in the field, he won out over both the other men. Building a dredge especially designed to operate in the canal, he had it in operation on the scene in 1884. After digging through the Scusset soil for about a mile, the dredge stopped and was never started again! Lockwood did not have the money to keep it running, and died, after various other attempts to obtain funds, a disappointed man, his lifetime ambition still a dream.

A company with a very pretentious name was chartered June 1, 1899, the Boston, Cape Cod, and New York Canal Company. Charles M. Thompson, engineer for Lockwood before the latter's death, was hired by the new group to act in a similar capacity. The most important date in the entire history of Cape Cod Canal activity was in 1906, when one of the incorporators, De Witt Flanagan, interviewed Mr. August Belmont. Belmont became deeply interested in the plans and engaged Barclay Parsons, a noted engineer who was a member of the Panama Canal Commission. Parsons, after considerable investigation at Sandwich, finally approved plans which had been drawn up, and the important canal between Boston and New York was started.

The first granite block was set in place for the breakwater June 19, 1909; the first water came through in April 1914; and the Cape Cod Canal was officially opened July 29, 1914, when eight vessels entered the new marine passageway.

By April 11, 1916, the canal was completed to a minimum width at the bottom of 100 feet, and a low-water depth of 25 feet. When the First World War broke out, the United States Railroad Administration took over the operation of the canal, and when the war ended, the owners refused to accept it back under the conditions offered by the government, so the canal was actually closed from March 1 to March 4, 1920, while the controversy raged. On the latter date it was reopened under a temporary agreement, but it was not until March 31, 1928, that the matter was finally settled. At that time the government paid the former owners $11.5 million, and abolished the toll system whereby vessels paid from three to ten cents per ton whenever they passed through. There is no charge today.

In 1931 a lock-canal project was suggested, but nothing ever came of it. Two years later the Public Works Administration ordered the construction of three fine bridges to cross the canal, one a vertical lift railroad bridge, and the others two high-level highway bridges. All three bridges were completed by 1935. At high tide they have a vertical clearance of 135 feet. The two highway bridges have a horizontal clearance of 550 feet and the railroad bridge 500 feet, according to the booklet on the subject issued by the War Department's Engineers Office in Boston.

Whenever I hike along the shores of the canal and watch the majestic liners as they sail effortlessly through the canal, or look far overhead at the steady line of cars which speed over the beautiful aerial causeways to Cape Cod, I think of the three centuries which passed before the canal and the bridges became a reality. What would Myles Standish have thought of the changes in the travel route which he pioneered back in 1623?

But there is a feeling of sadness which comes over me whenever I think of the few times I have been fortunate enough to watch the New York boats passing through the Cape Cod Canal. Those big, sleek, white vessels, sliding along toward their destination, were watched by thousands every night when they reached the canal, usually about 9:00 at night. The best place to observe the New York boat was down close to the water itself, where the suction caused by the 400-foot steamer actually made the tide go out for a brief time, and seemed to pull at the shoreline as well. Then the waters of the canal would subside, and the lights grew smaller in the distance. Our big moment was over.

One of the events associated with the passing of the New York boat through the Cape Cod Canal was the bugle playing each night of young Gilbert S. Portmore. Only ten years old when he began his evening playing, Gilbert would stand in front of his parents' new residence at Gray Gables, Bourne, and when the New York boat reached the State Pier at around 9:00, Gil would start playing "Taps." The beautiful notes echoed across the canal, and when they were finished the captain of the New York boat gave three blasts from his whistle, and raised and lowered his searchlight in farewell. Whenever fog or bad weather delayed the boat, the whistle was not used, as the residents complained that it disturbed their slumber.

The Cape Cod Canal (photo by Edward Rowe Snow)

One night a Metropolitan Opera artist was traveling on the boat, and after the echo of Gil's last note had died away, the artist repeated the taps. Those who heard it believed the music that evening the most beautiful to which they had ever listened.

In 1941 Gilbert Portmore entered the service as a fighter pilot, and after a fine record across the water in Australia and Asia, he returned to this country. He was killed in a plane crash in Kentucky. Thus the saga was finished, for the two New York boats, the *Boston* and the *New York,* were sunk by German submarines on their way to Ireland, and Gil Portmore's beautiful trumpet music was stilled forever in a tragic accident of the same war.

Not far from what is now the Cape Cod Canal lived Sarah McLean. A controversial book called *Cape Cod Folks,* which she published in 1881, was the center of terrific turmoil on Cape Cod because the author gave the characters in the book names of her own neighbors and friends. That was bad enough, for she had asked permission of no one, but when she introduced impossible and embarrassing situations into the book, making her actors perform deeds which they never would think of in real life, she found herself in trouble. She and the publishers then brought out a new edition, in which she changed the names of the characters to fictitious ones. But they still had several lawsuits on their hands from the original edition. A representative of the publishers visited Cape Cod and settled a majority of the claims for small amounts. In one case a settlement was known to have been made for less than $6.00.

In February 1884, Lorenzo Nightingale, whose name was used in the original edition of *Cape Cod Folks,* brought suit for libel in Plymouth Court. In the book, Nightingale, whose name in the later editions was changed to Cradlebow, courted Sarah McLean. He strenuously denied this romance in the suit. The newspapers of the day covered the trial fully, and one of the passages from the book war quoted in the *Boston Herald* to the effect that Nightingale was a "champion fiddler, inventor, whale-fisher, cranberry picker, and potato-bugger." The suit was finally settled amicably.

A character mentioned in the story, Consider Fisher, died on June 22, 1882, and it was said that her death was hastened by mental excitement brought on by the book. Another character, Bessie, who dies in the first edition of the volume under very sad circumstances, actually lived happily for many, many years.

Sarah Pratt McLean and her publisher printed several different editions, one of which was illustrated with scenes from her play, *Cape Cod Folks*, which had a successful run and was known all over New England.

My next destination was the Mashpee Indian church. Some years before, on getting off the train at Mandan, North Dakota, and walking along the platform, I saw several honest-to-goodness Indians, with full ceremonial regalia walking calmly by me. As I was not expecting any such happening, the very nearness of these heroes of my boyhood movie days actually made my hair stand up from the thrill of it. Regardless of where we are or what we happen to be doing, the very mention of Indians usually makes every American alertly interested.

And those were my thoughts as I hiked down the road which leads to Mashpee. I was about to visit the last survivors of one tribe of the noble race of red men.

In 1660 Richard Bourne secured a grant of 10,500 acres of land here for the exclusive use of the Indians. Twelve years later there were 237 Indians living in sixty-three wigwams in the vicinity.

It was about the time of the Boston Massacre that the first foreign strains of Negro and Portuguese blood reached the Indians of Mashpee, but by 1792 there were only fifty pure-blooded Indians still living there. Then many Hessian soldiers captured in the Revolution were sent to Cape Cod for hire at the saltworks. The Hessians married Indian girls in Mashpee, bringing names such as Hirsch and De Grasse to the town.

The Cape Cod Indians had been faithful to the white men during the dread King Philip's War, and there are many historians who believe that had the Cape Indians joined the general fighting, King Philip might have wiped out the white race in New England at that time. Richard Bourne can be thanked for teaching the word of God to the Mashpee Indians.

Although they remained faithful, the Indians were resentful of the fact that the white people thought them incapable of self-government. Protesting time after time about this treatment, the Indians were completely ignored until 1770, when one of their tribe actually crossed the ocean to reach London, where he complained in person to King George III himself. The Indian's name was Reuben Cognehew. As a result of his visit, the English treated the Mashpee Indians much better and Cognehew thus won a signal victory.

The grateful Indians fought valiantly in the Revolution for Massachusetts, as of course they did in 1917 and 1941. During the Revolutionary

War almost every able-bodied Indian joined the 1st Regiment of Massachusetts, and seventy of the Indians were killed.

After England was defeated, Massachusetts took away the Indians' rights again. Thus the Mashpee Indians, as a result of helping the Americans beat the British and win America's freedom, lost their own!

But the Indians did not give up. In 1833 they penned a set of resolutions. Headed by Ebenezer Attaquin, they asked for self-government, as "all men are born free and equal." Then came the ultimatum. After the following July 1 they would not allow any white man to take anything from the Mashpee Indian Plantation. The resolutions were sent to the Governor of Massachusetts.

The white men decided to try out the Indians on July 1, and those Indians who attempted to prevent the whites from cutting down trees on the plantation were promptly whisked off to jail. Benjamin F. Hallett of Boston heard of their predicament and came to the aid of the Indians. A great orator, he told the legislature the Indians were oppressed by the white men who had become rich by acquiring the property of the poor Indians and that the Indians were just as much justified as those Bostonians who brought about the Boston Tea Party. As a result of his impassioned oratory, the Indians were freed from jail, and the very next year an Act of Incorporation for the District of Mashpee was passed.

As the religious history of the Indians played such an important part in their lives, I have looked up the various ministers and their influence on the Mashpee community. Richard Bourne, one of the early settlers of Sandwich, saw the need for converting the Mashpee Indians to Christianity. It was he in 1658 who helped to establish a boundary line between the proprietors of Barnstable and Mashpee. We have already mentioned his enabling the Indians to acquire 10,500 acres of land. The Reverend Mr. Hawley said that Richard Bourne was a man "of that discernment that he conceived it was in vain to propagate Christian knowledge among any people without a territory where they might remain in peace from generation to generation, and not be molested."

Richard Bourne, after obtaining the deeds of the Indian reservation on August 17, 1670, was installed as pastor of the Indian church there. The ordination services were performed by the famous Indian Apostle John Eliot himself. It is of interest to note that Shearjashub Bourne, son of Richard Bourne, obtained from the court at Plymouth, after his father's death, a ratification of the deeds Richard Bourne had obtained, so that "no part or parcel of those lands might be bought by, or sold to, any white person or persons, without the consent of all the Indians, not even with the consent of the general court."

When Richard Bourne died, he was succeeded in the Indian pulpit by Simon Popmonet, a full-blooded Indian, who preached for forty years, dying about the time his successor, Joseph Bourne, was ordained. Bourne was in the pulpit from 1729 until 1742, when he resigned because of the ill-treatment and neglect the Indians suffered.

Solomon Briant, another full-blooded Indian, was the next preacher, and he talked to the red men in their own dialect. Although encountering considerable opposition in the county, he remained at Mashpee as preacher until 1758. The Reverend Gideon Hawley succeeded Briant. He had previously served in a similar capacity at Stockbridge and later among the Iroquois, having been a chaplain in the French Wars. He died at duty in 1807 at the age of eighty years.

The Reverend Phineas Fish took the pulpit in 1812 and ran into heavy seas of theological and political opposition, for in 1834 when the area of Mashpee was set off with partial self-government, the Indians at once retired the Reverend Mr. Fish. One of their brethren, who had been instrumental in bringing about the Indians' partial freedom, the Reverend William Apes, stepped into the vacant pulpit, but with their new freedom the Indians decided against any stable and settled pastorate, and changes were many from that period on.

In 1870 Mashpee was made a town without restrictions, but the state still showed its definite interest by keeping up contributions to the support of schools and highways.

Some years ago a gentleman from Boston was driving through Mashpee, and his hat blew off. A young Mashpee lad, who raced after the hat, grabbed it and ran back to the gentleman, who offered him a dime. "No, thank you," said the dusky boy. "My mother taught me not to accept anything for doing favors."

Samuel G. Davis, the gentleman from Boston who had offered the boy the ten cents, was strangely attracted to the lad for his commendable attitude. When Davis died shortly afterwards, his will revealed an unusual bequest to the town of Mashpee. It was a gift of real estate, stocks, and bonds, called The Kind Good Manners Fund. The entire income was to be used for medals and prizes for courtesy shown by the schoolchildren of Mashpee. The total cost of the prizes ran to less than $200, and after a few years the Mashpee citizens found the estate of

$50,000 increasing rapidly. About the same time they also noticed that a new school was needed. Therefore they petitioned the probate court for permission to use the surplus to build a new school, as the old building was badly in need of repairs. All was ready for the erection of the school, but suddenly came bad news. The court had denied the request of the people of Mashpee, because this would not be in keeping with the wishes of the donor, as definitely expressed in the will, so their plans were abandoned.

Of course, there will always be those whose loyal aim it is to extol the virtues of their own particular Cape Cod pond or lake, but the consensus of "on-Cape" opinion is that Mashpee Lake is the prettiest. Containing 770 acres, Mashpee Lake is not only the largest Cape Cod lake but one of the deepest, as only Snake Pond in Sandwich, sixty-eight feet deep, goes deeper than Mashpee Pond's sixty-one foot sounding. Cataumet Neck promontory comes out from the eastern shore, almost dividing Mashpee Lake into two parts. The northern portion, containing three islands, is known as Wakeby Pond. The islandless southern part of Mashpee Lake is called Mashpee Pond. For those who are cartographically inclined, I would compare the shape of Cataumet, or Conaumet Neck, as it is sometimes called, to a big-headed dog on a small rock, his tail northward at Cataumet Point, with jaws facing southward. The three islands of Wakeby Pond are called Jefferson, Keith, and Cleveland, but when Grover Cleveland fished around them during the last century their names were Cometoit, Stayonit, and Getoffit, in the spirit of other Indian names of Cape Cod.

Jefferson and Cleveland had many delightful fishing experiences here. A clever colored man piloted them around the lake in a homemade steamboat which he had built himself. More than a generation before this time, Daniel Webster had also spent many a happy hour wading knee-deep in Lake Mashpee, and it is Grover Cleveland who says that Webster, while fishing here, composed the famous "Venerable Men" passage of his Bunker Hill oration, presented when the cornerstone was laid.

Hotel Attaquin is associated with many great names in history. Built by Captain Solomon Attaquin in 1840, the hotel has had as guests Webster, Cleveland, Joseph Jefferson, John Drew, Richard Watson Gilder, Charles Dana Gibson, and many others. In 1910 the register with all the famous names disappeared from the hotel, just as the Minot's Light register with the names of Admiral Dewey and Henry W. Longfellow vanished from the great tower off Scituate. Probably the hotel register is reposing in some collector's private safe, to be brought out and enjoyed in secrecy.

Near the hotel is a little brook through which the herring enter Mashpee Lake. Every spring the crowds gather to watch the excitement. It is estimated that a single lady fish spawns 25,000 eggs annually. An average of only four reaches fishhood.

I was eager to reach the old Indian church in Mashpee, and I found it near the junction of Barnstable Road and Meetinghouse Road. Approaching the church I read an inscription from a bronze tablet on a boulder:

> Built in 1684. Remodeled in 1717. Rededicated in 1923.
>
> In memory of Friends who Labored Among the Indians. To the Ones Who gave more Crowded Hopes of Adoration to the Things of God in 1711, Daniel Williams Left a Trust Fund in Charge of Harvard College for the Perpetuation of Preaching to the Indians. Simon Popmonet, Solomon Briant, William Apes, Joseph Amos, The Blind Preacher. That it may Stand in All the Future Years the Indestructible Record of a Rugged Race to be Governed by the Word of the Lord in All Things. Now to Their Gentle Memory be Naught but Kind Regards and To their Quiet Ashes—Peace.

Walking up to the meeting house, I read the invitation on the door to enter, and did so. Inside were simple church furnishings, with twenty-nine pews, altar flowers, several Bibles and hymnals on the pulpit, and a visitors' book on the table. To the right of the book was a contribution box securely chained in place, with a message nearby which said:

> Visitors, you good folks. Will you please help this church to repair it the Hurricane done a lots of damage to it.

I made my offering and listened to it clink as it hit the bottom of the tin box. Then I went up into the gallery and sat down. There was not a single sound to interrupt my thoughts. I knew that Don Redfield, a friend of mine from Montana, was preacher here for several years, but had left three years ago. The pastor in April 1946 was the Reverend Cleveland A. Wilson. He serves churches at Osterville and Mashpee, preaching on Sunday in Osterville for the morning service, and in

Mashpee at 1:30. Although the old Indian church is always open, the Reverend Mr. Wilson gives his sermon most of the time in the new chapel at Mashpee Center, but is heard at the old Indian church at least once a month. A trust fund administered by Harvard College helps support this ancient institution of God.

I came downstairs again to put my signature in Visitors' Book Number 6, which had been started August 22, 1944. The day before I came, Chief Red Thunder Cloud from East Hampton, Long Island, had affixed his signature. I signed my name under those of several others, using ditto marks for the date, April 26, 1946.

As I went out into the vestibule, I looked at the tablet there erected in memory of Richard Bourne, missionary, who established the first Indian church at Mashpee in 1658. The tablet was placed by the Bourne Historical Society in 1934.

The graveyard outside the church extended for some distance in several directions. I noticed the name De Grasse, a descendant of a Hessian Revolutionary War prisoner who had married an Indian girl. Then I discovered the tombstone of Sally, the wife of Charles Lee, who died in 1833. The inscription follows:

> *In the silent tomb we leave her*
> *Till the resurrection morn*
> *Then, oh Lord, thy word shall raise her,*
> *And restore her lovely form.*

The Pells lot attracted me, for there was a special wooden fence built around four graves there. Several others of the same family were buried outside of the wooden fence.

My next call was at the home of Ambrose Asher Pells, whose tribal name is Rain-in-the-Face. He is perhaps the last descendant of King Philip himself. He put on his Indian regalia for me, and we posed for pictures together. Before I left I asked him how the recent fire affected Mashpee, and he said that it had burned three houses at the northern end of Mashpee Lake. Then he gave me his final message.

"There are about four hundred of us living in Mashpee. I am one of the three trustees of the old Indian church, and many of my people sleep in the graves around it. I wish to invite all people to visit our Indian church, for its doors are never closed. I am one of the last of the Wampanoag tribe of Indians. King Philip himself was my ancestor."

*Chief Rain-in-the-Face
(Ambrose Asher Pells)
and Edward Rowe Snow
(photo by William
Ayoub)*

Dean Tarbell tells us of the great powwow held at Mashpee on August 12, 1929, when several hundred Indians, dressed in full Indian costumes of many-colored head feathers, brilliant blankets, and beaded moccasins, met in observance of the 253rd anniversary of the death of the mighty King Philip, Wampanoag chieftain. At that time the Indian church was so overcrowded that many of the festivities connected with the celebration had by necessity to be held out of doors. Tarbell tells us that they were indeed a comely lot, well-formed, with smooth bronzed skins, erect carriages, and alert faces. He suggests that it was not an easy jump which the modern Indians took, this reenactment of their former tribal customs, for some of the costumes seemed of the mail-order variety, and a hot dog salesman seemed as out of place as did a pretty young Indian girl wearing silk stockings and high heels.

Traveling to the south of Johns Pond and Ashumet Pond, I reached the Falmouth-Sandwich Road, following it southward until I came to the Hatchville Road. I continued on this highway until Hatchville and the Falmouth Airport were behind me, and then I picked up Turpentine Road, which led northward for more than five miles. Soon I was out of Falmouth and into Sandwich again. I went by Camp Edwards, with its hundreds of buildings arranged in a huge square facing toward the center. On my left was the old CCC camp. About two miles beyond Camp Edwards I found an inviting road called the Pocasset-Forestdale Highway, which ran to the westward, so I followed it for half an hour before coming out on MacArthur Boulevard, which led me directly to the Bourne Bridge.

A few minutes later I was at that thriving community known as Buzzards Bay. I was anxious to meet Mrs. Lillian Small, the daughter of the Cape Cod Light lookout man, Isaac M. Small, who had watched the ships for more than half a century to report them up to Boston. The newspapers in 1898 claimed that Lillian Small had seen the *Portland* sinking off Highland Light that November night. Mrs. Small, wife of the Buzzards Bay postmaster, was not at home, but later I was able to talk with her on the telephone. She said that the 1898 report was not true, for she had not seen the *Portland* go down. I had come a long way to talk with this lady, so I was pleased to get my answer even if it was in the negative and by telephone.

Snow mentions comparing the pines of Cape Cod to those of Montana. His knowledge of this subject stemmed from his two years at Intermountain College in Montana, where he met his wife-to-be, Anna-Myrle Haegg.

There seem to be no end to the legends concerning the giant Mashope, or Moshup as it is most often spelled. He is said to have caught whales for food with his bare hands, which he would then cook over a fire using trees he ripped out of the ground. This is why there are now so few trees at Gay Head on Martha's Vineyard, according to the legend.

The Aptucxet Trading Post Museum is still operated by the Bourne Historical Society. There has been some debate in recent years about whether the building is on the location of the original trading post, but according to Eleanor Hammond, curator/site interpreter for the museum, "There is enough evidence to conclude the present building is on the site of that first business enterprise."

The name Wampanoag is used collectively for the indigenous people of eastern Rhode Island and southeastern Massachusetts. The Gay Head (Aquinnah) Indians of Martha's Vineyard are the only Wampanoag group officially recognized by the federal government. The Mashpee Indians are another of the best-known Wampanoag groups. Many of the current generation of Wampanoag are deeply involved in preservation of their traditional culture.

Mashpee's Old Indian Meeting House is the oldest church building on Cape Cod and is still used for worship, meetings, and social activities.

In 1677, after the death of King Philip (Metacom), the Wampanoag leader's wife and son were sent to Bermuda to live out their lives in slavery. Oral tradition on St. David's Island indicates that descendants of King Philip still live there. Mashpee Wampanoags were among forty American Indians who attended a reconnection festival at the St. David's Cricket Club in 2002.

The hull of the steamer *Portland* has been located in recent years in over 400 feet of water in the Stellwagen Bank National Marine Sanctuary, about twenty miles north of Race Point, further away from Cape Cod than where Snow and many others had believed it to be.

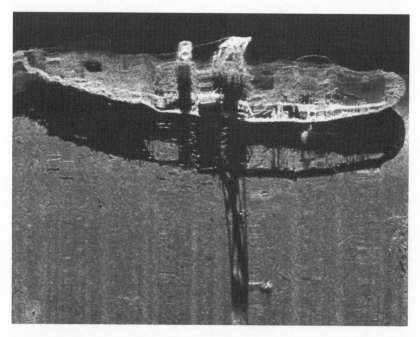

Side scan image of the Portland, *showing twin smokestacks and walking beam (courtesy of NOAA/Stellwagen Bank National Marine Sanctuary)*

CHAPTER 11

Falmouth and Woods Hole

Up early the next morning, I was soon ready for my walk to Falmouth and Woods Hole. After crossing the canal again, I passed through or around Gray Gables, Monument Beach, Bennets Neck, Pocasset, South Pocasset, and Cataumet, and crossed the Falmouth line at Megansett. A short time later I was in North Falmouth.

I wondered if I were approaching the battlefield where two Indian tribes fought a bloody war just before the period when Falmouth was settled. One tribe came from Martha's Vineyard and the other lived on the mainland in Falmouth.

On a cold day some years later an aftermath of the fight developed. A white mother and her son were stolen by the Indians, who came in from the sea and took them away by canoe. The boy stood up. "Sit down," the Indian leader shouted in his own language, but of course the boy did not understand and remained standing. The Indian clubbed him on the head and the lad sank to the floor of the canoe, unconscious from the blow. He carried the scars to his dying day.

Reaching their destination, the Indians allowed the boy to enter the warm wigwam, but the mother was forced to stay outside, where she froze to death before morning. After remaining for a long period of time with the Indians, who tried to bring him up in their way of living, the boy managed to escape and return to his home in what is now Falmouth. His name is not known, although his home was near the site of Solomon Davis's residence.

Around 1660 a group of Barnstable settlers removed to what is now Falmouth. The first night after landing, the pioneers encamped in the flag swamp at the southern end of Fresh Pond, and there the wife of Jonathan Hatch gave birth to a son. When asked what his name would be, she said, "He was born amongst the flags and his name shall be Moses."

Boundary lines are sometimes hard to relocate, and one which ran to a certain "great rock" half way up a hill marked the northeast boundary of Falmouth. Years afterwards no one could find the rock, so a very old Indian living some distance from the boundary line was interviewed. When he told the settlers that the rock formed the actual boundary termination, they replied by saying there was no rock there. He agreed to journey with them to the location and find it for them. Reaching the scene he quickly located a large pile of brush, and under the brush he found the rock.

"Here is the rock where people established the bound," said the Indian. "Every time they passed thereafter they put on a bough."

On the 23rd of July, 1677, the inhabitants of Succanesset agreed that land at Woods Hole, Little Harbor, should be divided equally among the inhabitants. As a blacksmith was badly needed at Woods Hole, twelve acres of upland were laid out or set aside for the encouragement of a blacksmith to come and live with them, and one was later found who took advantage of the offer.

On June 4, 1686, the plantation known as Succanesset, or Sachonesit, became a town, and was incorporated under the name of Falmouth. Woods Hole is now part of this town.

The most troublesome enemy of the early settlers was the blackbird, and literally swarms of these winged creatures filled the air when the farmers started their spring sowing. Crops were so greatly reduced by this bird that on March 25, 1701, it was agreed that "every house keeper should kill six old black-birds or twelve young black-birds, or four jay birds, by the 15th day of June next after the date hereof, and deliver them to the selectmen of this town or some of them, and they are to keep an account of every man's birds so delivered to them, and it is further ordered every house keeper that shall fail to kill their sum of birds by that time shall pay three shillings to be added to their tax."

During the Revolution a large British fleet visited Woods Hole and Falmouth, arriving off the coast in the year 1779. The principal rendezvous of the British cruising fleet was Tarpaulin Cove on Naushon

Island. On the night of April 2, 1779, several boats from the fleet landed along the shores of Falmouth Town, where the Britishers eluded the guard and committed many depredations before being driven off by the local militia. They barely failed in their attempt to steal twelve head of cattle from the farm of Ephraim and Manassah Swift. Getting the animals down as far as the shore, they were forced to leave without the cattle when the local militia charged them.

Returning in full strength the next day, the British fleet of two schooners and eight sloops stood off abreast of the town and bombarded the people of Falmouth with cannonballs, double-headed shot, bars of iron, grape shop, and small arms to which the local militia replied as well as they could. Encouraged by their apparent success, the British decided to make a landing at Falmouth and sent ashore ten heavily manned longboats, carrying in all 220 men. While the landing attempts were in progress, the battleships kept up a supporting fire from an hour before noon until 5:00, but in spite of this the men of Falmouth, fifty strong, drove the British back to their boats each time they tried to land. Finally the enemy withdrew and tried to get ashore at Woods Hole, where they were also repulsed.

During this visit of the British fleet one of the Falmouth housewives and a local wit made their own history. A small party of British soldiers confronted Manassah Swift's wife, demanding that she furnish them with cheese. Alone with her children, she told the soldiers that there was no one to defend her, but she presumed that the British leader was enough of a gentleman to behave himself under the conditions. He then asked to buy her cheese, and she replied that there was no cheese except that which she needed for her children. The soldiers roamed around the house until they found the cheese. Then two of their soldiers ran their bayonets into a cheese apiece. Mrs. Swift stationed herself at the door and as the soldiers walked out with their guns over their shoulders, she slid the cheese off their bayonets and hid them in the folds of her dress, at the same time giving the men such a tongue-lashing that she completely overwhelmed them. Rushing out to get away, they could still hear her scorching words as they fled down the road to the beach.

The Falmouth wag, Simeon Hamlin, was watching the enemy with the rest of the men of Falmouth, waiting for the right time to attack, when a small raiding party started for the beach with some farmer's stock. One of the British soldiers was having great difficulty getting a young porker into the longboat, and Hamlin sat down on a rock and began to cry. His comrades gathered about and asked him why he was crying. "Why, I hear that poor pig and can't help crying, to see how the English treat their fellow-beings."

Colonel Joseph Dimmick participated in one of the minor battles of the Revolution. A corn schooner taken by the British was anchored in Tarpaulin Cove, but the American captain escaped and made his way to shore, proceeding at once to the home of Colonel Dimmick to tell his story. Colonel Dimmick quickly organized a raiding party, appointing his brother Lot as right-hand man. Soon twenty alert men of Falmouth were aboard three whaleboats, ready to go to Tarpaulin Cove. Reaching the cove, they went ashore and built a fire behind a sand dune to keep warm. Then at dawn, they discovered the privateer and her prize in the cove.

Although both vessels began firing on them, the three whaleboats kept pulling through the shots to arrive at and capture the schooner, after which they ran her ashore at the west end of Martha's Vineyard. But the persistent captain of the privateer followed the men of Falmouth in and recaptured the schooner. Reforming their forces, the Americans made another raid, and the battle ended with the Falmouth men in possession of the schooner again. The flood tide floated them off, and they sailed the schooner back to Woods Hole. The joy of the inhabitants, who desperately needed the corn, knew no bounds.

A tragedy of the sea occurred in the year 1803, when Captain Joshua Crowell of Falmouth was lost in Boston Bay with his entire crew of four men. The wrecked vessel was later towed into Plymouth Harbor.

In 1806 a long-continued controversy respecting the passage of alewives or herring into Coonamesset Pond came out into the open. Some favored letting the herring come in, others felt the fish should be kept out. As the herring catch yielded substantial revenue, two parties were formed. General Dimmick himself sponsored the herring party. They believed that a passage should be opened to allow the fish free entry into Coonamesset Pond. Mill privileges and other rights interfered, so Thomas Fish was appointed to make a report on the matter, and subsequently decided against the herring group. General Dimmick then petitioned the legislature in Boston for this right. During the excitement caused by the action, the anti-herring group mounted a cannon on Meeting House Green, put in an overcharge of powder, and rammed in as wadding as many herring as they could. Then the gunner applied the match, and the poor man was killed when the gun was blown to pieces in the subsequent explosion. The final decision was that the herring were not to be allowed to get into Coonamesset Pond.

During the War of 1812 Falmouth was again bombarded by the British. On January 23, 1814, the brig *Nimrod,* carrying eighteen guns, anchored off the town at 10:00 in the morning and sent a flag of truce ashore demanding the possession of a vessel then moored at the wharf. The inhabitants indignantly refused to comply with their wishes, so the enemy returned to the *Nimrod,* which began a bombardment of the town. One of the Falmouth women had a very narrow escape. Alone at home, Ann Freeman sought refuge in her front room behind the chimney, and then decided it would be safer in another room. She was crossing the threshold when suddenly a thirty-two–pound shot crashed into the house, passing through the door casing to bury itself in a featherbed, where it was later recovered. The British did not win the battle, however, and soon moved off the coast.

At another time during the war, Captain Weston Jenkins, aided by thirty-two volunteers, went aboard the sloop *Two Friends* and made plans to capture the British privateer *Retaliation,* which was then commanded by Captain Porter. Becalmed at Woods Hole, the men rowed the sloop to Tarpaulin Cove, where the *Retaliation* was anchored. They were met by the Britisher's long gun fire, so the *Two Friends* anchored. Captain Porter of the *Retaliation* and five men, thinking they had an easy prize, rowed across in a boat to the *Two Friends,* where Jenkins and his thirty-two men easily overcame the Britishers. Then they rowed the sloop over to the *Retaliation* and after a short skirmish, captured the leaderless remainder of the British crew. Below decks they discovered two American prisoners who, needless to say, were overjoyed at the turn events had taken.

Falmouth is justly proud of the Paul Revere Bell, which W. H. F. Lincoln purchased from the Boston patriot on November 30, 1796. Sold at a price of forty-two cents a pound, it weighed 807 pounds. It still hangs in the belfry of the Congregational church, which faces the Falmouth Green. Dorothy G. Wayman tells us that it was later the custom for the leader of the church choir to tune his bass viol to the pitch of the original C-sharp, although when the bell cracked it is said the pitch changed to C-flat.

In 1799 it was voted to ring the bell every morning at 6:00, at noon for dinner, and at 9:00 for the curfew. In 1899 at the centennial for the Paul Revere Bell, Katharine Lee Bates, a native of Falmouth, composed a poem honoring the bell, part of which I quote:

> *Greetings to thee, ancient bell of our Falmouth by the sea!*
> *Answered by the ocean swell, ring thy centuried jubilee!*
> *Like the white sails of the sound, hast thou seen the years drift by,*
> *From the dreamful, dim profound to a goal beyond the eye.*
> *Ring thy peals for centuries yet, living voice of Paul Revere!*
> *Let the future not forget what the past accounted dear!*

The name Suckanesset means the black clam of the Indians, and clams are still a profitable business for many in Falmouth. Another industry doing well in Falmouth is the growing of strawberries.

Hiking along the road, I could see the Coonamessett Inn. It is a fine establishment. At one time the inn operated the largest ranch out to cultivation east of the Mississippi, but the government acquired land from it to enlarge Camp Edwards. It is a delightful location, with the Coonamessett Club, golf, tennis, polo matches, riding, and the airport all adding to the visitor's enjoyment. There are twenty-six houses in addition to the inn itself.

Visiting the public library on Main Street, I observed the picture of Elijah Swift on the wall. Swift, the leading townsman of Falmouth at the time of the War of 1812, suffered losses when his house was damaged by shots from the British warship *Nimrod*. Later in the war he built a schooner and launched it into the teeth of the British blockade, which he eluded to reach South Carolina. Six years after the war ended, Elijah Swift founded the Falmouth National Bank.

A visit to the Falmouth High School was my next project, for it is there that the murals of the modernist Karl Knaths of Provincetown are to be seen. Although they created considerable controversy at first, the Knaths Murals, which symbolize the various forms of education, are now accepted by most of the people of Falmouth.

It is said that the first summer residents in Falmouth were the Fays, who journeyed in 1852 to Woods Hole, where they purchased a home looking out over pleasant Little Harbor. Roses were in abundance at the Fay garden, and Michael Walsh was put in charge of their cultivation there. In the year 1893 Walsh delighted the Fay family by presenting them with his own creation, the rambler rose. Cuttings from this rosebush, the original one developed by Walsh, have been sent out all over the world.

I found the scientific institutions at Woods Hole fascinating. I had often seen the oceangoing ketch *Atlantis* tied up at the Marine Biological Laboratory wharf, and knew of the type of studies made here. It was in 1871 that Spencer F. Baird, in charge of the Bureau of Fisheries, decided to establish a laboratory at Woods Hole. Two years later Professor Louis Agassiz started his Anderson School of Natural History on Penikese Island, which was later moved to Woods Hole and renamed the Marine Biological Laboratory. In 1930 the Oceanographic Institution was brought into being, and the ketch *Atlantis* began its trips out to sea for exploratory work on the ocean bottom.

These three institutions work together in close harmony on the various problems which attract their mutual attention. The Bureau of Fisheries is studying migration and habits of fish and their food. A fish hatchery is maintained where millions of tiny fish are released yearly for food fish supply. Marine biology is the chief subject in which the experts at the biological laboratories concern themselves. The physiology, life history, and anatomy of the various forms of sea life interest the research workers. The Oceanographic Institution hunts in deep places at the bottom of the sea, studying light penetration, effects of winds and tides, and the character and shape of the terrain at the sea's bottom. During the Second World War these institutions were actively cooperating with the navy and the Coast Guard in carrying out very important work.

I also visited the Lighthouse Buoy Yard at Woods Hole, and then walked out to Nobska Point, where the lighthouse stands. I talked with the keeper there, who mentioned the fact that Nobska Light was first built in 1828 at the top of the lightkeeper's home. On clear days the chimneys of New Bedford can be seen, but I was unable to make them out that afternoon. Then I went down the hill from the lighthouse and started for my next destination, the site of an old whaling shop.

On the corner of Palmer Avenue once stood a small building through whose doorway probably passed every boy of Falmouth who ever went to sea. It was the whaling supply shop of John Jenkins, who could estimate the type and amount of supplies needed years in advance. The captain who depended on Jenkins' judgment could, many months later, far at sea, thank Jenkins for the supplies which still held out and were there when wanted. The needs were many, and went from sulphur matches and pea jackets to sea boots and casks of biscuits.

At the Newcomb Carleton estate I saw the old stone lookout tower, one of the watch towers of a former day, the age when signals were

Historic postcard of Nobska Light (from the collection of Jeremy D'Entremont)

flashed by semaphore right up the coast from station to station until the news arrived. From this very tower the arms of the semaphore once sent their signals that certain vessels were then in Vineyard Sound and were about to beat around the Cape and sail across Massachusetts Bay to reach Boston.

Falmouth has an interesting newspaper history, for it was in this town that the very first newspaper on Cape Cod began its publication in 1823. Its name, aptly enough, was the *Nautical Intelligencer.* The Old Stone Dock building, then at its peak of activity, was the home of the first Cape newspaper. Dorothy G. Wayman tells us that in 1873 a Seaside Press was active. By 1886 the *Falmouth Local* was covering Cape Cod news, while nine years later Charles S. Burgess founded the *Falmouth Enterprise.* By 1930 Miss Wayman, now with the *Boston Globe,* was the editor.

Several well-known people have lived in Falmouth. I have already mentioned Katharine Lee Bates. Born in Falmouth in 1859, she was a nationally known poet, best remembered for her song, "America the Beautiful," which I believe should be this country's national anthem. Professor of English at Wellesley College, she often revisited the house where she was born on Main Street in Falmouth, and a year after her death in 1928 a bronze tablet was placed there.

Edward Herbert Thompson, famed Yucatan archaeologist, lived in Falmouth for many years. He descended to the bottom of the Well of Sacrifices in Yucatan to recover the gold, jade, and incense from the bottom of the well. Two actors, Joseph Jefferson and Joseph Jefferson Holland, were well known in Falmouth, and a tablet in the local library honors Holland.

Many years ago the Indian queen on Falmouth Heights at Great Hill was known as Awashonks. A Cape Cod whaling ship named for this Indian queen was given one of the worst receptions ever suffered by a Massachusetts whaler. She was the unfortunate ship *Awashonks* of Falmouth, Massachusetts. The 5th of October, 1835, she was anchored at Baring's Island in the Pacific. Aboard the *Awashonks* at the time were three Nantucket officers, Captain Prince Coffin, First Officer Alexander H. Gardner, and William Swain, the second mate. Silas Jones of Falmouth was the third mate and another Falmouth boy, Thomas Gifford, was one of the twenty-four members of the crew.

By the 1st of October the cruising *Awashonks* had 400 barrels of sperm oil aboard, and Captain Coffin announced his intentions of sailing to Japan and then to the Sandwich Islands. At sunrise on October 5 the lookout sighted Baring's Island, and several hours later the ship reached a lagoon at the island. Seeing three canoes full of natives, the captain told Third Mate Jones that he was going ashore to get some fruit, and gave orders to heave the ship to.

Shortly afterwards the three canoes reached the *Awashonks,* and trading began. Coconuts and plantains were exchanged for iron and ivory, after which the natives were allowed to come aboard. The chief of the natives was the first man to come up the side. He was decorated with a string of fish's teeth, and had enormous ear lobes into which were bored holes two inches in diameter. In each hole he had placed a yellow plantain leaf. He wore a grass skirt. The other men were stark naked.

Captain Coffin then ordered dinner served, and went below with the two officers, leaving Third Mate Jones in command of the deck. At noon Jones took an observation with the quadrant, which seemed to frighten the natives who supposed that it was an instrument of warfare. Shortly afterwards he noticed several more canoes coming toward the ship. When Captain Coffin and the others finished dinner, the third mate went below to eat. Jones ate dinner and when he came up on deck again, he found that about thirty canoes were nearing the *Awashonks*.

From the first the natives appeared fascinated by the fifteen-foot cutting spades with their shining steel blades used for cutting up the whales, so Captain Coffin took one down from the box and showed them how the spades worked. One by one the curious natives came over the side to join their countrymen on deck until they outnumbered the white men. Looking over the side, Mate Jones detected one big native carrying his war club up the gangway, and shouted the information to Captain Coffin who ordered his crew to drive the natives off the deck. Jones grabbed the war club from its owner and threw it overboard, and then saw another war club being brought aboard. Starting for the second war club, the mate was frozen with horror when he saw several of the natives making a rush for the spades. Jones then made a run to get one of the spades before it was too late.

By this time spades, war clubs, and all dangerous weapons available were flying through the air in a complete bedlam of noise and confusion, but Jones miraculously reached the spade box, obtained a spade, and ran over the main hatches to the other side of the quarterdeck. There he met and wrestled with one savage, who was joined by another. Grasping the spade with one hand, Jones hit the savage with several well-directed blows of his clenched fist. The native loosened his grasp to run away in search of another weapon. Before Jones could handle the other man holding his spade, a new danger presented itself. He caught sight of a third native advancing on him with a murderous spear. At this Jones gave up the fight for the spade and ran forward. As he made his way by the mainmast, a weapon came flying at him through the air, but he dodged it and jumped down into one of the hatches, landing on the lower deck in the forehold where he found several other seamen making preparations for defense.

Third Mate Jones then thought of the weapons stored in the cabin on the other side of the bulkhead and began to break through a passageway at once. On the other side of the partition was the blacksmith, who immediately began to break through from his side. Within a relatively short time a passageway was forced through, and it was an easy matter to make their way through the steerage and into the cabin, where to their joy they found no savages. Obtaining a pair of large pistols from his own sea chest, the mate gave them to the blacksmith and ordered him to stand guard until Jones could get the muskets ready. The two men were then joined by Charley, the young Negro boy. Several muskets were shortly afterwards loaded and made ready for quick use.

All this time they could hear the joyous shouts and cries of the victorious natives on the deck above. Finally, discovering the men in the cabin, five or six of the savages began to organize for an attack, but Jones stepped out and discharged his gun into their midst, and the hilarity and noise stopped at once. Every few seconds from then on one or the other of the men in the cabin fired at the savages, and each time the natives threw something in retaliation, a spear, a spade, a harpoon, and even the spyglass. Jones then fired out of the stern window at a canoe-load of natives. By this time two others had joined the group in the cabin, a man named Lewis and a boy called John Parker. Lewis had been the lookout at the fore topgallant head, and had jumped to the deck when hearing the shots, severely hurting himself in the leap. Before he could get away, several of the natives had wounded him, but he kept on, dragging a terribly injured leg after him until he finally reached the cabin.

After Lewis arrived, Jones took account of the situation. The blacksmith, who had been sick, could not be counted on, but the four men able to fight had in their possession four muskets, two pistols, and two boarding knives. They were shortly afterwards joined by a fifth man, Daniel Wood, who was so weakened by his wounds that he was of no help at all.

Noises heard at this time convinced Jones that the savages were smashing the helm, so he discharged a musket up through the floor, trusting it might injure those trying to destroy the wheel. Actually, he later found, the shot had taken effect, the charge striking one of the savages. All Jones knew at the time, however, was that no more noise came from that direction.

Shortly afterwards the blacksmith reappeared, having rested so that he would have strength to come to the aid of the besieged group in the cabin, and a consultation was held. There were then six men, three of whom were either injured or sick. Just as Mate Jones was directing the able-bodied men to their posts, he heard the sound of shoes on deck, and Helmsman Perkins came running in to them.

"Oh! Mr. Jones, I didn't know you were alive. They are all gone, they are all gone!" he cried, and sank to the floor. After Perkins recovered his self-possession, Jones passed him a weapon, and they mounted the toprail to see the natives about sixty yards from the ship. All the crew members then came topside and fired at the departing men before they sat down to take stock again of what had happened. Jones could only tell what had befallen him, but he was now to learn the horrible outcome of the deck battle.

Only about two-thirds of the ship's company were on deck when the attack came, for there had been two men in the mastheads and the remainder of the crew in the forecastle. The natives had secured eleven of the fourteen spades to drive the white men before them. Almost at once Captain Coffin was killed by a blow of the cutting spade which practically severed his head, and in the fighting which followed the first and second officers were killed.

Jones realized for the first time that he was the captain of the *Awashonks,* for all the officers outranking him were dead. Reaching the forecastle, they found four wounded men lying in their own blood. Bestowing great praise on Third Mate Jones who now became Captain Jones, one of them then shouted, "My God, Mr. Jones, we are glad that you are left us!" The others praised Captain Jones highly, which caused him to reflect later to himself, "By what sudden impulse the mind of the sailor is often turned, as I was well aware that one or two of those very men who were the most lavish in bestowing praise on me and show-ing gratitude to their Creator for my preservation, would but a very short time before this have swung me on the yardarm with pleasure. And these different feelings all sprang from the same cause, which was my endeavoring to do my duty."

Collecting his company, Captain Jones ascertained that six had been killed aboard ship, the second officer was killed in the water, and another man was drowned. The other two men lost had been seen swimming away from the ship in the distance, but without question they were set upon by the savages when they reached shore, and killed. In any case, they were never heard from again.

The wounded now claimed the attention of all, and Captain Jones was forced to make the unhappy decision in his mind that four of them would probably die soon. Cut in many places, the men seemed beyond the aid of what limited help Jones could give them. Only Jones could keep at the nauseating work of sewing up the cuts and open wounds, for his assistants had to rush constantly to the deck for fresh air. Jones did not finish administering to his patients until the early morning hours of the next day.

At the close of that day the crew all assembled forward and commit-ted to the ocean the remains of their captain and first mate. Afterwards Jones said, "If one were there who did not sincerely thank his Creator for the preservation of his own life, he deserves not the name of man."

Sailing away from Baring's Island, Captain Jones directed his course to the north, where late at night several islands known as the Elmore Group came in sight. The next day a number of canoes started out, but Captain Jones would not permit them to come alongside. Angered by this rebuff, the natives made frightful grimaces and pursued the ship. Captain Jones wisely prevented the crew from firing at the natives, however, and the savages tired of their pursuit and paddled back to their own shores. The *Awashonks* then reached the Mosquito Islands. The days went by, and finally on November 25 the *Awashonks* entered Owhyhee Harbor, now Honolulu. Meanwhile Lewis had died, and a seaman named Wood developed gangrene, which Captain Jones was forced to burn out. Wood and the other patients eventually recovered.

The successful return voyage of the *Awashonks* created much favorable comment in Falmouth, and Captain Silas Jones was highly praised for his courage and wisdom.

May 20, 1836, Captain Jones returned to Woods Hole, where he was given a reception at the Village Reading Room. He later made another voyage in the *Awashonks,* and after several other trips was aboard the *Commodore Morris* when the Civil War began. The *Morris* was chased by the *Alabama* but managed to elude the Southern raider. At the time of Jones's death in 1896 he was president of the Falmouth National Bank.

The *Awashonks* had been built at Woods Hole and was later lost with thirty-three other whalers in 1871 in the Arctic Ocean. The story of the *Awashonks'* encounter with the savages was taken with the permission of Dorothy G. Wayman from the original account written by Captain Silas Jones.

One of the stories I enjoy telling about men from Falmouth is the tale of Andrew Jackson's figurehead, which graced the famous battleship *Constitution,* also known as *Old Ironsides,* at one time in her remarkable career. Mad Jack Percival, who had such a fascinating career, played a small part in the story.

In the War of 1812 the figurehead of the *Constitution* was a billet-head scroll, which replaced the figurehead of Neptune, chosen by Captain Hull. In 1833 when the ship was being overhauled, President Andrew Jackson visited the Navy Yard in Charlestown and was received with much acclaim by Captain Elliott, commanding officer at the Navy Yard. Captain Elliott asked President Jackson if he would allow his form in wood to grace the bow of the *Constitution.* Jackson acquiesced and posed for the statue the following week.

However, Captain Elliott had not figured on the local Sons of Liberty. Most of these men were Whigs and objected to "this Old Roman" being given prominence on a battleship built and launched at Boston, because Jackson, a landlubber and member of the opposition party, hailed from the South and was a Democrat. Various methods of bringing pressure to bear on the wood-carver who was making the statue failed to succeed, and the Whigs suffered the embarrassment of watching the *Constitution* floated again in 1834 with the hated figurehead in place.

At the height of the excitement Captain Samuel Worthington Dewey of Falmouth, Massachusetts, arrived in Boston Harbor with a cargo of sugar from the West Indies. Reaching Central Wharf, he noticed the other sea captains sitting around rather unhappily and asked them what the trouble was.

"Oh, it's that damned figurehead," was the reply, and the others soon told Dewey the particulars of the case.

"Well, if that's all that's worrying you, I'll take care of it myself," swaggered Dewey, and the others pestered him with questions until he revealed his plan. "Some rainy night I'll row over and cut the head from Andrew Jackson's shoulders," Dewey declared, "and then we'll show the Democrats what kind of Whigs we are," he finished.

"That's just a lot of talk," another captain spoke up, "I'll bet you a hundred dollars you'll never do it." "Done," said the Falmouth native, and the wager was made. Several days later, on the morning of July 2, 1834, a heavily overcast day indicated rain before nightfall, and surely enough, a pelting, driving rainstorm, accompanied by occasional flashes of lightning and boomings of thunder began at dusk. Dewey knew it was the night for his attempt.

Reaching the North End waterfront, Dewey pushed a small punt into the water and began sculling his way across the harbor to Charlestown. In a gunnysack at his side was a saw, a hammer, and a file. After fifteen minutes' sculling, Dewey pulled up under the bow of the famous *Constitution*, which was then moored between the seventy-four-gun battleships *Columbus* and *Independence*. There were many sailors aboard the *Columbus,* and a sentinel was placed where he could see the figurehead at all times. A light from an open port aboard the *Columbus* fell full on the wooden face Dewey had sworn to sever from Jackson's body.

Captain Dewey then secured his skiff and worked his way up into the manropes, finally reaching the object of his journey, the figurehead of President Andrew Jackson. Sliding himself in under the figurehead, he lay stretched out on his back and began to saw at the neck of the figure. As he lay there, time and again he noticed the alert sentry apparently staring directly at him, but the beating rain and wind helped obscure the sentry's vision, and Dewey was not detected.

Unfortunately, Dewey found a huge copper bolt at the base of the neck, and had to saw again, this time at the chin. Finally the severed head of Andrew Jackson's effigy was in Dewey's hands, and he dropped it into his gunnysack before he climbed back down the man-ropes into his skiff. By this time the punt was almost swamped with water from the storm, but he bailed it out, sculled back to Gray's Wharf in Boston, and returned to his home on School Street.

The subsequent results were many and varied, with rages of disappointment coming from the South and jubilation parades held in the North, all because of this daring act of a Falmouth sea captain.

Years later Dewey had the temerity to show the wooden head of Andrew Jackson to Secretary of the Navy Dickerson, who at first threatened to have Dewey arrested, but as there was no law at that time against what the captain did, Dewey was never punished.

The present whereabouts of the noted figurehead is not definitely known. Down at Annapolis, it is said, parts of the figurehead have been preserved, but another story is told that Jonathan Bowers of Tyngsboro obtained the figurehead and placed it on the shore of Lake Mascupic, where a pleasure resort known as Willodale was located. In 1925, we are told, the figurehead was sold at auction for $10,000 to a man by the name of Max Williams.

There I was at the southwestern corner of the Cape, and my journey around the land of my Pilgrim ancestors would not be complete until I reached Chatham, the southeastern corner of Cape Cod. From Falmouth it seemed quite a distance away, but I started out for my final objective, Chatham's Outer Beach, where the bones of unnumbered shipwrecks lie exposed to the elements.

An hour later I had left Falmouth Heights, and was hiking toward the narrow strip of land between Great Pond and Vineyard Sound at Mara Vista. Turning north at Acapesket, I crossed over Green Pond to reach Davisville on Davis Neck, continued eastward, and was soon in Menauhant. I realized that there was an important turn to the right ahead to avoid the peninsula which juts out into Waquoit Bay. After following Center Avenue to reach Highway 28 at East Falmouth, half an hour later I arrived at Waquoit Village and Bourne Pond. I crossed the

Quashnet River and entered Mashpee going to Pine Tree Corner, the interesting circular intersection of five Cape highways. Heading due east after I reached the junction of Falmouth Road and Quinaquisset Road, I followed the latter to cross Quaker Run, reach the mouth of the Cotuit River, and enter Cotuit itself.

The Paul Revere Bell at the Falmouth Congregational Church is inscribed "The living to the church I call, and to the grave I summon all. Revere Boston 1796."

Karl Knaths' paintings are no longer displayed at Falmouth High School; they were removed when the building was rebuilt.

The *Constitution*'s Andrew Jackson figurehead was eventually reheaded and stayed in place until 1848, when it was replaced by a new Greco-Roman–style carving of Jackson. The second Jackson figurehead by Boston carvers J. D. and W. H. Fowle is on exhibit as a statue at the Naval Academy.

CHAPTER 12

Along the South Sea of Cape Cod from Cotuit to Harwich through Hyannis

Cotuit has been referred to as Coituit, Coetuit, and Coatuct, while the original agreement of 1658, in which John Alden and Josiah Winslow represented Barnstable, mentions "all the lands lying westward of Satuit River" as well as certain lands on the eastern side. Those certain lands comprise what is Cotuit today.

The burial ground in Cotuit has an interesting stone, that of Azubah Handy, the first wife of Bethuel Handy, who died in 1819. I quote part of the inscription:

> *Husband and children here I lay*
> *Stamp on your minds my dying day*
> *Come often here and take a view*
> *Where lay the one that loved you*

Cotuit had a large and well-known fleet of coasting vessels, and her vessels and sailors were recognized up and down the Atlantic Coast. In 1866 twenty-five vessels wintered at Cotuit Harbor.

Here at Cotuit near the Osterville line occurred the famous Phelps treasure hunt. In 1849 a convict named William Phelps pretended that he had hidden his loot of $50,000 at Cotuit, so Warden Robinson from

Charlestown and Charlestown's City Marshall Nichols took Phelps to Cotuit. After digging for some time Phelps pretended to become tired and was helped out of the pit for a rest. Nichols jumped down into the deep pit and continued shoveling. When Robinson leaned over to see how Nichols was coming along, Phelps pushed him into the pit and ran away. Phelps said later that he ran six miles without stopping, and four days later was befriended by a Mashpee Indian. It was not until three months afterwards that he was captured. The general sentiment in Boston regarding Phelps' apprehension was summarized by a statement in a local paper that "out of respect for the skill with which he affected his escape, there was a strong feeling of regret manifested yesterday when his recapture became known."

Guided by Jack Frost's picture in his *Cape Cod Sketch Book,* I found the approximate location of the pit where Phelps had his moment of triumph. Frost tells us that the late A. Lawrence Lowell, former president of Harvard College, gave him exact directions on how to find the site of the pit between the Coleman and Robbins oyster houses.

Crossing the Santuit Golf Course, I followed the old King's Highway until it met Putnam Avenue. I was soon standing by the Mill Pond in Marstons Mills. That precinct of Barnstable known as Marstons Mills was named for Benjamin Marston, who moved to Cape Cod from Salem in 1738. Running the mill for many years, he developed it so that it not only fulled but dressed and carded cloth. There is an interesting story about John Goodspeed, who lived here in 1754. Shipping aboard a privateer during the French Wars, he was a crew member when the privateer captured a Spanish vessel carrying a rich cargo of gold. Five thousand dollars was the share he brought back to Marstons Mills.

Those who gather to watch the herring run at Marstons Mills River are always certain of having plenty of excitement. In 1851 the price for herring was set at three cents a dozen, "salted and struck."

I had in my notes accounts of two citizens of Marstons Mills, who were aboard shipwrecked vessels. The first was Edwin Fuller, chief mate on the *City of Columbus,* who lost his life with a hundred others in 1884 when the steamer hit the dreaded Devil's Bridge off Gay Head, Martha's Vineyard. The other was Captain Frederic Hinckley, who was sailing on the ship *Living Age* when she hit a reef in the Pacific. Escaping aboard a raft to Pratas Island, he was rescued by a British steamer to return home safely. Hinckley later started an insurance business in Boston.

A delightful story is told by Chester A. Crocker illustrating the courage and stamina of the older members of the Jones family of Marstons Mills. Nye Jones, ninety-five years old, went hunting with his grown grandsons and the hound dog, Sukey, a little more then a century ago. It was a bitter December day and no game was sighted before sundown. The grandsons decided to go home before they froze their feet, but just then their dog could be heard nearly a mile away near Satuit Pond. Grandfather Jones continued with the hunt and the boys all went home.

They ate their supper, and waited for the old man to return. But he did not come and the hour grew late. Toward midnight, when they were getting ready to go out and search for him, there was a noise on the porch and Grandfather Jones threw open the door. Walking into the room with a 120-pound doe on his shoulders, Grandfather was flushed with victory. His eyes showed scorn as he addressed his grandsons.

"See if you can stand the cold in the barn long enough to dress the deer while I have supper."

Years later a descendant of Nye Jones, Edmund Hamblin, was lost overboard during a snowstorm from a Gloucester fishing vessel after he had become practically frozen at the wheel. The schooner was hove to and flares were lighted. The crew knew there wasn't much chance of finding him, but they kept up their search for a half hour. When they were about to give up, they heard his powerful voice coming across the water, rowed over to him, and got him in the dory just in time, for his strength was rapidly failing. Hamblin lived on to become one of the few men ever rescued from sea during a night snowstorm.

I found a good supper and lodging for the night at Marstons Mills. The next morning began another rainless day, and there was much talk of forest fires in Marstons Mills. I started along the road which led to Osterville, and half an hour later had reached that precinct of Barnstable. The early settlers here named the vicinity Lovell Neighborhood, because there were so many Lovells residing in Osterville.

In 1788 Benjamin Hallett of Osterville established a line of packet vessels between Boston, Albany, and Troy, New York. It was Hallett who brought the marble to Boston for the state house. In 1808 he built a sloop which he named in honor of his ten living daughters, the *Ten Sisters*. He was an earnest Baptist, and when the *Ten Sisters* was anchored in Coenties Slip, New York, he held a religious seaman's service which was the beginning of the Seaman's Bethel movement.

One of his daughters married Captain Samuel Dewey of Falmouth. Their son, Samuel Worthington Dewey, figured prominently in the famous Jackson figurehead episode which I told when visiting Falmouth.

The history of the Cape Cod catboats started in Osterville. Andrew Crosby, assisted by two sons, Worthington and Horace, designed and built a new type of craft never seen before on Cape Cod. At the time, he was dabbling in spiritualism, and his wife, Tirza, became a medium. He claimed that the spirits helped design the new craft, which had the mast up in the eye, was without a keel, and carried only one sail. In spite of the fact that everyone scoffed at his plan, he went ahead. Andrew Crosby died before the new boat was finished, but his sons launched it, christening the new vessel *Little Eva.* A large crowd which had gathered to make fun of the boat remained to admire it, as she "would sail three inches to their one," and come about "as quick as a cat." So catboat it became, and a very popular design it proved to be.

Every section of Massachusetts has its legend or ghost, and Cape Cod is no exception to the rule. There is a tradition concerning Hannah Screacham, or Hannah the Screacher as she was called. Two centuries ago Hannah watched a band of pirates bury a treasure chest on lonely Oyster Island. As the buccaneers were lowering the treasure chest into the pit, Hannah became frightened and started to leave the vicinity. It was too late, for as she ran away she was caught by one of the pirates, who dragged her back to the pit where the gold was being buried. The pirate captain (some say Kidd, but as Kidd was not a pirate we'll suggest the name might have been Blackbeard), ordered her killed at once, and her body was thrown into the pit on top of the treasure. Then the hole was filled and the buccaneers sailed away forever.

Ever since that day over two centuries ago Hannah's spirit has dwelt near the spot where the gold was buried, and if anyone should venture too near the location of the buried treasure chest, Hannah warns them away by a weird, piercing screech. Many in Osterville are said to have heard the screech, and once was usually enough, for no one who heard the sound would ever go near the island again. Today, however, there are few who claim to have any knowledge of Hannah the Screacher, the poor girl killed by pirates from the Spanish Main.

Leaving Osterville, I followed along County Road until I arrived in Centerville. Phyllis Bearse tells us that the name Centerville was changed from either Chequaquet, as the old maps indicate, or Wequaquett, as Amos Otis suggests. I was eager to see the place where Captain Dennis

Sturgis lived, as he was the only man I ever heard of who had a mahogany pigsty. One day he unloaded some beautiful mahogany logs on the Centerville beach while sailing from the West Indies to Boston with his cargo. As the weeks went by people began to wonder what type of furniture Captain Sturgis planned to make of the mahogany. Finally Sturgis returned to Centerville and for the next few weeks was busy cutting, splitting, and sawing. A month later the captain invited his neighbors over to see his latest creation—a mahogany pigsty.

Captain Sturgis might have been a candidate for the Cape Cod Tall Story Club of which I appoint Captain Ready, former town crier of Provincetown, a charter member. When Sturgis was older, he used to relate the details of a storm he went through on the Great Lakes when grindstones came sailing through the air because the wind was so strong.

I continued south from Centerville to reach Craigville Beach, a beautiful stretch of sand bordering Centerville Harbor. It was there one August night some years ago that Dr. Mark M. Burke of Boston was standing on the beach. It was a moonless night and the beach was more or less deserted. As he stood there smoking a cigarette, Dr. Burke observed someone walking toward him from the edge of the water. As the person came closer, the doctor saw that he was a fairly young man with sandy hair which actually came down over his shoulders, and that he was attired in the simplest garb.

"Who is in charge of this beach?" the blond stranger asked Dr. Burke in a foreign accent. "I would like to keep my boat here for the night."

Dr. Burke told the man that he probably wouldn't have any trouble if he left the craft on the beach until morning. The doctor was strangely interested in this character who landed on a foreign beach long after dark, and questioned the man to satisfy his curiosity. It was an amazing story which Uno Eaverson, for that proved to be his name, told to Dr. Burke there on the Craigville Beach. Starting for Vineyard Haven from Nantucket in his fifteen-foot sailboat, Uno found that the wind was taking him off course, and so he decided to let the wind carry him to the mainland and go to Vineyard Haven the next day.

Uno Eaverson, a minister's son, was born in Greenland shortly before the turn of the century. He sailed away from Greenland at the age of fourteen in a fifteen-foot sailboat, using a piece of bamboo for a mast! From Greenland he went all the way down the Atlantic Coast on his first trip, stopping at almost every lighthouse, inlet, harbor, and island on the way. Cruising along by New England and the Middle Atlantic

States, he reached Florida, lived two and a half years with the Panama Indians, and later crossed to the West Indies.

It was his custom to pull his craft up above the waterline and sleep on the beach. He used a bamboo pole because it would bend and not break. His very first marine expedition landed him in Panama, and by the time he reached Craigville that night he had spent fourteen years sailing up and down the Atlantic in his fifteen-foot flat-bottomed rowboat!

Uno Eaverson's first visit to New York caused him much unhappiness. With great anticipation, he anchored in the East River and went ashore. But as his hair had not been cut for four years, Uno became the object of merriment to a gang of playful boys, who decided to chase him around New York because he was such a curiosity. Pulling his hair and bothering him in other ways they chased him in one end of the Pennsylvania Railroad Terminal and out the other. He finally took refuge in an undertaking parlor where a man befriended him, giving him a chance to rest for a period of time. The outcome of his New York adventure was that he sold his hair for fifty cents, and received a free haircut as well! By the time he sailed away from New York, Uno was a good friend of the undertaker, and promised to communicate with him once a year. As the years passed Uno made it a habit to sail in the winter around Florida and between Vineyard Haven and Portland, Maine, in the summertime.

When he met him on Craigville Beach, Dr. Burke listened intently as Uno continued his tale. The doctor tried to puzzle out this unusual character. It was an almost unbelievable story, but there Uno was beside him. Many questions came into the doctor's mind, and he decided to ask Uno several of them.

"Why don't you get a larger boat, Uno?" was the first.

"If you recall, when people on large boats get into trouble and have to leave them for safety, what do they do? They get into smaller ones. So I am in a small one already, and don't have to worry about getting into a safe boat, for I am there already, too."

It seemed logical the way Uno worked it out in his mind, so Doctor Burke risked another question. "Why don't you have a keel on your boat?"

Uno explained that the only purpose a keel had was to allow you to steer a straighter and faster course. He had no use for a keel for the very reason that he was not in a hurry to get anywhere. Somehow, to the doctor sitting on the beach, that also seemed a logical statement.

"Where do you sleep?"

"I sleep on the beach wherever I am," was the answer.

"What happens if it rains?"

"I just wait until the rain stops—then I dry out."

"By the way, Uno, were you ever shipwrecked in your fourteen years at sea?"

"Yes," was Uno's reply, "but just once, three years ago, when I was cast upon a rock in the Bahamas for thirty-six hours during a storm, but that was the only time, and I did not suffer much from it." Uno went on to tell Dr. Burke about his experiences on his trip to Cuba, when he lived ashore eating wild berries and fruit for eleven months at a total cost of sixty-three cents.

"What do you do for a living?"

"I paint smokestacks, for no one seems to care how long I take and that is the kind of work I like."

"Do you go to church?" asked Dr. Burke.

"Oh, yes," was the reply. "Any denomination at all, but I always sit up back because of my looks and dress."

Lighthouses were his favorite places, however, for he always seemed to become good friends with the lonely keepers, and besides, his newspapers were newer than any the keepers had. They would give him a moderate amount of food but he never accepted meat, for he was a strict vegetarian.

Dr. Mark Burke then invited Uno Eaverson to his home to enjoy a late supper, but it was only after constant urging that the man from Greenland accepted. The next day, when it came time for Uno to sail away, there was quite a large group gathered on the beach to wish him success on his venture, for the news of the sailor from Greenland had traveled fast. Dr. Burke made him promise to send a postcard from time to time, and as Uno sailed out to sea, the doctor called after him, "Don't forget your promise."

Months later Dr. Burke received a card which read, "Just a line before heading south." The card was dated September 10, 1931. He never heard from Uno again. Several months afterwards there came a letter from Anna Lang of Martha's Vineyard to Dr. Burke, enclosing a clipping from the *Vineyard Haven Gazette* of February 9, 1932, which gave an explanation of what probably happened to Uno.

The account told of an incident which occurred on the Virginia Capes. A woman watching a storm at sea from the security of her home caught sight of a small craft being buffeted by the waves. She telephoned the Coast Guard at once, and they went out and brought the craft in. There was no occupant, but in the boat, attached to the thwart, was a small envelope addressed to Uno Eaverson, General Delivery, Martha's Vineyard. There was nothing more in the sailboat, and Uno's body was never found. Thus Uno Eaverson probably died as he wished in a storm at sea.

A short time later Dr. Burke noticed a small article about Uno in the *Boston Post,* and the weekly newsmagazine *Time* mentioned this lone mariner who had foundered at sea. Dr. Burke decided to notify Uno's father up in Greenland, so sent the clippings and a letter northward. A long time later the letter came back unopened, marked "Address Unknown."

After spending some time on the Craigville Beach I headed east again, reaching West Hyannisport. (One may call it Hyannis Port or Hyannisport.) Following County Road I passed the Hyannisport Golf Club and crossed Hall Creek to reach Sunset Hill. A certain Hyannisport whaler, Peleg Nye, once had an experience which put him almost in the class of Jonah, who also knew his big fish.

In March 1863 Nye fired his bomb lance into a sperm whale, and everyone aboard the longboat assumed that the whale was killed. Nye prodded the huge mammal with a hand lance, and suddenly the whale slapped his tail and crashed his lower jaw into Nye's boat, causing Nye to fall forward directly into the whale's mouth. Scrambling to get out of the way, Nye found himself caught in an almost unbelievable manner as the whale closed his great jaws. A sperm whale has teeth only in its lower jaw, teeth which fit into upper jaw sockets. Nye was actually caught by the whale's jaws just below his knees, but the space between the whale's teeth and sockets was roomy enough to prevent Nye's legs from being crushed. However, the whale soon sounded, and Nye said afterwards he thought the huge beast reached the very bottom of the ocean with him before everything went black. Then Nye opened his mouth, breathing in seawater, and lost consciousness.

Luckily, at approximately the same time the whale gave up the struggle and floated to the surface, dead. Just before the mammal appeared, Nye's body came to the surface and was taken aboard the whaler. It was a long time before he could be revived, but Nye finally came to, and recovered completely before reaching home. Living to the good age of seventy-nine, Peleg Nye was known as the Jonah of Cape Cod.

On leaving Hyannisport, I saw the Hyannisport Breakwater on my right as I reached Gosnold Street, and turned left at Ocean Street to cross Snow's Creek. I passed the Hyannis State Teachers College building on my left, and was soon in the center of Hyannis itself.

Donald G. Trayser had told me that the name Hyannis comes from the gentle and courteous Indian sachem Iyanough, who helped the Pilgrims find young Billington and later died hiding from them. The name Yanno first appeared in Barnstable records in 1664. Nicholas Davis was the first settler and the first business man of Hyannis, coming to Cape Cod's "South Sea" in 1666.

When I arrived at the railroad station, I walked almost a block and then turned right looking for the offices of the *Barnstable Patriot* and the printing establishment of F. B. & F. P. Goss. Not very far down the street I found the building and went inside to meet the *Patriot*'s editor, Percy F. Williams, Jr. He told me that there are at present seven Cape Cod newspapers. They are the *Barnstable Patriot,* of which he is the editor, the *Cape Cod Standard Times,* the *Falmouth Enterprise,* the *Yarmouth Register,* the *Cape Codder,* the *Provincetown Advocate,* and the *Harwich Independent.* The *Patriot* has had some hard uphill work in the last few years, and credit for its fine standing today belongs without question to two men, Donald Trayser, who was editor during a difficult period of readjustment, and Percy Williams, its present editor.

"In the days when Major Phinney ran the sheet there were some great battles between the Whigs and the Democrats down here," said Editor Williams. "The verbal contests between a Yarmouth editor and Major Phinney often attracted the attention of the great Boston dailies, and Major Phinney was frequently quoted in the pages of the *Boston Post.*"

Editor Williams escorted me around his efficient printing plant and publishing house, and then I left the premises for my next adventure.

I headed westward again to visit Aunt Betty's Pond and Fossett's Pond for I had been told both had interesting stories about them. The first was named for Aunt Betty Bearse, the widow of Lot Bearse, who in 1830 had a pleasant orchard which extended to the pond. The second pond was called for Dr. Thomas Fossett, who lived nearby. I visited the Cobb's Hill Cemetery to read the inscription on his tomb, written by the doctor himself before he died. The inscription tells us that he practiced in three states for more than fifty years and lost an average of less than a patient a year! Fossett said that he had "conversed with the spirits of the dead for forty years, as with the living."

The earliest known harbor on the "South Sea" was utilized hereabouts in 1747 by Elisha Lumbart, but by 1800 there was only a small village where Hyannis now is. Trayser tells us that of the 3,000 persons living in Barnstable in 1800, one thousand were scattered along the southern shore between Cotuit and Hyannis. The saltworks became a thriving industry shortly afterwards, and when business was good, Lot Crocker and his three sons turned out 3,000 barrels of salt a year.

In 1826 Congress appropriated $10,500 for a breakwater, and between 1827 and 1837, $70,000 more was obtained to complete this project. Barnstable people were not in favor of this breakwater, Major Phinney in the *Patriot* calling it a "monument of human folley."

The last windmill in Hyannis stood at the junction of what is now South and Main Streets. "Uncle" Oman Bacon, the miller, allowed the children to play about in the mill, and one day a girl named Hepsibeth tried a dangerous stunt which some of the boys had accomplished successfully. They would cling to an arm until it was a substantial distance off the ground and then drop. Hepsibeth held on too long, and was carried fifty feet in the air.

"Hold on, Hepsie," the boys cried at her, and she did, completing the arc and reaching the ground safely. The slogan, "Hold on, Hepsie" became a watchword in Hyannis for years afterwards.

Hyannis, without question, has forged steadily ahead until today it can be called one of the most enterprising of all Cape Cod communities. With the Hyannis Airport, the Cape Cod Hospital, the *Barnstable Patriot,* the Massachusetts Maritime Academy, and scores of other activities, the precinct of Hyannis has outstripped its mother Barnstable. The first land boom here was during the 1870s, but since then it has been busier almost each successive year. The population has increased yearly until in 1946 it is the largest village on Cape Cod, and the greatest business district on this "bended arm" of Massachusetts.

Wandering out by the Hyannis Airport, I met Floyd Van Duzer, who breeds Morgan horses and runs a dude ranch in the summer at Cummaquid. He has an ideal combination on his ranch, for it is located near a fine beach where the horseback riders can gallop along the shore. The summer of 1946 will be his second season at Cummaquid. The day I saw him he had his famous western stagecoach team, and it added much color to the day to see his horses drive up with a flourish and come to a stop at the airport.

Leaving Hyannis, I passed the Mill Pond in West Yarmouth to reach Englewood. Parker's Neck was ahead, and Bass River in the distance. Ten minutes later I was in South Yarmouth.

As I hiked up the road, I noticed great columns of smoke billowing across the Cape, and it filled my heart with a strange chill, for I knew it came from a forest fire. For several days afterwards that section of the Cape around Sandwich and Barnstable was swept by the blaze.

Knowing that my good friend Alton Hall Blackington would surely be in the vicinity because of his interest in fires, I decided to suspend my historical activities and find out from him what had happened. One of Blackie's rendezvous at Cape Cod was Sheriff Crocker's office in Barnstable. I telephoned across to Sheriff Crocker and found that Blackington had been reported in the vicinity of Peter's Pond that very morning, directly in the path of the flames, which were even then sweeping through the Wakeby section of Cape Cod. I decided not to attempt to locate Blackie that day.

The fire was well under control several days later when I finally reached Peter's Pond and the Wakeby area, but Blackie was nowhere to be seen. Walking up to a hard-working fireman, I asked him if he had seen Alton Hall Blackington. As he wiped his perspiring brow, he replied, "Yes, he and Sheriff Crocker left here for Barnstable Courthouse three hours ago."

This was one of the times when I wished I could steal a ride. But I didn't. Two hours later, however, I reached the courthouse and there was Blackie sitting with the sheriff in his office. They both seemed almost dead from exhaustion, and the stories they told made me realize that the blaze had been one of the worst in the entire history of the Cape.

"Did you make any air pictures of the fire?" asked Blackie, and of course my answer was no, for I had hardly seen an airplane since landing almost three weeks before in a Provincetown field. "Well, they probably wouldn't have been too good anyway," said Blackie. "In an air shot the smoke hides the fire and the men. But you should have been with me last Sunday morning."

The Yankee Yarnster, holding his beloved pipe in his hand, continued, "I was standing diagonally across from Peter's Pond, looking over at some cottages in Wakeby. I saw the blaze rolling down to strike the cottages, which seemed to melt into flames. I talked with Chief Bernard Ames of Osterville. He was standing right in front of the house when the fire hit. A few embers landed on the roof and the veranda, and the heat was already so intense from the advancing wall of flame that the whole house just burst into flame and disappeared."

"Yes," said Sheriff Crocker. "You get an ordinary fire, and it takes two or three hours to destroy a house. But these forest fires generate such a terrific heat, and everything in the house gets so extremely hot, that the whole house burns at the same time in less than half an hour."

Sometime later I called on State Fire Warden Joseph Peabody, who told me that the fire had burned over approximately 15,000 acres on the Cape side of the Canal. Sad to relate, the fire which destroyed so much of the beauty of Cape Cod was without question of incendiary origin. At the height of the blaze, the authorities had to call out 2,000 men, including representatives of the State Guard and the American Red Cross.

Back down Phinney's Lane and Iyanough Road I went, passing the Hyannis Airport on my left. After crossing the railroad tracks, I soon reached the junction of Main Street and Iyanough Road in Hyannis. Again passing the Mill Pond, I continued through West Yarmouth and South Yarmouth, crossing Bass River to go through West Dennis and Dennisport. The town of Harwichport was only two miles away, and there I stopped for the night.

The next day I continued to Harwich, the community which was so determined years ago that it should not be absorbed by Chatham. I had done considerable hiking because of the forest fire, and so was amused to learn that Harwich itself had been founded in 1694 by Patrick Butler, who walked all the way from Harwich to Boston to obtain the Act of Incorporation. Incidentally, Harwich is named for a seaport and market in Essex County, England.

Eighty-one years after the incorporation of the town of Harwich, news arrived that the Revolution had started at Lexington and Concord. Ebenezer Weekes of Harwich said to his son Ebenezer, "Eben, you are the only one that can be spared; take your gun and go; fight for religion and liberty." The son left at once with many others from Harwich, and fought valiantly in the Battle of Bunker Hill. The days of the Revolution were hard and bitter for Harwich, but her men did their share to help bring American victory.

There is much conflict in the religious history of Harwich. When Baptist Elisha Paine came here in 1744 he held several open-air meetings and made many converts, stating afterwards that the "pine woods of Harwich ring with Hallelujahs and Hosannas," and that when he rose up and "exhorted them to come to Christ . . . there was a screeching and groaning all over the multitude." Paine made so many converts that a meeting of ten Cape Cod ministers was held in Harwich in February 1745 to determine what action should be taken. Finally they set their thoughts down in a booklet. Admitting that Whitfield and Paine had "done some good," the desperate ministers declared that the evangelical preaching substituted schism and discord for peace and unity, and therefore the ten ministers of Cape Cod went on record that they could not give any "encouragement or countenance" to Whitfield and his followers. We must realize that it was pretty hard on the poor Congregational minister, whose duties included school teaching and doctoring, to have outsiders come in end emotionally arouse his parishioners so that many left his flock and joined the "New Lights" or the "Come Outers." Nor did the converts stop there, for many returned to the church of their former religion to stand up in meeting and attempt to disconcert the poor minister.

The Reverend Mr. Stone of Harwich was probably as upset as any other preacher on Cape Cod. All had been going well with him. In 1739 his salary had been voted as £150 and in 1742 it was raised to £200, but the very next year came the Great Awakening with all its dissension, and the brief peace of mind which the Reverend Mr. Stone had enjoyed was over. From that time on the ministers and congregations of other denominations made life hard for him.

Harwich, says a wit quoted by Dean Arthur Tarbell, is the place where you can "see the Sound and hear the sea!" In my opinion, the world's prettiest harbor is located on this same Nantucket Sound and is a man-made port. I refer, of course, to delightful Wichmere [usually spelled Wychmere—*Ed.*] Harbor, originally a freshwater pond, which has had a remarkable history. On the Department of the Interior's geological survey chart of Harwich, the spelling is "Witchmere Harbor." As far as we know, no witches were ever associated with this pleasant haven of refuge. We cannot, however, entirely ignore the possible influence of the Devil here, because many years ago it was the custom for the old sea captains to race their horses around this freshwater pond in Harwichport, and there were many thrilling encounters in which as much as fifty bushels of oats was the gambling stake.

Gambling, however, was using an instrument of the Devil, so the good ladies of Harwichport looked askance at the developments down at the pond. To add to their consternation, the Sea View Hotel was erected on the northern side of the pond, and it became the custom for

Wychmere Harbor (photo by Edward Rowe Snow)

groups to gather on the broad veranda of the hotel to watch the outcome of the races. Activities of various and sundry nature were said to have taken place in the hotel after the races were over. All in all, the good people of Harwich, South Harwich, West Harwich, and Harwichport frowned on the rapidly developing situation at the pond.

Two events then occurred, although not at the same time, which made the ladies of Harwich believe that their prayers at the Millennium Grove had been answered. The hotel burned down and the ocean broke through into the freshwater pond. Shortly afterwards a Brooklyn group said to have been led by a Doctor Wichmere purchased land around the pond and developed it. Then a man-made canal was cut through to the sea and the pond was dredged out for a harbor. Now there is a substantial breakwater which pushes its way out into Nantucket Sound and protects the inner harbor from everything but hurricanes.

Today, a visitor coming upon the harbor for the first time receives the impression that he is in fairyland, and that the harbor is really a miniature representation with tiny vessels and yachts riding at anchor. I shall never forget the first time I flew over Wichmere Harbor and looked down to see the symmetrical curves of the old pond, the opening to the sea, and the community built around the harbor. It was a distinct thrill, for to me fairyland had come true.

This time I walked around the harbor and watched the seagulls as they circled and wheeled over the bay. How free they seemed, without a care. The freedom of those gulls reminded me of another freedom which a Harwich man considered vital to his conscience over a century ago. His name was Captain Jonathan Walker. Born on a Harwich farm in 1799, he went to sea at the age of seventeen. While master of a small craft at Pensacola, Florida, in 1844, Walker was approached by seven unfortunate slaves who had run away from their masters.

"Take us to the West Indies, where we can be free," they implored him, and Captain Walker, thinking how he enjoyed his own freedom, decided to run the risk and sail for Nassau with them. Rounding the Florida coast, the captain unfortunately took ill, and also ran short of water. In a difficult position, he hailed another vessel, supposing that it was a fishing schooner. The vessel actually was a wrecking craft, the *Eliza Catherine*. Captain Phillips of the *Catherine* knew about the escape of the seven slaves, and was aware that a handsome reward of $1,000 would be paid for the capture of northerner Walker.

Captain Jonathan Walker was seized, landed ashore, placed in the pillory on the public highway, and then branded with a hot iron on his right hand with the letters "S S," indicating that he was a slave stealer! As if this were not enough, Walker was then imprisoned for eleven long months, weighted down all that time with twenty pounds of iron. Finally returning to New England, Captain Walker told his story, and so aroused the Yankees that John Greenleaf Whittier wrote his famous poem about the branded hand.

Captain Walker soon became the friend of abolitionist William Lloyd Garrison, and lectured with this great man for several years. About 1900 the house where Walker was born was moved across the town line to South Chatham. Few passersby, however, ever realize that it was there where Whittier's hero lived, about whose branded hand the poet said:

> *Hold it up before our sunshine, up against our Northern air;*
> *Ho! Men of Massachusetts, for the love of God, look there!*

Many residents of Harwich knew Barney Gould. He has a niche all his own in Cape history. Barney was the self-appointed messenger boy of Cape Cod. He would make deliveries miles away for as little as ten cents, but whenever he met anyone on the road, he would endeavor to collect a road tax from that person, and he usually succeeded, for it only amounted to two cents a year. One day a friend gave him a dime, and Barney exclaimed, "That pays you up for the next five years!" Barney ran and walked a considerable distance every day, usually starting at a dogtrot and making a grandstand finish in the same fashion, but without question he walked a good part of the way.

I visited the Brooks Library at Harwich Center. In the building there is a permanent exhibition of small statuettes originally sculptured in clay by John Rogers, who was born at Salem in 1829 and became an outstanding sculptor of his day. At about the time of the Civil War his Rogers Statuettes, as they were called, came into prominence, and for many years the little statuette groups were seen in parish houses, parlors, and public buildings. They were very popular as wedding gifts.

The Brooks Library has forty-six of these plaster casts. Miss Susan Underwood, the librarian, told me that some of the more famous groups are Lincoln, Stanton, and Grant; three of Rip Van Winkle for which Joe Jefferson himself posed; various scenes from Shakespeare's plays; Civil War battles; and one group called Checkers at the Farm. Should you believe you have a statuette by Rogers, glance at the base. If it is genuine, there will be Rogers's name on the bottom and the date he finished the statuette.

In 1880 the forty-six statuettes were presented to the Town of Harwich by Pliny Nickerson, and they now occupy an honored place in the library. Incidentally, the library is usually open one day a week, on Saturdays from 1:30 to 5:30. During July it is also open on Wednesdays at the same time.

The statuettes form one of the largest collections of Rogers's work in the world, and collectors would be willing to pay high prices to obtain them. The collection is a worthy rival to the secret collection of an important Rhode Island man. I have promised never to reveal what I saw in his museum.

The next day was Saturday. I found my friend Tom Johnson, with whom I had grown up, staying for the weekend at a home on Freeman Street. I was soon telling stories to his three sweet little daughters, and the time sped rapidly by. Finally, it was their bedtime, and I gave them my last story, that of Oscar the Whale. After they were all tucked away for the night, I spent the rest of the evening with Tom and his wife, Jean, and then went to bed around midnight.

I was now prepared for a long hike. Leaving Harwich early the next morning, I turned to the northeast on the Old County Road to Orleans, stopped at Orleans to eat, and an hour after lunch I was in East Orleans, heading for the Outer Beach, known officially as Nauset Beach on the map. Travelling steadily southward along the shore, I passed the Orleans Coast Guard building and soon could see the Old Harbor Station in the distance. I was then in the vicinity of the place where the *Sparrowhawk* had been wrecked. The *Calvin Orcutt* also met her doom nearby.

Hyannisport is, of course, often associated with the Kennedy family, and visitors today can learn about that aspect of the village's history at the John F. Kennedy Hyannis Museum.

A life-size statue of Iyanough sculpted by Davis Lewis can be seen today at the entrance to the Hyannis town green. It is believed that the chief sachem's actual name was "Yanno," but when asked his name by the Pilgrims he replied "I Yanno," which was recorded as "Iyanno" or "Iyanough." As Snow wrote, the name "Hyannis" was derived from "Iyanough."

A few years ago members of the Harwich Women's Club cleaned and restored the collection of Rogers Statuettes at the Brooks Free Library in Harwich. Rogers's works are still considered highly collectible Americana.

CHAPTER 13

Chatham, the Southern Anchor of Cape Cod

Arriving at the Old Harbor Life-Saving Station, found it deserted and evidently abandoned by the government. I walked around the structure, and thought of the many times the surfmen had plodded their lonely way along the beach to and from this structure. It was quite evident that the station would never be reestablished. Continuing along the beach southward, I finally came to the wreckage from the *Edith Nute,* which made me realize that I was just across the bay from the shipwreck mansion of "Good Walter" Eldridge on the mainland. I thought over the possibility of getting across the bay. Perhaps I could swim it.

It then was May, and the water was much warmer than when I had landed at Provincetown. But I was pretty tired, having hiked over twenty miles that day, some of it the hardest going possible, through the soft sand of Cape Cod's Outer Beach. What should I do? It was getting late, the sun was about to go down, and I had no desire to share Nauset Beach with the scores of skunks which roam there at night. I couldn't retrace my steps to Orleans, for it would be pitch dark before I'd get halfway there. After thinking it over carefully, I decided to wait for low tide, which came in half an hour, and then swim to the mainland. I scooped out a hole in the sand, placed my clothes and knapsack into a large box I found, and put it in the hole. I then donned my swimming trunks. The knapsack, incidentally, was considerably lighter than it had been six weeks before at Provincetown, for I had mailed home all my books, and many of my other belongings. Covering the box over with sand, I went down to the inner beach facing

Chatham, and waded out as far as I could. The Coast Guard station at Morris Island and Chatham Light tower were across from me as I began to swim. I didn't try to break any speed records, for I was afraid I might get a leg cramp after the long hike. I swam, drifted, and then floated on my back. Halfway across I decided that it was rather a foolish stunt, but five minutes later I had finished the 250-yard swim and was resting on the beach.

Negotiating the cut-through without difficulty, for it was dead-low water, I was soon walking north abeam of Chatham Light, which the keeper had just turned on. Good Walter's dory was there in shallow water, and after considerable effort I pushed and pulled it into deep water and began to row across to my belongings.

Landing on the Nauset Beach which I had left an hour before, I retrieved all my possessions, dressed, and returned to Walter's dory, which I rowed rapidly across to his shipwreck house in Chatham. Good Walter invited me in to warm up in his kitchen, but after a short time I decided that I should make my plans for the night, and set out for the main part of town. The night wind chilled me to the bone as I walked across town to the Wayside Inn, so after a brief meal, I engaged a room and turned in for the night.

On awakening the next morning, I read completely through Part I of William C. Smith's *History of Chatham,* which I had borrowed the night before. After breakfast I began Part II of Smith's interesting history of this town, which stands as a sentinel to protect the southeasterly part of Cape Cod.

The people of Chatham are rightfully proud of their superior location, the town's intriguing history, and the personalities associated with Chatham's activity today. Many visitors to Chatham from all parts of the country agree that the town has one of the best locations on the entire Cape.

When I went to the local library, I found several more books which included Chatham history. However, the town is especially unfortunate in this respect, for not only were most of its records burned in the great Barnstable fire of October 22, 1827, but the Congregational parsonage fire of 1865 took many more. There are, however, local records which escaped both blazes, and William C. Smith preserved much of interest in his *History of Chatham.*

In 1602 Bartholomew Gosnold visited what is now the area around Chatham near Point Gammon, where a company of Indians wearing no clothing except their loincloths came out to the *Concord,* Gosnold's bark.

Coming prepared to trade, they offered in exchange tobacco, skins, and other small articles. Nevertheless, Gosnold decided that the Indians seemed suspicious of the white men, and so sailed away and landed at Cuttyhunk Island instead, where he stayed for several weeks.

On September 5, 1606, Jean de Poutrincourt sailed from Port Royal, Nova Scotia, on a voyage of exploration and discovery, accompanied by Samuel de Champlain, an Englishman named Daniel Hay, and more than twenty others. On October 2, Champlain's vessel anchored off what is now Chatham Village. Observing many Indian fires along the shore, the white men manned a boat to go ashore, but the heavy Chatham surf breaking on the white sands so frightened them that they returned to their vessel. Thereupon, the Chatham Indians launched a canoe right into the highest waves of all, negotiated the huge combers with an ease which bespoke long experience, and safely reached Champlain's craft. Singing and making signs of happiness, they paddled around the French vessel. Through the Indian interpreter aboard the boat, they informed the Frenchmen that there was a safe way into the shore further south. On the next day Champlain's group barely crossed the dangerous shoals, dragging bottom several times.

Daniel Hay was now sent on ahead in the shallop to see if the vessel could come in the harbor, now called Old Stage Harbor. As they approached the shore a solitary Indian called to them, "Yo, yo, yo," and beckoned them to land, whereupon they did so. By sign language the Indian explained that the ship could come in and anchor without danger. Champlain and de Poutrincourt then weighed anchor, sailed into the harbor, and anchored off what is now Harding's Beach in six fathoms of water.

Champlain left us a fine sketch of Chatham in the year 1606, and it is amazingly similar to the present Chatham. Morris Island and its pond, Harding's Beach, the Oyster Pond, the Mill Pond, Monomoy, and Great Hill are almost unchanged today.

Champlain was attracted to the location, and the only objection was the dangerous sea approach to Stage Harbor. He saw more than 500 savages, dressed like the inhabitants of the oft-reported but seldom-seen Cape Cod nudist colony, with the only dress of any sort a small loincloth made of sealskin. Champlain then spoke of the farming which the Indians accomplished, and of their methods of planting corn and beans in the same hill so that the beans could use the cornstalk to climb on. Tobacco and other crops were also grown.

Champlain and de Poutrincourt attended to the repair of their rudder, which had become seriously damaged while running over the shoals. The Indians, at first, gathered around and bartered their fish, raisins, bracelets, arrows, quivers, and beans with the Frenchmen, and a friendly as well as profitable trade ensued. Finally, word of the white visitors traveled so far that literally swarms and droves of savages appeared all around them and many became troublesome. De Poutrincourt decided it would be wise to give a display of French armament strength. Swords were brandished and flourished, but it was the guns of the Frenchmen shooting through wood which their own arrows failed to pierce that amazed the Indians to the utmost and kept them in order.

This exhibition of the white man's supremacy lasted for ten days, but then trouble began in earnest. One of the Indians had stolen an axe, whereupon a Frenchman fired two shots after the fleeing natives. Shortly afterwards Sieur de Poutrincourt noticed the Indians taking down their wigwams and sending the women and children into the woods, as if something was about to happen. The Indians, evidently disturbed by the gunfire, had decided to take matters into their own hands.

Champlain tells us that in spite of this, Sieur de Poutrincourt fearlessly visited one of the cabins where the old people and the women were quartered, and freely passed out hatchets, knives, bracelets, and rings to relieve their possible fears. But it was too late. Sieur de Poutrincourt had already ordered every man aboard ship before night but several Frenchmen disobeyed, and unknown to their leader remained ashore.

Early the next morning, October 15, 1606, the savages attacked in what was actually the first known Indian onslaught against the Europeans on the New England coast. Four hundred savages, surrounding the white men who had not taken refuge on the ship, sent a deadly volley of arrows toward the camp, so that "to rise up was death," according to Champlain. The Frenchmen fled toward the bark, but it was too late. Every man was pierced with arrows. An account of the death of one follows.

> It was caused by the folly and disobedience of one whom I will not name, for that he died there; he was wont to play the braggart and because they would not let him get drunk, he had sworn, as was his fashion, that he would not return to the long boat, nor did he, for this very man was found dead face downward, with a little dog upon his back, both transfixed and transpierced by the same arrow.

Champlain and the others on the ship tried to get aboard the shallop and row it ashore, but they struck a shoal and had to wade the rest of the distance. Then the savages, seeing the Frenchmen with their guns, fled into the woods. Four Frenchmen had perished. Their dead bodies were buried on the beach, and a cross erected. Then the Frenchmen returned to the boat, and the Indians came out of the woods, tore the cross down, and disinterred the bodies. The Frenchmen again went ashore, and the Indians once more fled into the woods. The Frenchmen reinterred the four bodies.

The very next day Champlain's company sailed away from Chatham, a location they originally had named Port Fortune, but which they changed to Port Misfortune after the battle.

They later took terrible revenge on the Indians. Going ashore, they attracted a group of red men to them. Drawing their swords, the Frenchmen butchered seven Indians, cut off their heads, and took the heads aboard the vessel. A friendly chief of the Sagamore Indians, Secouden by name, was a passenger aboard the vessel, and returned to Port Royal with Champlain, of whom he was very fond. The head Secouden had captured dropped overboard, and Secouden "wept openly and aloud." The other six heads were taken ashore at Port Royal, where the vessel landed November 14, 1606.

Champlain under attack at Chatham

There were several others who called at Chatham shore before the Pilgrims came. It is almost certain that Henry Hudson, Samuel Argall, and Edward Harlow all sighted Monomoit (the old name for Chatham) as they sailed along our shores, and very probably Harlow went ashore there in 1611, for we know that he stole three Indians from their tribes somewhere in this vicinity. One of the Indians got away, cut Harlow's boat from his ship, and went ashore in it, and Harlow never did get it back. Coming just a few years after Champlain's encounter, Harlow's kidnapping of the Indians gave the relations of the English with the Cape Cod Indians a further setback.

Three years later the illustrious John Smith sailed off Chatham, but did not explore Monomoit at all. He says that "toward the south and southwest of this cape is found a long and dangerous shoale of sands and rocks, But so farre as I encircled it I found thirtie fadome water aboard the shore and a strong current . . . But the Salvages say there is no channel," so John Smith never found out, taking the Indians' word for it. Unfortunately, his lieutenant, Captain Thomas Hunt, disgraced the memory of John Smith by kidnapping Indians near Plymouth and again at Nauset, selling them into slavery at Malaga.

Then Admiral Adrian Block sailed by Chatham in 1614, followed two years afterwards by Captain Edward Brawnde. Block chartered and named Monomoy Point and Stage Harbor, calling them Vlacke Hoeck and Ungeluckige Haven. Another visitor in 1616, a French fishing captain, was wrecked with his crew, and the Indians killed them as they were caught. Finally there were only five Frenchmen left, and they were transported all around Cape Cod to the various sachems, where they were miserably treated, being fed the food of dogs and experiencing a fate worse than slavery.

That same year, 1616, brought a terrible plague to the Indians, decimating them rapidly. When Captain Thomas Dermer arrived at Cape Cod, he rescued the two survivors from the French fishing vessel, using an Indian named Squanto or Tissquantum for interpreter. Squanto, one of the Indians captured by Hunt, for some reason had never been sold into slavery, arriving in England as a person on equal footing with the other sailors, and became a servant to an English gentleman. Later he reached Newfoundland, where Dermer found him.

In the autumn of 1622 Governor William Bradford with a small crew sailed along the outer coast of Cape Cod aboard the ship *Swan*, exploring as he went. Accompanying him on this voyage was Squanto, acting as interpreter and pilot. If Squanto had not been along, Bradford and his party undoubtedly would have been massacred, as the Indians were in no mood for either kidnappings or trickery, and were ready to take revenge on any and all white men. Governor Winslow tells us that the Pilgrims "made for a harbor not far from them at a place called Man-amoycke, which they found, and sounding it with their shallop, found the channel, though but narrow and crooked, where at length they harbored their ship." Historian Smith of Chatham believed that the harbor was the old harbor opening into Pleasant Bay, closed now for many years. Squanto went at once to the rulers of the Indians there, explaining who the Pilgrims were and why they were exploring. Convinced that the Pilgrims were friendly, the Indians came out of hiding and associated with the whites, but on finding that Bradford wished to stay ashore all night, became suspicious again. Squanto quieted their fears by further discussion, and thereupon the chieftain allowed them to stay ashore that night. But they were still treated with care and suspicion.

Shortly afterwards Squanto fell ill with a bad fever, which was accompanied by a bleeding nose. He never recovered. His last words to Bradford were for the Pilgrims to pray that he might be allowed into the white man's heaven. Somewhere on a Chatham hillside is buried the remains of a great and good Indian, without whose skillful and diplomatic activities the early Pilgrim colony might have received a damage from which it would never have recovered, the massacre of Governor William Bradford and his entire party.

The further division of land on Cape Cod was prevented in March 1641 when the Pilgrims reserved this area for the "Oldcomers" of the Colony. Thus any Pilgrim who came on one of the first three vessels, the *Mayflower,* the *Fortune,* or the *Ann,* was entitled to Oldcomers' privileges. The reservation was all inclusive, extending across the Cape from sea to sea. Most of the Oldcomers also joined a group known as the "purchasers," or those who in 1627 banded together and bought from the London merchants for £1,800 their half-share in the Pilgrim colony. This allowed the Pilgrims for the first time to own outright their land in America. When I read the list of purchasers in the Chatham Public Library that May day I was pleased that two of my Pilgrim ancestors, Nicholas Snow and Stephen Hopkins, were included one after the other in the Pilgrim group which then owned the entire colony.

Of course, another ancestor, William Nickerson, knew nothing of all this when he arrived in America at Salem in 1637. Moving to Yarmouth in 1640, he represented that town on the grand jury a year later. About the year 1656, William Nickerson entered into a bargain with Mattaquason, the sachem of Monomoit, exchanging a boat for a parcel of land in what is now Chatham. When the Pilgrim fathers found out about it, they claimed it a direct violation of the rights of the purchasers, or the old comers, and ordered him to court, where he pleaded ignorance of that particular law. He was found guilty, and allowed to keep only a small part of his purchase. Year after year he continued his demands, but it was not until 1664 that he actually moved into what is now Chatham with his family. The Plymouth court decided to fine him £200, but the chief marshall, arriving at Monomoit, could not locate any property belonging to my ancestor, William Nickerson, so he returned to Plymouth and explained his failure.

The very next year the King's commissioners sat at Plymouth to hear Nickerson plead his case, and decided that his claim to a "farm of four miles square" seemed a little large, but authorized the colony court to remit his fine and allow him 100 acres. This action limiting him to 100 acres instead of a tract four miles square bitterly disappointed Nickerson, but the Pilgrims had been determined from the first to prevent his getting the full benefit of his trade, thus escaping the punishment they considered rightfully his. But there was no other way out, so he made the best of an unfortunate situation.

When Nickerson settled at Monomoit, there were forests of huge oak trees and pines covering the hillsides, while the swamps were dense thickets from which high cedars grew. In the clearings near the shore were pitched the wigwams of the red men. Here it was that sixty-year-old Nickerson moved and worked for the next thirty years. Josiah Paine of Harwich said that Nickerson lived near the head of Ryder's Cove, where Kimball Howes later built his house. We know that William Nickerson was buried on the hill above his house when he died around 1690.

Ancestor Nickerson was involved with pirates as well as Pilgrims. In the Plymouth records of October 28, 1684, I read that "William Nicarson and Samuell Bryant" were bound over to the court to explain why they helped pirate John Graham escape from Nantucket Island. As sufficient evidence was not produced against them, they were cleared. But I like to think that in the sands out on Fox Hill Island or Strong Island, there may be treasures which my ancestor, who had to answer for carrying off a pirate from Nantucket Island, might have buried.

By the time of William Nickerson's death the settlement was growing rapidly. In 1706 the residents were negotiating for a "coleg man as
cheap as they can" for a preacher. On June 11, 1712, Governor Dudley
signed an order passed in council that the "Village or District now called
Monomoit be erected into a Township and the Town called Chatham."
Thinking of Chatham in England, the residents so named the town,
probably at the suggestion of Mr. Adams, then the minister.

It is of interest to note that since Harwich would not agree to become
part of the new settlement, Chatham thus came into being with exactly
the boundaries of the original Nickerson purchases and claims, without
the addition of a foot of soil outside William Nickerson's grant.

As I walked along the Chatham streets toward the ocean, my attention was taken by a quarter board which read *Lamartine*. I could not possibly pass up such an intriguing object, so I went up on the piazza and
rang the bell. Answering the door, Miss Virginia A. Harding invited me
to come in and hear the story of the *Lamartine*. I was soon seated in the
presence of Virginia, her mother, Mrs. Heman Harding, and believe it or
not, the strangely attractive figure of a lady in a painting, whose eyes
seemed to follow me around the room. "Oh, you'll get used to that,"
said Mrs. Harding, "for we have. I'll tell you her story later. Now, what
would you like to know about the quarter board?"

My answer was typical. "Everything you can tell me."

"Well, you have come to the right house for that," proudly stated Mrs.
Harding, "for Virginia here is president and treasurer of the Eldridge
Public Library, and is on the committee which is completing Smith's
History of Chatham."

"Now mother, don't scare the man," said Virginia, but she quickly left
the room to return with a sheaf of important-looking documents.
"Here's what I have on the *Lamartine*. She was a two-masted schooner
launched at Belfast back in 1848. Registered December 23, 1848, she
sailed from New Haven to Belfast. Eight days later she took a gale from
the west northwest and rode it out. On January 10, 1849, she shipped a
sea and went over on her beam ends. They cut her masts off and she
righted. The bark *Maria,* bound for California, took off her crew, and
the ship *Angelique* picked up much of her wreckage. How the quarter
board arrived at Chatham is more or less of a mystery, but it probably
drifted ashore." I finished my notes, and then looked up at the girl with
the haunting eyes. Mrs. Harding saw that I was looking at the painting.

"Now I'll tell you about the lady with the eyes which follow you around the room," said Mrs. Heman Harding, turning slightly in her chair. "She was the sister-in-law of Captain Zenas Marston, for she married Russell Marston, Zenas' brother. Captain Zenas was a famous Hyannisport sea captain, and his brother, Russell, started the Marston Restaurants in Boston. If you look across the room, you'll see old Captain Zenas himself." Turning in my chair, I glanced behind me, and surely enough, there was a painting of a substantial-looking gentleman across the room from his sister-in-law. Incidentally, Eleanor Early says that when Captain Zenas went on a long voyage he took more than 300 shirts with him, every one of which had been carefully made at home by his wife! Then there was Captain Sumner Pierce, who brought home 700 shirts for his wife to launder.

"What about this girl with the haunting eyes?" I asked Mrs. Harding.

"Well, I don't know too much, but her maiden name was Sarah Crosby and, of course, she married Russell Marston. There is something about her, isn't there?"

I agreed at once, for Sarah Marston fascinated me. It seemed too bad we knew so little of her life.

Mrs. Harding went on with her thoughts. "There's an interesting bit about Chatham Light I have," she reminisced. "One day in the 1880s my husband, Heman, and Captain Josiah Hardy's son, Samuel, were playing near the light, when the veteran white-whiskered light keeper strode over to them. He had just finished calculations for the day, and there was a pleased expression in his face. 'I want you two boys to remember this day as long as you live,' said the captain. 'I have seen as many ships today as there are days in the year.'"

The boys never forgot it, and later when Heman married Mrs. Harding, he told her about it. It must have been a wonderful sight, those 365 barks, brigs, schooners, and ships as they sailed to all ports of the world by Chatham Light. Today, when a sail is raised from Chatham Bluff, it is considered an event, and there are almost a score of days every month when no white sail lends its enchantment to the horizon.

"Virginia, why don't you take Mr. Snow over to the old Atwood House?" suggested Mrs. Harding. "I must tell you about Mr. Atwood, before I forget it. When Captain John Atwood proposed to Aunt Marjorie, he promised her a beautiful new home if she would only become his bride, so she finally accepted his proposal and married him. Unfortunately, his talk of a new mansion seemed temporarily shelved when they moved into the old house, now the oldest in Chatham. His grandfather,

Joseph Atwood, had built it in 1752 with the help of neighbors. Marjorie asked him about the new mansion and he made the remark, now a classic, 'Margy, that was only courting talk.' But Marjorie was a determined young lady, and although she forgave him she never forgot the beautiful home of her dreams. Years later Captain Atwood allowed an ell to be built, and it is said that the lady spent most of her time in the ell of her home, thus accepting her 'new mansion' in a compromise fashion."

When we reached the Atwood House, Virginia Harding unlocked the side door and we entered. It was cold and had an unlived-in feeling, but there was much inside to interest me. A small model of the old saltworks was on the table and I spent some time figuring out how the windmill worked to pull the salt water over into the drying vats. Then the hair wreath of Rebecca Atkins caught my eye. She and her eleven children were represented there.

We went into the front room where I saw a good painting of a vessel at sea. A little faded card stuck in the frame told me that it was painted by William Mack, drowned in the *Wadena* disaster in 1902. Virginia Harding told me that Mack's mother once came to the old Atwood home and sat on the sofa in that very room. Thinking of the days when she sat on a similar sofa at home while her son was painting his picture, she decided to send the chair he used while painting to the Atwood home, and later sent the picture as well.

It was very cold in the Atwood House that May afternoon and we both kept our coats on. Soon I was examining the old records, placed there by the local historical society, for I was particularly anxious to find reference to the *Orissa,* the galley of which is in the parsonage of the Reverend Mr. Kimball in Orleans. Every mention of a shipwreck took my attention, and then suddenly I found what I was after.

"Here it is," I shouted. "It's the *Orissa,* all right, but look at the way it is spelled." We read together the entry made in 1857:

The spelling *Oricea* did not seem the same as the *Orissa,* so I determined to find out for myself just what the newspapers of the period said about the incident. But I didn't get the newspaper of that particular year until the following week at the Harvard College Library, where I found out that the *Oricea* and the *Orissa* were the same vessel.

Little is known today about the ship *Orissa.* I have mentioned elsewhere the voyages which Captain Joshua Sears and his wife took on her. Built at Medford, she was owned by Atkinson, Rollins, and Richards. Frank T. Rollins of that firm sailed from Calcutta as supercargo, but was saved when the shipwreck occurred at Nauset Beach. First Mate Prentiss of Marblehead and three other sailors were drowned. Captain Sears of the *Orissa* said afterwards that Mr. Prentiss was a "gentleman and a good sailor." The storm in which the *Orissa* was lost was the greatest since Minot's Light had crashed into the sea six years before. All up and down the coast there were terrible shipwrecks which caused great loss of life. The *Tedesco* came in at Swampscott, and the *Emeline* near Highland Light, with not a single soul saved on either ship. The *New Empire* and the *California* hit at Cohasset, and the *Judge Hathaway* piled ashore at Scituate. More than thirty vessels were completely destroyed in this 1857 gale.

The next interesting entry in the old diary was an item about the weather:

Jan. 23 1857. Cold Friday 15° below zero.

A few lines below was a remark about the lighthouse:

December 15, 1879. The Old South Lighthouse went down the bank between 12:00 and 1:00 O'clock.

Then the final line which I copied:

July 13, 1880. Harding's Beach light lighted for 1st. time today.

Enoch Eldridge was the first keeper of the Harding's Beach Light. He was succeeded by George Folger, who remained at the beacon for sixteen years. Other keepers were Alfred Howard and a Mr. Gunderson, whose son took his place. Several people told me that one of the last keepers committed suicide at Harding's Beach Light, but his name was not known.

In the Atwood House we made another discovery—a short poem of four lines written in 1823 by Captain Zenas Nickerson in his book:

Steal not this book my honest friend
For fear the gallows will be your end
This book is one thing, hemp is another
Take not the one for fear of the other.

We spent another twenty minutes browsing through the old records filed in the Atwood House, and then we found an old picture of Chatham Lights.

"Perhaps the record books of some of the old keepers are here," I wondered aloud, but Virginia Harding told me that there were not any in the building. However, she did remember there was a journal or diary kept by famous Captain Josiah Hardy, the same lighthouse keeper who years ago told her father Heman of the 365 vessels sighted in one day. And so the home of Captain Hardy's granddaughter became my next objective. After putting the papers and pictures back in order, we locked up the Atwood House and started for the home of Grace Hardy. Ten minutes later we arrived at Miss Hardy's home.

"Oh, yes, I remember your book on lighthouses," said Miss Hardy. "Well, why didn't you say something about my grandfather in your lighthouse book?" was her question. I explained that in every book

Captain Josiah Hardy
of Chatham Light

which I had written, there were always a few parts which would have been better had some missing diary or absent journal turned up in time. After the book was published, it would be read by the unknown party who had the missing information. The party was willing and even pleased to furnish it, but, of course, it was then too late, as the book was printed. I had not known of the diary or journal or where to find the information in time.

"I'd be glad to include your grandfather's career in my Chatham section of the Cape Cod book," I replied, and in this she readily acquiesced.

"Grandfather was keeper of the light from 1872 until 1900, and I have his diary, although it is falling apart and going to pieces from my lending it to so many people. I'll show it to you, however," and her eyes flashed as she got up to bring back the precious journal of Captain Josiah Hardy. Yes, indeed, the little book was in need of rebinding, but I spent a happy hour reading the pages of the interesting lighthouse diary.

Keepers of other years were Samuel Nye, Joseph Loveland, Samuel Stimson, and Simeon Nickerson. Nickerson's widow took over the duties of keeper at his death, and she was followed during the Civil War by Captain Charles Smith. In 1871 Josiah Hardy became assistant keeper at Chatham Twin Lights, and on December 6, 1872, he assumed his duties as head keeper, a post which he was to retain until the end of the century. Just before Hardy had come to Chatham Light, a great physical change occurred in Chatham.

In the days after the Civil War there were many houses built to the eastward of Chatham Light, and there was at one time a store half a mile to the eastward. But on November 15, 1870, a terrific northeast storm hit the Cape causing extremely high tides and a dangerous surf. As the day lengthened, the storm grew worse, and fishermen everywhere feared for their craft. Suddenly the serious news reached Chatham Village that the beach had broken through, with waves washing under the piles of Hardy's Wharf. It was the beginning of the end, as far as the two old lighthouse towers were concerned. At the time of the breakthrough, the edge of the cliff was 228 feet from the brick lighthouse towers.

Four years went by. Keeper Hardy wrote that the 23rd of November, 1874, was "a day of storms, ushered in by a northeast wind and high course of tides," adding that the bank had suffered severely during the storm. Ten days later Hardy measured the bank to find it 190 feet from the South Tower, commenting on the fact that since 1870 thirty-eight feet had been lost, or "an average of not quite ten feet a year." A more serious note is seen in the next entry which we quote, that of November 15, 1875: "It has washed away on an average of fifty feet a year opposite the house of Captain Josiah Hardy and abreast of the Lights just thirty-one feet a year."

Each month Keeper Hardy faithfully made his measurements of the doomed bank. Each month Hardy reported it to the lighthouse authorities, but nothing was done to shore up the banking. "On February 17, 1877, Mr. Lunt, a member of the Harbor Commission visited this station today to ascertain the extent of the washing away of the shore line." Just eleven days after Mr. Lunt's visit the distance from the bank to the South Tower was only ninety-five feet, and on March 31 eleven feet more had fallen! This so discouraged the government that it was decided to abandon all future efforts to save the lighthouse station.

On April 25, 1877, Frederick Tower, assistant engineer of the Lighthouse Board arrived in Chatham to arrange and lay out the grounds for the new lighthouses across the street on the west side of the road. Begun in May, the towers were built rapidly, for by then the cliff had reached a point seventy-seven feet from the old South Tower. Forty-two feet high, the new towers were one hundred feet apart, with the keeper's dwelling located between. The work was finished September 6, 1877, when the lenses were moved from the old towers to the new towers, and were lighted the same night.

The lights finished, work was rushed on the keeper's dwelling, and his family thankfully moved into the new house in November, when the hungry bank had reached a point less than fifty feet from their old home.

The next year the lighthouse tender Myrtle sent ashore two barrels of kerosene and new fixtures to supplant the old fixtures which burned lard oil. On the night of July 4, 1878, kerosene oil was used for the first time in Chatham lighthouse history, and all the fishermen and townspeople rejoiced at the great improvement in the glow.

But the relentless Atlantic Ocean's tricky currents accelerated their activities, and on June 30, 1879, Keeper Josiah Hardy wrote in his diary that the old South Tower was only seven feet, four inches from the bank, having washed away more than twenty-three feet in less than a year.

On September 30 that same year the South Tower stood twenty-seven inches from the edge of the cliff, and exactly two months later one-third of the same lighthouse was out over the edge. The townspeople visited the scene daily, speculating on the exact time when the great tower would drop over the bank, and it is said that many bets on that subject were placed by the fishermen sailing up and down the coast.

The spectacular event took place at exactly 1:00 in the afternoon of December 15, 1879. There had been a terrible storm that year, and while it helped the destruction of the South Tower, it seemed to aid in the formation of a new barrier beach. The old cistern went over the bank the following July, but after that the cliff fell away at a slower rate. It was not until March 26, 1881, that most of the North Tower fell over, leaving a small cone-shaped pile of red bricks and mortar. The complete lighthouse foundation never did go over the cliff, for in the presence of Miss Virginia A. Harding, on that May day of 1946, I located several of the red bricks at the top of the cliff.

The reason for the cliff's halting its rapid pace of washing away can be found in Captain Hardy's remarks of 1881. He tells us that the barrier beach was then making down from the north to reach a point nearly opposite the lights, which if continued would protect the shore. And so it did, for today the sand stretches out substantially in all directions from the foot of the old lighthouse. A brave soul has even built a house on the east side of the same road which many considered doomed back in the 1870s.

Old Chatham Lights, around 1865

Retiring in 1900, Captain Josiah Hardy was succeeded by Captain Charles Hammond, who died in service at the twin lights. Keeper Allison was in charge at the twin lights when the northern light was moved to Nauset in 1923.

The last regular keeper of Chatham Light was George T. Gustavus, who retired October 20, 1945. I located his home a few streets from the lighthouse, but he had moved the month before to East Harwich, where he was then living on Queen Ann's Road. After a long journey I found his house, and we talked for more than an hour. There were many dates and experiences he wanted to make sure of, so he wrote out an account of his career in the service.

George T. Gustavus, last regular keeper of Chatham Light (courtesy of Joan Kenworthy)

I was born September 1, 1884, in Vinland, Wisconsin. I enlisted in the U. S. Navy on February 5, 1903, at the age of eighteen, served four years as Yeoman on the old Battleship Iowa. *After coming out of the Navy I worked on a Government Boat in Wisconsin. This work did not appeal to me so I came East again to be near the salt water which I had grown to love. I went to Rockport, Mass., where I was married to Miss Mabel G. Norwood, a young lady whom I had met while the Fleet was anchored off Rockport in 1905. We were married July 1, 1907. I entered the Lighthouse service April 1, 1910, going to Tarpaulin Cove, Naushon Island, and our second child was born on April 5, 1910. Later I was transferred to Eastern Point Light, Gloucester, Mass. Two children were born at this station, then I was transferred to Thatchers [Thacher or Thachers] Island Light Station, Cape Ann, Mass. One child was born while at Thatchers Island— while on Thatchers we had to board the school children on the main land during school season. From Thatchers Island was transferred to Cuttyhunk Light Station, where we spent seven years. Three children were born here. Then I was transferred to Bird Island Light Station, East Marion, Mass. Our last son was born while at this station. When Bird Island Station was discontinued, I was transferred to Dumpling Rock Light Station off Salters Point, New Bedford.*

From there we were transferred to Prudence Island Light Station, Sandy Point, Prudence, R. I., at which station I lost my wife and youngest son in the hurricane of 1938. The station dwelling was on the low level at the Sandy Point. Many summer folk had cottages near and around the Light dwelling; our nearest neighbor, retired Keeper Thompson, who had been stationed at this light for 25 years, had a nice little cottage next to the Station dwelling called the "Snug-Harbor." On the day of the storm, he and Mr. and Mrs. Lynch, summer folk, came rushing into the Station dwelling. Mr. Thompson said that he had lived there for 25 years and that the house would stand any blow that would strike. Those folks, my wife and son and I were caught inside by the tidal wave and after two 17-foot seas of water along with plenty of wind hit, we were caught like rats in a trap. We all rushed up stairs, when the house broke up we were all thrown into the rushing waters—I found myself inside a cottage on the Island about ½ mile from where the station dwelling had been. A lad living on the Island followed me down the shore. When he saw me near the cliffs, he stuck a timber down into the water and I clamped the death grip on it. Then he and others hauled me out. I was the only member that got out of that dwelling alive—my wife was found a few days later on the beach near Newport. I never found the boy. Keeper Thompson, Mr. and Mrs. Lynch were found on the Island shores about a week later. The first thing we done after getting out, was to see that the light was attended. We strung a wire from the Electric Light building that was near the light station and got a light going; then I began looking for the wife and son, whom the neighbors informed were safe and taken care of. I knew better. They told me the next day how things really stood.

I was transferred to Nobska Point Light in 1939. From there I was transferred to Chatham. In April 1943 I enlisted as C.P.O., U.S. Coast Guard, still remaining on as lightkeeper. I was in the Brighton Marine Hospital for an operation in 1945, where I met my good pal, Arthur A. Small, who also lost his wife in the same September 1938 hurricane. Queer world this is, for Small was the keeper I went into service with and later on he came to Thacher's Island with me as my assistant. Maurice Babcock was also my assistant at Thacher's Island.

I retired from service October 20, 1945. I guess the world does not owe me much; have to make the best from now on. I was married again in 1943. My wife Edith is my good companion to look after things. The children are all in other parts, I'm grand-daddy quite a number of times.

George T. Gustavus

Chatham residents and summer visitors as well have a place in their hearts for the familiar lighthouse on the bluff. Long may its flash warn the mariners off the coast as well as make happy the hearts of those who see its gleam from the shore.

Here is a fitting conclusion to our remarks about Chatham Light, a quotation from Carol Wight's poem, "The Lights O' Chatham Town":

Over the world wherever I fare
Sea-roving up and down
Forever in my heart I bear
The Lights Of Chatham Town.

I hiked out of town to South Orleans to visit the well-known John Kenrick's cottage, said by many to be a perfect example of Cape Cod architecture. John Kenrick built the house in 1792 after returning from a voyage on which he discovered the Columbia River. Leaving Lieutenant Robert Gray to explore the Columbia, he returned home, circumnavigating the globe. It was John Kenrick who began the fur trade for the United States. After studying the lines of the cottage, I returned to Chatham itself.

Over in another part of town, down a road which ends at the Mill Pond outside the home of Mrs. Joseph Shattuck, stands a valiant lady, in winter and summer, snow, rain, and sleet. She is the figurehead of the old *Altamaha,* wrecked years ago. The figurehead was originally on the *Altamaha* when she was known as the *Gypsy Queen.* At that time the figurehead had two arms, one of which held a black cat. That arm is at present missing from the figurehead. Mrs. Shattuck told me that the *Altamaha* was wrecked about thirty-five years ago on Monomoy Beach. The figurehead was acquired by her father, E. Frank Lewis of Lawrence, Massachusetts. I respectfully stood by the side of the figurehead for a few minutes before I turned back for my journey to the lighthouse cemetery.

There was the sharply pointed Mack monument, standing perhaps thirty feet high, in memory of the twelve men who perished in the Monomoy disaster of March 17, 1902. Two barges, the *Wadena* and the *Fitzpatrick,* had been stranded on Shovelful Shoal off Monomoy Point. All of the crews were taken ashore, and later when wreckers went aboard the *Wadena,* another storm caught them unawares. The men became frightened and flew a distress flag. Captain Eldridge of the Monomoy Life-Saving Station went out with his crew in the rough seas and managed to reach the *Wadena,* where he took the frantic wreckers off. When a wave broke right into the surfboat, the wreckers became panic-stricken and in the confusion the surfboat overturned. One by one the various occupants of the lifeboat went to their death, until only Surfman Ellis remained on top of the overturned lifeboat. His account written later is one of the stirring epics of the sea, telling how he found courage and strength to hold on until rescued by Captain Elmer F. Mayo, who rowed a makeshift dory to the scene and later landed Ellis safely on the Monomoy Beach. The drama of this disaster and rescue caused nationwide interest, and $36,583.52 was raised for the families of those drowned.

The monument was put up in 1908 by members of the Mack family in memory of the Mack boy, his four associates, and the seven members of the Monomoy Life-Saving Station who perished with them.

Standing at the graves in what Good Walter calls the "potter's field," I was told by Virginia A. Harding that in 1899 her father as selectman of Chatham authorized the last burial here, for the undertaker told him there was no more room. The bodies of so many shipwrecked sailors had been buried here that one might say the sea had claimed every burial plot for its own.

The only gravestone in the mariners' cemetery behind the Mack monument marks the place where Peter Cambell of Turk's Hill was buried. The inscription tells us he was from the brig *Oriska,* and died in February 1846. I was interested in whether or not this might be the same vessel which ran ashore about that time, the galley of which is still preserved as part of the Reverend Mr. Kimball's parsonage at Orleans. I later discovered that it was not.

One of the most unusual gavels in all the world was presented to Captain Oscar Nickerson on the occasion of Captain Nickerson's twenty-fifth anniversary as town moderator. The gavel is made from the bark *Elizabeth,* the bark *Owhyhee,* the schooner *Calvin B. Orcutt,* the pilot boat *Haddock,* and a cedar stump.

The head of the gavel is from boxwood, part of the cargo from the Swedish bark *Elizabeth.* The rest of the cargo was castile soap and wine. When the men from Chatham Village got out to the wreck, crew members were breaking open the wine to let it run out of the scuppers and lighten the ship. Tinkham, one of the Chatham Villagers, stood up as the Chatham dory was rowed alongside, and noticed the scuppers pouring wine. He put his southwester underneath the stream, filled it, and shouted, "Here, boys, let's have a drink." Afterwards a schooner came in to investigate and also ran aground. Both the *Elizabeth* and the schooner were later got off.

The handle of the gavel is from a red cedar stump from the old forest where Crab Ledge is today. A metal plate around the handle is made from copper taken from the famous brig *Owhyhee,* which came out of the sand about thirty years ago after having been buried since around 1826. When she was coming out of the sand Captain Herbert Eldridge sent word up the beach to Good Walter, and he and others secured many copper spikes and considerable metal from the keelson, which was twelve by thirteen inches in size.

The *Owhyhee* is the oldest wreck on Chatham Beach of which modern records actually exist. Built at the Mystic, Connecticut, shipyards at the turn of the century, the *Owhyhee* came ashore on Chatham Beach about 1826. One of her earlier captains had been Josiah Richardson, who later went on to greater heights while master of the McKay-built *Stag Hound*. In 1853 Richardson went down with his ship, the *Staffordshire*.

The gavel also has an inscription on the handle made from a spike of the *Calvin B. Orcutt*. Another ring was taken from the old pilot boat *Haddock*. The gavel is indeed an interesting bit of Cape Cod shipwreck history.

My next visit was at the Wight home. Dr. Wight invited me in. His wife was fixing a huge, bulky, rocking chair and before I left, the doctor and I carried it out into the kitchen so she could work on it properly. On my way back from the kitchen he took me into their large parlor or studio, where their son Frederick's painting hangs. One life-size painting of his mother is balanced by a fine character study of one of the last sailmakers of Chatham, Charles Andrew Howes. The doctor has written many poems concerning the Cape and its traditions, and we talked about several of them, including the one about the Chinese bride who returned to Cape Cod with her husband, the man whose life she saved. Nevertheless, she was snubbed by her neighbors and died of a broken heart.

"How did the hurricane affect you?" I queried.

"The storm of 1944 was about twice as bad in Chatham as the blow of '38," said Dr. Wight. "We had a terrible time at Stage Harbor with the tidal wave sweeping right across our property. The wind was like the teeth of a rake, certain parts of Stage Harbor getting it severely and other sections seemingly ignored. The wind hit 105 miles an hour that evening. This house was not affected at all, but the roof went sailing right off our barn, and the barn was built just as strong as the house. The wind traveled in streaks. The building where my wife has her murals now was badly wrecked, but I jacked it up and it's all right today."

"Are those your lobster pot buoys down on the fence?" was my next question.

"No, they belong to Harry Bearse next door. He paints them the way no fisherman would ever do, believe me. Let's take a walk over to the Champlain marker and down the road."

We walked across the road and over to the Champlain monument. I was pleased to see it and think that here, back in 1606, the great

Champlain stood. "I built that marker myself," proudly stated Carol Wight, "and I remember the various things we had to put in it. It was getting pretty hard, mixing all that cement, so my wife gave me a dozen bean pots and in they went. I suppose some future archeologist will find the crumbling ruins and deduce that Champlain introduced bean pots in Chatham."

We crossed over the old break in the road where the 1944 hurricane had ripped it apart, and went into the little Wight shack. Here was a varied assortment of objects saved from the tidal wave which swept in that September afternoon. A typewriter, a bit of chain from Admiral Byrd's vessel, a life preserver from a torpedoed London steamer, the *M.V. Sebastian,* the shattered fragments of an Indian's skull found on the property, possibly one of the natives killed by Champlain's men, and a shelf containing an inscription in Greek, ΧΡΟΝΟΣ ΑΙΩΝΑ ΜΙΜΟΥ-ΜΕΝΟΣ, which translated means "Time, the imitator of eternity," a quotation from Plato.

I then walked across to see the Bearse lobster buoys, and certainly found them an impressive collection. They were also pushed far and near during the gale, but the collection now seems as large as ever.

Walking back to the house, I asked Mrs. Wight if I might visit her rightfully famous murals, and she suggested that I go over to the special building which now houses them. Formerly the murals were placed in the Congregational Church, but certain members of the congregation objected and the murals were removed to the Wight building at Stage Harbor. The murals are truly inspiring, and I was deeply moved by the symbolism of Christ addressing the people from a Chatham dory. Mrs. Wight, who paints under her maiden name of Stallknecht, has included many of the Chatham residents in her modern-day interpretation of the return of Christ. Thus she has it appear that Jesus would not be dressed in the conventional white garments of Biblical times, but would come to us in everyday modern clothing.

Among other impressive murals in the building are paintings of various Chatham selectmen, Joseph Lincoln, Mr. and Mrs. Heman Harding and their daughter, Virginia, Abraham Lincoln, Franklin Roosevelt, Leverett Saltonstall, and various characters depicting the Boy Scouts, Girl Scouts, and the Masons. Taken all in all, the entire exhibition will be long remembered by anyone who visits it.

Dr. Wight and I walked around his house. "My garden is in the center of an old Indian camping ground," said the doctor. "I would often get my boy to weed the garden by suggesting that he might find arrow-heads." The flint probably was brought down here from Maine by the red men. They would heat the flint and then allow drops of water to fall on the flint to chip it off.

I recalled a question I had planned to ask. "Dr. Wight," I began, "I heard a story once that I believe comes from you about a marriage of convenience. As I remember it, in your poem you speak of an old Cape Cod widower who married late in life, and his new wife reminded him of his departed comrade. Could you tell me a little more about it?"

"Well," said the good doctor, "I don't remember all the details after so many years, but as I recall it a Cape Codder named Winston, over eighty at the time, was getting sick of keeping his own house, and of course missed his wife dearly. Finally he decided to marry again, choosing a lady of seventy-eight. After they were married he still mourned for the first wife, but his second mate was philosophical about it." Dr. Wight later gave me a copy of the poem he wrote about Winston and his wife, and I quote two stanzas of it below:

We called on the bride who was seventy-eight
And neat and sweet and dear
And the house was just immaculate
But Winston didn't appear.
"He's up in the bedroom," she said, "poor lad,
He'll be down when his tears are run;
I let him alone when he's feeling bad;
He's crying for number one."

About a century ago Isaiah and Simeon Harding had a store over by the beach. They sold out their business in 1865 to their brother, Andrew Harding. The previous year Andrew Harding had started a store on Water Street, but combined the two when he bought out Isaiah and Simeon Harding.

Anxious to find the original building where Andrew Harding had his famous general store, I went down Main Street until I reached a building which Good Walter Eldridge told me was formerly the store. It had been changed some years ago into a residence.

Two generations ago, however, the general store of genial Andrew Harding was one of the landmarks on all Cape Cod. Around it Chatham Village was built. Out in front was a long plank, where the sea captains

Men of Chatham at Uncle Andrew Harding's store, July 1911

and others would sit and swap stories. Andrew Harding called it his "Anxious Seat," for reasons known only to him. In the evening, after the last yarn had been told, the men would go home one by one, until only Andrew was left to close up the store. Then, on stormy nights the shout often echoed up and down the streets of the village, "Ship ashore, vessel ashore," which meant that every able-bodied man in the town should get up and go down on the beach. Late one day there was a fearful wreck, and ten or twelve colored men were brought in, frozen and cold, but no one was willing to put them up. Kindly Andrew Harding placed blankets and pillows on his parlor floor, and there the poor Negroes spent the night.

I returned to Good Walter Eldridge's house on the beach. The visit which I made to this Cape Cod man's home was a never-to-be-forgotten experience. He lives on Chatham Beach perhaps 250 yards to the northward of the lighthouse itself in a two-story house which he built from the wreckage of seventeen different shipwrecks. Renting dories and sailboats in the summer keeps him busy, but in the winter he hibernates most of the time, coming out occasionally at low tide to dig clams for his cat and himself.

As he is among the last of Chatham's real mooncussers, I asked him if he had ever heard of Edward Holman, probably Chatham's first

Good Walter Eldridge (photo by Edward Rowe Snow)

Eldridge's home, constructed of seventeen shipwrecked vessels (left to right: Josselyn Eldridge, Walter Eldridge, Donald Snow) (photo by Edward Rowe Snow)

beachcomber. Good Walter had to admit Holman was unknown to him, so I told him the story of this earliest of all Chatham mooncussers, who made his find on the beach in the fall of 1641.

Edward Holman discovered a chest of goods thrown up on the Monomoit shore from some unknown shipwreck. An honest beachcomber, he took the chest to Yarmouth, and later to Plymouth where it was turned over to the public authorities, but not until Holman had presented a strange bill for his and others' services in connection with the shipwreck chest. Besides charging five shillings for transporting the chest to Yarmouth, his bill was eight more shillings for landing it at Plymouth. His fee for an Indian "at boat side" was six shillings, and a hatchet which he gave the red man came to one shilling, six pence. To a Mr. Simpkins, "for washing & drying of the goods," sixteen shillings were allowed. Thus he set the example followed by the next three centuries of Chatham history—he saw that his experience on the beach in finding shipwreck goods paid him something substantial for his trouble.

We stood there talking about shipwrecks, and from time to time Walter would bring in pieces of driftwood which he poked into the kitchen stove. Somehow we both agreed that it should have been a little warmer that May afternoon. Good Walter soon had the temperature warm enough inside, but I thought of my walk over to the Wayside Inn, and it made me shiver. Good Walter poked at the fire a little, and then came over and sat at the table across from me, glancing significantly around him.

"Getting dark, isn't it?" he began. "I always go to bed when the sun goes down."

But I was not to be defeated so easily. I knew that he wanted me to leave, but I had much to ask him.

"Haven't you any candles or lamps?" I asked him.

"Well, yes, I bought a candle a few months ago. Got it here somewhere."

"How about lamps?" was my next question, and he showed me a row of lamps on the shelf.

"Got enough lamps," he said, "but you have to have oil for them. I haven't had any oil for years. But I'll try to find the candle for you," and he disappeared into the parlor of his shipwreck mansion. Five minutes later he returned, bearing a long, tapered candle and a tarnished candlestick.

"Here, this ought to do," he suggested triumphantly, and lit a match. A substantial glow illuminated the kitchen, and I turned hopefully to my notes. "Say," said Walter, "I just remembered a story about the last lumber craft to come ashore here. After she hit, Wes Eldridge was eating dinner and saw something waving in the water. It was a man's hand from the wreck, and Wes didn't finish his dinner.

"I put so many parts of wrecks into this building that I've lost track of the number. I guess there are about seventeen. There was the *Wyoming*. In your shipwreck book you say no one ever saw what happened to her, but I did. She was a big six-master and I saw her anchored out there with the *Cora Cressy*. The *Cora Cressy* got under way and beat out to sea, but the *Wyoming* was caught in the northeaster. There was no rain the first day, and we could see her out there with the seas going over her, four miles from us. That night she broke up and all the crew was lost. The next day we could see the masts sticking up like buoys. The coal sank to the bottom and even now there is a lot of it around. The anchors, chain, and windlass are still out there."

Walter seemed quite willing to accept the novelty of the lighted candle when his bedtime had come and gone, but suddenly he rushed for the window and yanked down the shade. "They'll think I'm sick or counting my money if they see a light here," was his explanation. Just then there was a scratching at the window.

"Oh, that's Tom Tiger," said Good Walter. "I'll let him in," and a moment later a large cat jumped across to the kitchen table on the other side of the room. "Tom Tiger only eats clams," said Walter, "but right now Tom's going catting, and I'm feeding him beef for strength. I got him two years ago from Mrs. Stebbins.

"But we were talking about wrecks. I was in the Chatham Life-Saving Station when the *Calvin Orcutt* was lost, serving in place of Dan Harding for a month. I had the first watch from four to eight up in the station, and heard them talking about the wreck. Then Frank Hamilton found the boat. We went over the next morning across the harbor and landed on the beach. What a mess it was! Braddy Bloomer found a man the next morning. Poor Braddy, they found him dead later on the beach himself. Well, they kept looking for the *Orcutt*'s bodies until one man got jumpy and had to quit. (The wreckage from the *Jason* looked just like a man's body when it came ashore.) I guess they found six bodies from the *Orcutt* altogether, and most of them are up in the potter's field near the Mack monument. There are about sixty or seventy drowned sailors buried there, and only one has a gravestone. They say he was a cook.

"When the *Orcutt* was wrecked someone found the captain's letter and read it. He said in his letter that he wasn't going to sea anymore. And he never did. The other bodies are in the great hole out there. There's a deep hole out off the bar where all the bones seem to go. We never find the skulls, though, for they seem to roll away."

The men who watch the Chatham beaches, Good Walter and many of the others who live near or along the beach, believe a ship or vessel sanded in periodically comes out of the sand. Such a craft is the *Emperor,* lost a few years before Good Walter was born in 1870. When she came up on the beach, Andrew Harding and George Andrew Taylor built a house from her hull on the shore. The wreck was due to be coming out of the sand again, according to Good Walter.

"Say, I got pieces of the *Wentworth,* the *Albertina,* the *Edith Nute,* the *Dorothy Palmer,* and the *Owhyhee* in this house," reminisced Walter, as he fed his cat large helpings of cut-up beef cubes. "The *Dorothy Palmer* was quite a sight, but no one drowned aboard her. She came ashore at Monomoy about thirty years ago and I got the whole top of her house. I built the house the year after the *Nute* came in, just about twenty-three years ago.

"Over a century ago, the *Owhyhee* was wrecked. People talked about it for years, and about twenty-five years ago we decided it was due to come out. Ellis telephoned up one day she was on her way out, and we went down. All copper fastenings, and we got there in time. Here's a present for you," and Good Walter handed me a long copper spike, part of the *Owhyhee* itself.

"There was a funny one when the Italian bark came in, loaded with wine. The crew knocked the barrels in to float the bark off, and our boys went out there just as everything was going on. The Italian mate came out with a gun, for he thought we were pirates. Then another Swedish brig went to pieces and everyone got some brandy and gin. My uncle got acting a little foolish from the brandy, and mother says, 'Father, come here, John's acting foolish.'

"One night everyone was up in Andrew Harding's store on Main Street. It was full of men in southwesters, all of them talking at once. My older brother, Josselyn, ran into the store and yelled, 'Boat ashore.' The store emptied at once and they'd all run out to find that their oars had been hid. There really wasn't any boat ashore, but if there was, we'd get there ahead of the regular life-saving crew most of the time.

"One day Anson Bloomer, a big powerful man (nothing could stop him), arrived a little late and most of us were in the dory. He tried to take a short cut to the beach, over Uncle David Gould's property. Uncle David had covered his henhouse over with a big fish net so the hens wouldn't escape, and Anson ran full tilt into the coop and net and kept on going. Arriving at the beach, his movements were somewhat hampered, so we yelled at him, 'What the devil are you doing?' He finally crawled out of the wreckage and came along. The life-saving days are gone now, though. They've got young boys in the Coast Guard and some of them turn over dories like girls do.

"Sometimes it's a lonely walk along the beach. We stir up a loon and what a strange cry they make! We'd think it a ghost if we didn't know. One poor boy years ago bumped into a giant seal which weighed all of eight or nine hundred pounds.

"One night another surfman, resting in the halfway house, felt a strange rubbing against the house, which scared him badly. Finally he mustered up enough courage to go outside and look, for he couldn't stay in the shack all night, and to his surprise he found that it was an old horse, wandering along the beach. Another source of possible fright at night on a lonely beach is the grass, which rolls itself into a ball and sometimes comes tearing along the beach to scare you. Many times barrels and baskets chase each other during a heavy wind, and if you hadn't a flashlight you might imagine almost anything is after you."

It was then really late, and I felt ashamed of myself for keeping Good Walter up so many hours beyond his accustomed bedtime. Gathering my belongings together, I said goodbye. I then started back toward Main Street in Chatham, and shortly afterwards went into the Eldridge Taxi Stand where I met Mrs. Josephine Starkweather. Also in the Taxi Stand was Ralph E. Cahoon, who was on crutches. He was interested in the fact that I was writing a book about Cape Cod.

"Don't forget the *Onandaga*, which was wrecked on the beach about 1906 or 1907, in the winter," said Cahoon. She stayed there for many a week. The cargo was gradually unloaded on the shore in the daytime and would disappear in a strange fashion at night. A man known as Wicked Walter worked on the cargo.

"Everyone has to watch everyone else at a shipwreck or any other unusual activity on the beach. When the sardines were coming in, I remember watching one man crouching over a pail dropping sardines in and a man behind him reaching between the other's legs in front and stealing the sardines as fast as his unknowing neighbor filled the pail.

"All sorts of cargoes come ashore here. I remember the potatoes we got from the ocean. Once when we tried to bring a big load of hay across the bay, it capsized and all our efforts were in vain.

"I used to be the telegraph operator in the tower on the hill. We would report for all owners of ships, but that was before the canal went through. We always had a man in the cupola. The house is still standing at the corner of Main Street and Millpond Road, but the cupola was torn down just a few weeks ago. I went there in 1899. The treads to the tower were worn thin as paper by the climbing we did on them year after year. By the way, you've heard of the two Walter Eldridges, and their nicknames, Good Walter and Wicked Walter. Why, I remember a third Walter Eldridge who committed suicide while captain of a steamer from Boston to Baltimore."

The next day I went out to the West Chatham Airport, where I met the airport manager, Wilfred J. Berube, and Pilot Ted Weinz. Ted took me up on a tour of Chatham, Monomoy Beach, and Nauset Beach. Flying out over the Chatham beach, I glanced down at several remains of shipwrecks showing up through the clear water. The old timbers of the British privateer, if privateer she had been, interested me. Already an anchor and a chest of money had been pulled up to the surface from her wreckage in the 1870s. The money fell into the sea again when a line parted and was buried by a subsequent storm, but two cannon, now on the estate of James Stuart Smith at North Chatham, were tangible reminders that probably much more of value remained down in her hull, now about fifteen feet below the surface. Flying out over the cut, I spied more timbers on the beach there, possibly the wreckage of one of the ships which Good Walter is waiting for.

Pilot Ted Weinz told me of the day he landed on the beach at low tide with George Bearse, who purchased the Monomoy Point Light property when the government gave up the lighthouse there some years ago. On entering the house they noticed evidence that navy planes had machine-gunned the old building, for several bullets had penetrated right through the dwelling. One bullet had come down through the wall to knock out a rung from a rocking chair. Another shot had gone through the building to lodge itself in a four-by-four beam. They cut the bullet out and thus identified it. Ted told me that there were several places along the beach where cub planes could land without any trouble. We returned to the West Chatham Airport and I walked back to town thinking of my plane trip over the nearby area. If you wish to see a different Chatham, one you can understand from the mapmakers' viewpoint, take a flight over the village in a plane. You will never forget it.

The next morning my cousin, Captain John G. Snow, arrived from Rockland, Maine, for I was to take him over to the wreckage of the *Edith Nute,* on which he had many strange adventures as quartermaster some years ago. An hour later John, Good Walter, and I were rowing, across the bay. We landed on Nauset Beach and started across the sand. First we found one of the hatch covers of the *Nute,* which John identified. Then we saw the big boom, and that put John in a reminiscent mood.

Captain Snow sat down on the boom to tell us the *Nute*'s history. The vessel was built as a four-master in Rockland by I. L. Snow & Company with Richard and Israel Snow the active builders. When she was partly in frame, Herbert L. Nute arrived at Rockland to announce that plans had been changed, and the four-master became a two-masted diesel-motor ship. The *Nute* was raised from her original model so that when she was fully loaded the schooner lines were under water.

Launched in 1917, the *Nute* was rigged with two masts, square sails, trysails, and jibs. With two yards, one on each mast, her queer rig caused considerable comment in Rockland.

Launching of the Edith Nute *at Rockland, Maine, 1917*

John G. Snow, showing Edward Rowe Snow and Bill Bennett the timbers of the Edith Nute
(photo by Richard Kelsey)

At the time, John Snow had just graduated from Rockland High School, and saw the *Nute* alongside the wharf. He had already skipped school to make a voyage on the *Hugh De Paynes,* and so he now asked the captain of the *Nute* if he could sail with him. The skipper signed him on as quartermaster. When the vessel was five days out to sea, the wheel ropes of the *Nute* stranded and parted. Emergency repairs were necessary, and the wheel was rigged with a luff tackle. The *Nute* became practically impossible to steer. After discharging part of the cargo of coal at Para, the *Nute* seemed to handle better, and they arrived at Rio Grande du Sol, January 6, 1918, making fast to a big buoy off the dock. Here the remains of the coal was unloaded. Four days later, against orders, the master decided to load lumber for Montevideo. About this time the owners of the coal discovered that they had not received the complete cargo of coal, and accused the captain, whose name Captain John decided not to mention, of removing it from the *Nute* as he had actually done at Para. The owners of the coal then libeled the vessel. The captain fired the mate for drunkenness the next day, and the third mate decided the *Nute* was a trouble ship and left. Things were in a merry state.

Twenty-four days went by with the ship tied up under the libel, and then the captain made a private settlement with the coal owners and was able to sail the lumber to Montevideo. When he landed there, the captain was arrested on an old charge of stealing a vessel, and stayed in jail for three days. Getting free in mysterious fashion, he ordered the *Nute* brought into the pier, and spent a week discharging the cargo.

Back on the Chatham shore we unwrapped some sandwiches and ate them as John Snow continued his story. "Trouble began in a big way then," he went on. "We took on 16,200 bags of linseed and then waited for diesel oil. The oil was too heavy, but the skipper refused to change it, as he had taken his rakeoff. After several arguments about the oil, the captain ordered the *Nute* anchored out in midstream. Finally the *Nute* sailed for New York, using the small supply which still remained of the good oil."

The very next day the *Nute* passed a convoy of eleven ships, escorted by a British cruiser suspicious of the *Nute*'s unconventional lines, but after a time the cruisers and the convoy disappeared.

Finally the engineer announced that there was only a twenty-four hour supply of oil left. "When that is gone," he said, "I'm done. I can't ruin my engines and you'll have to use sail."

The captain, worried for his safety, headed for the nearest port, Rio de Janeiro, where he arrived April 16. After a wait of twenty-one days they obtained fifty cases of suitable oil and sailed away. By this time the bottom of the *Nute* was foul with marine growth, because of the long periods of time spent waiting in various ports. The speed was actually only three knots, and this worried the captain, who declared that "the engine is no good, and there's no slip to the wheel."

On May 10 the *Nute* was back in Rio, as her speed was too slow. Seven days later the second mate was paid off, so the ship was without any officers except the captain. Men deserted almost every day, and still the *Nute* waited. Then a temporary mate was hired, and a trial run caused the inspectors to condemn the engine. The third engineer, who had helped build the engines, complained to the American Consul and prevented the German-influenced board from getting the engines.

"I was getting uneasy by this time," said John. "When Captain Drisko came into the harbor July 1 with the *Ella Pierce Thurlow,* I had a chance to go home as second mate aboard her. I was certainly happy about it. The old man would have none of it, however, and influenced the American Consul to refuse permission for me to change ships."

The *Nute* became so slow and heavy that she had to be dry-docked in August. The mussels, kelp, and seaweed extended for six feet from her bottom to touch the floor of the dry dock itself. "To anyone but a sailor it was a pretty sight, with all the mussels glistening in the sun," said John.

Back in Rockland, Maine, John's father, Captain John I. Snow, was getting very suspicious of the whole affair when months went by and the *Nute* still remained in South America. He wrote to the authorities, but it was a long time before they acted.

It seems that the captain got into trouble because an old charge of taking a vessel was still held against him, and the coal which he had unloaded caused further delay. Finally, matters became so involved that the United States Navy received orders to take action.

The final showdown came November 20, when seven sailors and three officers from the *Pittsburg* came aboard during the captain's absence and seized the *Nute*. Shortly afterwards the captain arrived at the gangway by bumboat. One of the officers pulled out his forty-five and shouted at the captain.

"Captain, don't step your foot on that gangway!"

"Who has charge of this ship?" the captain asked, enraged at the turn events had taken.

"The United States Navy," was the reply, and then the captain realized that he would have to change his plans. He never went aboard the *Nute* again, and on November 27, 1918, Captain Bert Magee from the States took charge of the *Nute* as master. Four days later the *Nute* was on her way home, but making very slow time, as her bottom had again become heavy with seaweed and mussels. On January 29, 1919, the *Nute* reached New York after one of the queerest trips on record, and John was soon sent home with $1,000 in his pocket for his long trip and stay in South America. It had been eighteen months since he had left Rockland!

After a stay at Portland Harbor, the *Nute* sailed again, and was constantly going aground at various places according to her logbook, which was later found on the Chatham Beach by Harry A. Bearse. Finally she started out from Boston with no cargo, and was wrecked on Nauset Beach late in 1922, approximately opposite Good Walter's shipwreck house at Chatham. At the time Bearse, the underwriting agent for the insurance companies, was notified about the wreck. He found out that in the opinion of the Boston wreckers, the *Nute* was not worth pulling off the shore, so later he auctioned off what he could of the fittings. The *Nute* gradually went to pieces.

Good Walter, John, and I walked around the beach and found many other fragments of the *Nute*. It was a strange adventure for John, locating fragments of a vessel on which he had undergone such unusual experiences. John took one of the bolts from the hatch coaming as a souvenir.

But the sun indicated the day was over, and half an hour later we landed on the Chatham shore near Good Walter's shipwreck house. John's car was parked on Andrew Harding's Lane nearby, and we soon said our farewells. He was off for Rockland, Maine, the memories of the *Edith Nute* and her strange career still with him.

The following morning I was ready for my hike southward along Monomoy Beach. I started out at low tide, for at that time one may get across the cut-through without too much trouble. Proceeding southward, I came to the wreckage of a great ship whose timbers were outlined in the sand, but there was no way of telling its name. Then I uncovered another wreck, but it was also unidentified. I finally came to the old Monomoy settlement and its abandoned lighthouse. After resting briefly and exploring the lighthouse grounds, I walked down to the beach and looked out to sea at the Stone Horse Lightship, anchored just a short distance offshore. I started northward again; it was two hours before I returned to Good Walter's shipwreck house.

He was standing in the doorway when I arrived. "Say, Professor," he began, "Did I tell you about the wreck of the *Grecian*?"

"No you didn't," I replied, and grabbed my pencil and some note paper. "Did it take place recently?"

"No, it was back long before I was doing much on the beach, in 1885. Of course I was around, and knew about it, but George Bloomer and Ben Patterson were the boys to remember that December night." Good Walter then told me the complete story.

One of the little-known exploits of the men of Chatham town who often frequented Andrew Harding's store was the rescue of the sailors from the schooner *Grecian,* wrecked in the early morning hours of December 6, 1885. The men had all gone home from the store the night before, little dreaming that they would be called upon before daybreak the next morning.

While they were sleeping at about 6:00 A.M., word was shouted through the village that a ship was ashore. At the time it was raining, a big sea was making up, and the storm seemed about to get worse. But two boats were manned within twenty minutes, one commanded by George W. Bloomer and the other by Ben Patterson. The others in the crews of the two surfboats were Andrew H. Bearse, Zenas W. Hawes, Otis C. Eldridge, Zenas H. Gould, Francisco Bloomer, Willis I. Bearse, and Wilbur H. Patterson. The two captains steered the surfboats in the general direction of a huge flare in the distance to the south. Reaching the location, they found the schooner partially sunk and surrounded by angry waves. The men were faced with a perilous undertaking, as the dories would have been swamped had they tried to run in close. Ordering the five members of the crew to jump one by one from the deckhouse into the water, the Chatham sailors rescued each in turn. Finally, with all the crew of the *Grecian* aboard the two dories, Bloomer and Patterson directed their crews to row for shore, and a short time later everyone was landed safely on the beach. While on their way back, they were met by the crew of the Chatham Life-Saving Station rowing to the aid of the *Grecian*. The life-saving crew turned back upon finding that the Chatham men had rescued all aboard the schooner.

When they were safely landed ashore, the crew members of the *Grecian* told their sad story. Anchored off Chatham the day before in a large fleet of vessels, the *Grecian,* heavily loaded with coal, got under way again in the early morning hours. Encountering a heavy gale of rain, she lost some of her sails, became unmanageable, and struck on a bar about 5:00 in the morning. The crew members fired their shotguns several times, and then lighted a fire on the deck. But shortly afterwards the schooner began to go down, striking bottom when about 400 yards off shore, with her deckhouse partly under water. They all huddled on the deckhouse to await rescue, and it came shortly afterwards in the manner described. For this fine feat of daring the nine members of the two rescue crews were all awarded silver medals.

The best thing about hiking around Cape Cod is that you never know when you will stumble on a gold mine of information. I remember one afternoon I noticed one of the quarter boards of the *Edith Nute* decorating an attractive Chatham barn, so I knocked at the back door of the nearby home to meet Miss Ann Bevins, whose parents are the owners of the property. After discussing the quarter board, which she told me her father purchased from Harry A. Bearse at the "strippings" auction held after the vessel was wrecked, she showed me a fine list of wrecks and accounts kept by Thomas Holway, an old fisherman and wrecker of the last century. The list had been given her by T. W. Holway, his son, and some of the more important wrecks are listed below:

Edwards, 1851; *New York*, 1851; *Lightfoot*, 1852; *Virginia*, 1852; *Mary Ann*, 1852; *Two Brothers*, 1854; *Eben Herbert*, 1854; *Czarina*, 1854; *R. S. Miller*, 1856; *Bin Tultan*, 1857; *S. F. Lewis*, 1858; *Virginia Voyage*, 1859; *Mary Pierce*, 1860; *R. B. Forbes*, 1860; *Emperor*, 1861; *James Henry*, 1862; *Wolcot*, 1862; *Mary Millihen*, 1862; *James Martin*, 1863; *Mary* and *E. English*, both in 1864; and the *Perit*, 1877.

I later showed Good Walter the list and he told me he had heard of many of the vessels mentioned. Those he did not know were wrecked before he was born.

There are many who had told me of the romance in Good Walter's life, but he has never mentioned it to me, so I must be silent in that respect. He is quite talented as an artist, having painted his own picture from the reflection in a mirror, while his paintings of clipper ships, barks, and brigs are good likenesses. His ship models are outstanding.

One day he was standing with the underwriter's agent, shortly after the *Orcutt* disaster. The underwriter told him that if he could get the huge bollards or iron bits off the hull of the *Calvin Orcutt* he could have them. A day later he brought them ashore to the amazement of the underwriter, and ever since then they have stood in the yard of his old house. It was a remarkable feat, but Good Walter never told how he managed to do it. Another accomplishment of Good Walter was his gasoline boat, one of the first on Cape Cod. He built the boat himself, calling it the *Mariner*.

The sea lingo clings to the sailor, and crops up in the most unusual places. Good Walter was an usher at the Methodist Church during the summer, and some out-of-state ladies entered the church one Sunday. Good Walter smilingly came up to them, and asked, "Where would you like to sit—forward, aft, or amidships?"

The next day when I returned to Good Walter's house he was cleaning fish, but soon finished so that he could walk down the beach with me. "Yes," said Walter, "I guess I know almost every piece of wreckage which we can see on the Outer Beach. I remember the *Wentworth*. No one talks about her now, but she was one of the worst of all. You'd better look her up in the records sometime." I promised to get the official report when I next visited Washington, and then asked him to tell what he could remember about her. The following story is partly from Walter's recollection and partly from the official government records, filed in Washington.

Sometimes a particular storm or wreck, well-known at the time, becomes completely forgotten after a few years have elapsed. The October Gale of 1904, which lasted for two days and caused heavy loss of life from Cape Cod to Florida, was just such a gale. In addition to the wreck of the *Wentworth,* another vessel was lost at Peaked Hill.

The storm was particularly trying for the lifesavers of Chatham. The disaster which befell the *Calvin Orcutt* in 1896 influenced the government to erect a new life saving station which they named the Old Harbor Station on Nauset Beach across from Chatham. Now, with the new station active, another sad event was about to occur in the vicinity.

On Tuesday, October 11, 1904, the three-masted British schooner *Wentworth* sailed from Hillsboro, Nova Scotia, bound for Newark, New Jersey, with a cargo of plaster. On board was a happy crew and captain, for the "old man" had his wife and three children along. Captain Esau Prindle owned a quarter share in the *Wentworth,* and looked forward with pleasure to the arrival of the schooner at the New Jersey port. But the *Wentworth* was not destined ever again to come into the harbor of Newark, New Jersey, or any other port of call. The vessel ran into heavy weather while off the coast, and Captain Prindle was caught on Chatham Bar before he knew his position. We cannot tell what his actions were then, for to this day no word has been heard from the captain, his family, or his crew of seven.

On Orleans Beach the south patrolman had left the Old Harbor Station at 5:00 P.M. on the afternoon of October 13, to walk his beat as far as Chatham Inlet. The weather was squally, with light drizzling rain coming at intervals, but a heavy northeast wind all day long had built up some nasty breakers which were booming with ceaseless regularity in the surfman's ears as he forced his way southward. Not a single vessel had been sighted all day long, and it looked like an uneventful evening.

Reaching the end of the beat, he paused a moment. Then he heard a faint sound, which was shortly afterwards repeated—a distant foghorn. He turned his ear in the direction where he had heard the horn, and then it came again. There was no mistake; a vessel was in trouble. Running to the telephone hut, he called the station and told Keeper Hezekiah F. Doane the news of the wreck. By this time the horn could be heard louder than before and the lifesaver ran down toward the surf as near as he dared. There before him he could faintly make out the outlines of the *Wentworth*. He burned a Coston flare to let the sailors know they had been observed and went back to telephone that the vessel in distress was right off the beach.

He had seen a gaff swinging off against the rigging, as the halyards were already carried away.

The sound of flapping sails came to his ears distinctly even above the roar of the waves and the wind. No sidelights were visible on the vessel, but the cabin lights were shining. Then, without warning, the fog horn suddenly stopped.

At the Old Harbor Station the men climbed the watchtower. By straining their eyes through the darkness they were able to make out a black shape off the beach, which they decided must be the schooner, and burned a Coston flare from the station. The keeper telephoned both the Orleans and Chatham stations that there was a ship ashore and then ordered the beach apparatus car manned. By this time the south patrolman had reached the station, and with the exception of the north patrol, the men, six in number, were ready for the difficult task of wheeling the beach wagon through the soft sand to the scene of the wreck.

It was a bitter fight the men waged with their three foes, wind, sand, and tide. The north patrolman, who had seen the Coston flare, joined them halfway down the beach, and through their combined efforts, they reached the scene of the wreck by 8:30 P.M. The outlines of the hull and spars of the *Wentworth* could barely be discerned in the blackness of night, but the crackling and flapping of the sails could not be mistaken. Although the faint flicker of the cabin lights was visible, no sign of life could be made out, no distress signals nor any other indication that those aboard were anxious for their own safety.

Setting the beach apparatus up on the sand, the men fired a number nine shot line with a six ounce charge of powder. Shortly after the shot line reached the schooner, some of the surfmen believed they detected shouts coming from the vessel, and the megaphone was used to try to communicate with the *Wentworth*. There was no response, but the keeper thought for an instant that he saw the feeble flicker of a light, although it was not repeated. The cabin lights were still on. When the shot line began to jerk, as though it were being hauled aboard, the whip block was bent on, and an effort was made to send it out. Of course the men ashore could not tell what actually was happening aboard the schooner, but after waiting a reasonable length of time for the whip block to be tied to one of the masts, they bent on the hawser and started it out. It went off for several yards, but then stopped. Keeper Doane realized that something was wrong, and so he hauled in the hawser and found it hopelessly fouled with the whip.

Evidently, for reasons we can never know, the sailors aboard the *Wentworth* made no response as they did not at any time make fast any line sent out to them. Of course, we cannot say this with certainty, but the captain, his family, and crew might have made a desperate effort to reach shore in the jolly boat. All probably perished as the boat was caught in a giant breaker. Or it is possible that they might all have been trapped in the rigging, for the seas, by this time, were making a clean breach of the entire vessel, roaring several feet deep over the deck with terrible fury. The storm increased as the hour neared midnight, until it seemed no surfboat could possibly have survived for a moment. Returning with heavy hearts to the station, the keeper and crew saw the southern patrolman from the Orleans Station coming toward them. When he had not met the northern patrol from Old Harbor Station, the surfman continued along the beach to the deserted station. This made him realize there was trouble to the southward. He kept on walking and joined in helping the Old Harbor crew to get out the surfboat and haul it to the scene of the wreck.

By this time the townsmen of Chatham knew of the disaster, and three of the braver ones had crossed the harbor in a dory to land on the outer beach. All experienced lifesavers, they joined the others who were pulling the surfboat.

Reaching the scene again, the men observed that the surf was worse than ever, and decided, in their desperation, to send out another shot. A number seven line was used this time with the same charge of powder. When the line had landed across the schooner, a Coston flare was burned, and the men took turns shouting through the megaphone. No reply ever came. Reluctantly the men hauled in their shot line, to find the shot still attached. Just after this, the cabin lights went out, either because of the sea's engulfing the cabin or because of the collapse of the cabin itself.

Keeper James H. Charles from the Orleans Station arrived with his men shortly afterwards, bringing with him a new type of Wells light. He ordered the searchlight set up on the beach, and the rays were directed out at the wreck. The *Wentworth* could easily be made out by the light, but her position, whether she lay head on or stern on, could not be determined as the waves were burying her with foam every few seconds. Another shot line was prepared and fired, but hauled back without result. A final conference was held on the possibility of a surf-boat's reaching the schooner. The rolling billows, breaking ten and fifteen feet high right in front of them, convinced even the more adventuresome of the watchers on the beach that an attempt at launching would not be successful, so a fire was built on the shore and plans were made to stand by and await developments.

As the tide set to the southward along the beach, surfmen were dispatched to cover the entire distance of the patrol. The others waited by the fire, constantly lighting new Coston flares in vain efforts to get answers from the doomed schooner. Nothing happened until long after midnight, however.

Around 3:00 in the morning a loud crash was heard and what appeared to be fire flashing from the schooner's mastheads was seen by the watchers on shore. One of her masts had gone by the board. Then, above the noise of the surf and wind, came what Keeper Doane always claimed was a woman's piercing shriek of despair. The beach patrol continued their search, and shortly afterwards pieces of the cabin began to wash along the beach, indicating the vessel was starting to break up.

Word then came across from Chatham that a board with WENTWORTH on it had been found on Chatham Beach by people from the village, and thus the name of the schooner became known for the first time.

It was a sad wreck which the first rays of dawn showed the discouraged surfmen on Orleans Beach—the *Wentworth* lay stern on with her hull almost submerged. Her foremast alone remained upright, for her mainmast was broken off at the step and was hanging by its spring stay against the forerigging, and the mizzenmast was in the water alongside with a great mass of other wreckage. Her stern was split open and the after deckhouse gone. The bowsprit and jibboom were standing. There was no sign of life whatever on the *Wentworth* as the men looked out at her. The seas washed over and through her. The schooner was beaten—out of action forever.

But what of her crew, the captain and his family? Had any of them reached shore alive, to be discovered later? The surfmen were not very hopeful of this, but still, one never can tell at sea.

At 6:00 that morning the patrol saw an object floating in the water down near the south point below the wreck. He waded out and brought in a woman's body. Appearing to be about twenty-five years of age, the woman, fully clothed, was clutching a blanket which was loosely knotted about her body as though it had bound a child to her. Shortly afterwards the remains of a man were found on the beach, southward of the wreck. Those two bodies were the only ones ever found of the eleven who perished that terrible night.

On October 16 the brother of Captain Prindle of the *Wentworth* visited Old Harbor Station, where he identified the woman's body as that of Mrs. Prindle, the captain's wife, and the man as Thomas Pergerson, a seaman. Her remains were sent to Nova Scotia, while the body of Pergerson was buried in the Chatham Cemetery.

In writing the story of the unfortunate disaster, the investigating officer closed his reports with the thought that had "the whole Life-Saving Service been on the scene the result must have been the same." Everything which human power could do had been tried in a vain effort to save the unfortunate people who left Hillsboro, Nova Scotia, on Tuesday, October 11, 1904, aboard the luckless schooner *Wentworth*.

The sun had already set in the west as we finished our discussion of the disaster which befell the *Wentworth*. An hour later I was climbing the stairs of the Wayside Inn on my way to bed, for I was tired and worn out, and had decided to leave Chatham and the Cape the next day.

When dawn came, however, I decided to make a final effort to climb the Jenny Lind Tower in Truro. It had been on my conscience as an uncompleted mission and as such was bothering me, for I had definitely failed to carry out that particular objective. Calling my good friend Dick Kelsey on Main Street in Chatham, I found that he was willing to fly up with me and render any assistance needed.

Three hours later we were standing outside the door of the old tower. Unfortunately it had been heavily barricaded since my last visit, and the only entrance was through the transom. My 200 pounds proved quite a problem until we found the old flagstaff lying in the blueberry bushes nearby. We lifted the flagstaff up and through the transom, and with the aid of wooden props I climbed the outside of the heavy oak door. Then Dick pushed the flagstaff all the way in, and it came to rest against the cast-iron staircase.

Using the flagstaff for a hold, I inched through the transom, and made a grab at the railing of the circular ladder in the middle of the tower. In a moment I was inside. I then asked Dick to hand in the end of the 100-foot rope I had brought along, and climbed to the top of the iron ladder.

Tying the rope to a piece of piping, I threw it over my head through the trapdoor in the roof of the tower, and Dick grabbed it later from the ground below. I then went up hand over hand on the rope, and soon grabbed the projection around the trapdoor, pulling myself to safety. I had accomplished my objective!

After spending a half hour making pictures from the unusual vantage point at the top of the tower, I signaled to Dick that I was ready, and he held the end of the line while I went down the rope to the top of the iron staircase. We returned to Chatham well pleased with the results of our journey. A picture which Dick Kelsey took while I was on the tower is in this volume.

Early the following morning I telephoned to Boston for a seaplane to come down to carry me back to Boston. It was with a feeling of sadness that I took my last walk along the Cape beach. At 10:00 I was leaving Good Walter and all that he stood for. He walked along with me, for I had told him that I was leaving by plane.

"Don't forget to circle out off the Brant Stand and look for the privateer," he reminded me, for we had a project the following summer to bring up the treasure which went down more than 200 years ago off the shore there.

"I'll be sure to look," was my answer. Within a few minutes we heard a roar in the sky and my plane landed a short distance offshore and taxied over to the beach. I jumped aboard with my belongings.

"When are you coming back to go down and get the treasure?" were his last words, but the roar of the engine cut off any further attempt at conversation.

A few moments later we circled around to give him a final greeting, and there he was, standing outside his shipwreck house with his dog Mandy. As we came flying by he raised his hand to a level with his eyes and held it there. And in that fashion this man of Chatham bade farewell to his friend the "Professor" on a May afternoon in 1946. He knew that I'd be back for another try at that privateer off the beach. He was sure that there was around $5 million in gold in the wreck, but the Professor wasn't too interested in whether it was pirate gold, privateering cannon, or pieces of eight which might be found fifteen feet down in the blue waters off Monomoy, for he had in mind a still greater treasure—just another visit to Cape Cod.

Five minutes later we were circling over the ancient wreck which lies in fifteen feet of water some distance south of the bell buoy, and could see its timbers against the sand. Yes, I was coming back to explore what still remained on that old hulk the following summer, but I also thought of the many other unfinished missions which I had not accomplished.

My quest to locate a story about a giant sea horse off Chatham had failed; the actual date of the wreck of the *Owhyhee* was still undecided; and I had not met Mrs. Small of Buzzards Bay nor the lighthouse family of Howards at West Chatham. However, I had accomplished most of my objectives, and in addition had enjoyed seven delightful weeks on Cape Cod.

But I was leaving it all too quickly. We sped across Pleasant Bay and turned up the coast. Orleans, Wellfleet, Truro, and Provincetown passed under us, and then we began the water jump between Race Point and Plymouth. A short time later Boston and the custom house were outlined against the horizon, and then I saw, off to the left, the tall Myles Standish Monument in Duxbury. I wondered what the Pilgrim fathers would think if I could tell them of my visit to Cape Cod. Would they be happy, if they, too, returned to the land they left three centuries before? Ten minutes later, when we landed in Boston, the Pilgrims were still in my thoughts.

I would tell them that Cape Cod was in safe hands. Yes, Pilgrim Fathers, your descendants at Cape Cod are carrying on for you, fulfilling your aims and living up to the ideals which you had when you landed in the New World from the *Mayflower* and the other early ships. The dreams which you treasured when you reached Cape Cod's wilderness have not been forgotten by your descendants and all those who came after them from every land. Here, in America, and especially on Cape Cod, the inspiration "to strive, to seek, to find, and not to yield" will never be forgotten.

Squanto eventually came to be regarded as an enemy of the Wampanoag, and he is now regarded as a somewhat controversial figure. But there is no doubting his importance to the survival of the Pilgrims.

Harding's Beach Light is also known as Stage Harbor Light. The keeper who committed suicide was Mills Gunderson, who went to the station from Boston Light in 1916. In 1918 Keeper Gunderson committed suicide, hanging himself in a shed for reasons unknown. His son, Stanley, took over as keeper and stayed at the light until it was decommissioned in 1933.

A new tidal inlet formed at Chatham in 1987, as the north beach was breached by a winter storm. Since then a number of homes along the shore have been lost. The parking lot at Chatham Lighthouse was undermined for a time.

In 1969 the Fresnel lens and the entire lantern room were removed from Chatham Lighthouse. Modern aerobeacons producing a rotating 2.8 million candlepower light were installed, and a new, larger lantern room was built to accommodate the larger optics. The old lantern room and lens are now on the grounds of the Chatham Historical Society's Atwood House Museum, which is open to the public from early June through September.

The memorial obelisk near the Chatham Light Station was paid for by the mother and sister of William Henry Mack, twenty-nine-year-old owner of the *Wadena,* who perished in the Monomoy disaster. The inscriptions include Alfred Lord Tennyson's poem "Crossing the Bar." A ceremony was held at the memorial on March 17, 2002, the centennial of one of the worst days in Cape Cod's twentieth-century maritime history.

Mrs. Wight (1880–1973) painted under the name Alice Stallknecht. Her murals are now housed in the old Chatham Railroad freight shed at the Atwood House Museum, and there was a special exhibit of some of her other work at the museum in 2002-2003.

Monomoy Point Light today (photo by Brian Tague)

In 1964 the Massachusetts Audubon Society restored the lighthouse and keeper's house on Monomoy, and there was some further refurbishing in 1988. The infamous Blizzard of 1978 cut Monomoy into two islands, North and South Monomoy. Today both islands are managed by the U.S. Fish and Wildlife Service. The Cape Cod Museum of Natural History offers day trips to South Monomoy and overnight stays in the keeper's house.

Bibliography from the 1946 Edition

Bangs, Mary (1920). *Old Cape Cod.*

Beston, Henry (1928). *The Outermost House.*

Boston District Office, U.S.E. (1940). *Cape Cod Canal.*

Bowles, Francis T. (1924). *The Loyalty of Barnstable in the Revolution.*

Bradford, William (1890). *Of Plymouth Plantation.*

Brigham, Albert Perry (1924). *Cape Cod and the Old Colony.*

Carter, Robert (1864). *A Summer Cruise.*

Chatham, Dennis, and Marion Chatham (1920). *Cape Coddities.*

Dalton, J. W. (1902). *Lifesavers of Cape Cod.*

Dalton, J. W. (1911). *Cape Cod Canal.*

DeCosta, B. F. (1881). *Cavo de Baros.*

Deyo, Simeon L. (1890). *History of Barnstable County.*

Digges, Jeremiah (1937). *Cape Cod Pilot.*

Drake, Samuel Adams (1875). *Nooks and Corners of the New England Coast.*

Driver, George Hibbert (1930). *Cape Scapes.*

Dwight, Timothy (1821). *Travels in New England and New York.*

Early, Eleanor (1936). *And This Is Cape Cod.*

Edwards, Agnes (1918). *Cape Cod, New and Old.*

Freeman, Frederick (1858). *History of Cape Cod.*

Frost, Jack (1939). *A Cape Cod Sketch Book.*

Goodwin, John Abbot (1888). *The Pilgrim Republic.*

Hatch, M. V. M. (1939). *Provincetown and Truro.*

Howard, Channing (1941). *Little Journeys, Geographical and Historical, Boston Bay to the South Shore and Cape Cod.*

Howe, Henry F. (1943). *Prologue to New England.*

Irwin, Frederick T. (1926). *Story of Sandwich Glass and Glassware.*

Jenkins, Charles W. (1889). *History of Falmouth.*

Jennings, Herman A. (1890). *Provincetown, or Odds and Ends from the Tip End.*

Johnson, Jack (1944). *Stories of Cape Cod.*

Keene, Betsy D. (1937). *History of Bourne, 1622–1937.*

Kelly, Stanley (1936). *About Cape Cod.*

Kittredge, Henry C. (1930). *Cape Cod: Its People and Their History.*

Kittredge, Henry C. (1935). *Shipmasters of Cape Cod.*

Kittredge, Henry C. (1937). *Mooncussers of Cape Cod.*

Lincoln, Joseph C. (1930). *Cape Cod Ballads.*

Lincoln, Joseph C. (1935). *Cape Cod Yesterdays.*

Livermore, Charles W. (1865). *Ye Antient Wrecks.*

Massachusetts Department of Labor. (1922). *Population and Resources of Cape Cod.*

McCue, James W. (1941). *Romantic Cape Cod.*

Mourt, George (1865). *Mourt's Relation.*

Otis, Amos (1885). *Genealogical Notes of Barnstable Families.*

Paine, Josiah (1937). *History of Harwich.*

Perry, E. G. (1898). *A Trip Around Cape Cod.*

Phinney, S. B. (1840). *Cape Cod Centennial Celebration at Barnstable.*

Pratt, Ambrose E. (1890). *250th Anniversary Celebration of Sandwich and Bourne.*

Pratt. Rev. Enoch (1844). *Eastham, Wellfleet, and Orleans.*

Rich, Shebnah (1883). *Truro—Cape Cod, or Landmarks and Sea Marks.*

Small, Isaac M. (1928). *Shipwrecks on Cape Cod.*

Small, Isaac M. (1934). *Cape Cod Stories.*

Smith, William C. (1909). *History of Chatham Part I.*

Smith, William C. (1913). *History of Chatham Part II.*

Smith, William C. (1917). *History of Chatham Part III.*

Snow, Edward Rowe (1943). *Storms and Shipwrecks of New England.*

Snow, Edward Rowe (1944). *Pirates and Buccaneers of the Atlantic Coast.*

Snow, Edward Rowe (1945). *Cruising the Massachusetts Coast.*

Snow, Edward Rowe (1945). *Famous New England Lighthouses.*

Swift, Charles F. (1897). *Cape Cod.*

Tarbell, Arthur Wilson (1932). *Cape Cod Ahoy!*

Thoreau, Henry David (1864). *Cape Cod.*

Trayser, Donald Grant (1939). *Barnstable, Three Centuries of a Cape Cod Town.*

Wayman, Dorothy G. (1930). *Suckanesset, Wherein May Be Read a History of Falmouth, Mass.*

Index

About the Author

Edward Rowe Snow (1902–1982) was descended from a long line of sea captains. He sailed the high seas, toiled aboard oil tankers, and worked as a Hollywood extra—all before attending college. Later he worked as a teacher and coach, and as a reconnaissance photographer during World War II. His education and work prepared him well for his legendary writing career—which was part maritime history, part show business.

The Islands of Boston Harbor, his first book, was published in 1935. In all, Snow wrote nearly one hundred books and pamphlets, illustrated

with many of his own photographs. He also contributed newspaper columns to the *Quincy Patriot Ledger, the Boston Herald,* and the *Brockton Enterprise*. In the 1950s his radio show *Six Bells* was heard on dozens of stations, and he made many other appearances on radio as well as on television.

Snow is fondly remembered as the "Flying Santa." For forty years he flew in small planes and helicopters over the lighthouses of New England, dropping Christmas parcels for the keepers and their families. His efforts to preserve the islands of Boston Harbor as public lands are less well known. After his death in 1982, the *Boston Globe* lauded his support for conservation: "There are many political leaders and environmentalists who can justly share the credit for the preservation of the harbor islands, but among them Mr. Snow will hold a special place as a link to their past and a guide to their present."

Snow married Anna-Myrle Haegg in 1932. They had one daughter, Dorothy Caroline Snow (Bicknell), two granddaughters, and one great-grandson. The young people who grew up "at his feet," reading and listening to his tales of New England maritime history, are countless.